A Young Dutchman
Views Post–Civil War America

A Young Dutchman
Views Post–Civil War America

Diary of Claude August Crommelin

Claude August Crommelin

Translated by Augustus J. Veenendaal, Jr.

Edited with an introduction by
Augustus J. Veenendaal, Jr., and H. Roger Grant

INDIANA UNIVERSITY PRESS
Bloomington and Indianapolis

Publication of this book has been supported in part by a grant from the Department of History, Clemson University.

This book is a publication of
Indiana University Press
601 North Morton Street
Bloomington, Indiana 47404-3797 USA

iupress.indiana.edu

Telephone orders   800-842-6796
Fax orders   812-855-7931
Orders by e-mail   iuporder@indiana.edu

∞ The paper used in this publication meets the minimum requirements of the American National Standard for Information Sciences—Permanence of Paper for Printed Library Materials, ANSI Z39.48-1992.

Manufactured in the United States of America

Library of Congress Cataloging-in-Publication Data

Crommelin, Claude August, 1840-1874.
    A young Dutchman views post-Civil War America : diary of Claude August Crommelin / Claude August Crommelin ; translated by Augustus J. Veenendaal, Jr. ; edited with an introduction by Augustus J. Veenendaal, Jr., and H. Roger Grant.
        p. cm.
    Includes bibliographical references and index.
    ISBN 978-0-253-35609-3 (cloth : alk. paper) 1. Crommelin, Claude August, 1840–1874—Diaries. 2. Crommelin, Claude August, 1840–1874—Travel—United States. 3. United States—Social conditions—1865–1918—Sources. 4. United States—Economic conditions—1865–1918—Sources. 5. Reconstruction (U.S. history, 1865–1877)—Sources. 6. United States—Description and travel. I. Veenendaal, A. J. II. Grant, H. Roger, [date]- III. Title.
    E168.C93 2011
    973.8—dc22

                                                                    2010035372

1 2 3 4 5   16 15 14 13 12 11

For Jannie and Martha

Contents

Acknowledgments

This book is the result of a joint effort of two historians, one Dutch and one American. The Dutchman stumbled upon the diary of Claude August Crommelin while conducting research for another book project in the vast holdings of the Minnesota Historical Society in St. Paul. He grew enthusiastic about the text of the diary and the way Crommelin described America and Americans a century and a half ago. He then translated the Dutch text into English and asked his American friend if he shared his assessment of the diary for an American audience. When the answer came in the affirmative, they set to work to make the document understandable for an interested public.

During his travels to and in America Crommelin met many people. We have tried to identify most of them by using the usual biographical dictionaries, American, English, and Dutch, and other research works. The titles of the more specialized literature are provided in the endnotes to each chapter. Some names, however, proved to be elusive, but they are all listed in the general index.

We want to thank the staffs of the University Archives and the Cooper Library at Clemson University, Clemson, South Carolina, for research and interlibrary loan materials; the Royal Library of The Hague and the Institute of Netherlands History also in The Hague; the Minnesota Historical Society and the Amsterdam and Rotterdam City archives. We appreciate the generous financial support given to this project by the Department of History at Clemson and its chair, Professor Thomas Kuehn.

Of the many individuals who have assisted us in some ways, we first of all wish to mention Liesbeth Crommelin and her husband, Henk Visser, of Amsterdam. They were enthusiastic about the project from our first tentative requests for support. They helped with information about the complicated family history, and they made photographs of Claude August Crommelin available for publication. Govert Deketh, who lives in Geneva, Switzerland, and is webmaster of the "Stichting Familie Crommelin," also assisted us with invaluable information about the Crommelin family. We are also indebted to others, including Otto Schutte of The Hague, who identified Crommelin's travel partner Meder and located the diplomats named in the diary; C. J. de Bruijn Kops of Abcoude, the Netherlands, who identified the De Bruijn Kops family members met by Crommelin in New York City and Minnesota; Margriet Bruijn Lacy of Indianapolis, who provided the precise location of the former Asylum of the Blind in her hometown; John Hattendorf of Newport, Rhode Island, who supplied facts about that famous "watering place" in Crommelin's time; Eileen McCormack, St. Paul, Minnesota, who gave particulars of the churches in New York City; and Dick van der Spek of Emmen, the Netherlands, who kindly drew the beautiful maps of Crommelin's travels in America. They all contributed materially to this work.

Our long-suffering wives, Jannie and Martha, have endured too much Crommelinization over the years, especially Jannie, who had to hear about him since we don't know when. Nevertheless, they always supported us, and we thank them for their patience and critical remarks.

Augustus J. Veenendaal, Jr., 't Harde, The Netherlands
H. Roger Grant, Clemson, South Carolina

A Young Dutchman
Views Post–Civil War America

Introduction

During the nineteenth century the United States of America was somewhat of an enigma for Europeans. It was a country where democracy was in full swing, but with a popular sovereignty that frightened many Continentals. In European eyes it was likewise a place of unlimited economic and social possibilities, where an enterprising man could improve himself unhindered by ossified autocratic regimes. This New World Republic was also a developing industrial colossus, with factories and mines and an infrastructure bolstered by an integrated network of post roads and turnpikes, canals and railroads. By the 1850s American technical and business prowess had achieved a position of leadership, and a decade later railroad mileage soared from 9,021 to 30,626 miles, allowing the nation to claim more than half the railroad mileage in the world. At the same time it was a land of unsurpassed natural beauty, with mountains, waterfalls, wide rivers, deep forests, and broad prairies, and a paradise for sporting gentlemen who delighted in bagging wild game, whether passenger pigeons or American bison.[1]

Small wonder that travelers from Europe crossed the Atlantic to experience this American wonderland. It would be in 1831 that an observant young Frenchman, Alexis de Tocqueville (1805–1859), became arguably the most famous visitor from abroad. In his popular work, *Democracy in America* (1835), he captured the essence of American values and culture. His commentaries revealed much about the burgeoning Republic, noting that American democracy, while imperfect, was certainly the wave of humanity's future. His observations prefigured a concept that later became known as American exceptionalism. And Tocqueville's perceptive insights made much of the practical orientation of Americans; citizens warmly embraced the notion that an idea means what an idea does. In this democratic society shortcuts to wealth, labor-saving gadgets, and inventions that increased the comfort or pleasure of life "seem the most magnificent effort of human intelligence."[2]

While Tocqueville, Charles Dickens (1812–1870), Anthony Trollope (1815–1882), and others found a wide, appreciative reading audience with their thoughtful commentaries on America, mass tourism was still something of the future. Yet in the mid-nineteenth century well-heeled travelers from the Old World could afford to spend a few months in the sprawling new country. It might involve visits to major cities, hunting expeditions, or mostly travel on canal packets, steamboats, or railway cars that gave opportunities for intimate contact with Americans and an examination of the expansive landscape.[3]

It is clear that a transatlantic journey in the 1860s was still something out of the ordinary, indeed something adventurous and not to be taken lightly. Travel was fraught with discomfort, perhaps danger, when the traveler booked passage on a sailing vessel or a primitive steamship. Even though there were established commercial shipping lines to American destinations from British ports, and while Englishmen came in some numbers, Dutchmen did not commonly venture across the high seas. In the 1840s and 1850s, though, scores of Dutch families had made the trek for economic and religious reasons, settling mostly on the Michigan and Iowa farming frontiers. Emigrants were chiefly interested in their physical and economic survival and often were too poorly versed in their own language to write extensively, penning at best simple letters to relatives at home. A trip for pleasure or even for business was unusual. Small wonder, then, that well-to-do, better educated adventurers not only recorded their experiences in letters but generally kept diaries or journals of sorts. Some of their efforts appeared in print shortly after their return, but in the Netherlands a real market for these publications came only later in the nineteenth century.[4]

✳ ✳ ✳

Claude August Crommelin, author of this rare diary of an early Dutch visitor to America, was a scion of a well-established French-Dutch family. The Crommelins originated in northern France and the southern region of present-day Belgium. Being Protestants, some family members emigrated to the north at the end of the sixteenth century and settled in Haarlem in the Protestant Dutch Republic. A new wave of emigrants came after 1685, when King Louis XIV of France ended most rights of these Protestant Huguenots and attempted to have them converted to Roman Catholicism. Yet other branches of the family remained in France, and became useful business contacts for the "Dutch" Crommelins. At least one member of the family crossed the Atlantic and settled in British North America, again providing business contacts with kin in Holland.[5]

The Crommelins in Holland prospered and mingled with other French *émigré* families and with families of the ruling classes. Daniel Crommelin (1707–1788), born in New York City—the one-time New Amsterdam—where his father had settled, returned to Amsterdam, and in 1737 established a commodity business that soon expanded into banking and shipping. This firm developed contacts in America and in Europe and operated under the name of Daniel Crommelin & Sons. Soon it became a well-respected, solid, old-fashioned house, especially with its American relations. However, the business slump of 1848, partly fueled by widespread political unrest in Europe, meant a sharp downturn in the company's profits. In 1854 Claude Daniel Crommelin (1795–1859), great-grandson of the founder, announced his wish to end the partnership. Five years later at the time of the death of Claude Daniel, the company's books were closed. The financial operations were taken over by another Amsterdam firm, Tutein Nolthenius & De Haan.[6]

Claude August Crommelin, the diarist, was born in Amsterdam on March 1, 1840, and was the sole surviving son of the last partner, Claude Daniel. His mother, Alida Maria Wolterbeek (1802–1862), was the widow of J. J. Weymar. A daughter from this earlier marriage, Elisabeth (1825–1902), older stepsister of Claude August, married Julius Hendrik Tutein Nolthenius (1824–1889). Their offspring, Julie Elisabeth (1853–1939), will later play a role in the Crommelin diary. Young Claude August, called Gus by his mother but Aug or Auk by his friends, was of a sickly disposition, and received his basic education at home from Swiss governors, until he was sent to a famous and fashionable boarding school, Noortheij, near Voorschoten, south of Leiden, where he continued his schooling. At Noortheij he was in the same class as Prince William of Orange, the eldest son of King William III of the Netherlands. Apparently Aug had no desire to be taken into the family business, opting instead for a career in law and public service. He pursued legal studies at the University of Utrecht, a premier academic institution in the Netherlands, and on June 28, 1865, earned his doctor's degree with a thesis on land tax. His signature academic work was a fairly short book, only three chapters that totaled 114 pages. In it Crommelin focused exclusively on the taxation of landed property, not developed real estate, and made frequent comparisons with other nations, mostly European countries. But he also considered similar matters in the United States. In Dutch academic usage some concise propositions were—and still are—mandatory at the end of every thesis. In these Crommelin carefully discussed the rules concerning commercial transactions of several different kinds, such as buying and selling of goods, or buying and selling on commission without actually owning the goods in question.[7]

Before his visit to the United States, Crommelin likely had traveled extensively in Europe, at first chiefly with his affluent parents. It appears that on later occasions he sometimes joined a friend from his Noortheij days, Jerome Alexander Sil-

This photograph shows Claude August Crommelin and is dated 1865.
Liesbeth Crommelin Coll.

lem (1840–1912), scion of another Amsterdam banking family. This would not
have been unusual for a son of a well-to-do family. From scattered remarks in his
diary it becomes clear that he had at least been to Brussels and London in 1856,
and to Dresden, Vienna, and Prague in 1863, and that he had seen numerous mu-
seums and art collections and industrial concerns. In his writings about his American journey, he relates that while visiting the shops of the Illinois Central Railroad
in Chicago he did not see anything there that he had not viewed elsewhere. Particulars about these early visits are unfortunately lacking.[8]

Soon after obtaining his doctor's degree, Crommelin set out for America. The
purpose of his trip is not quite clear, but the diary that he kept faithfully from the
start of his journey indicates several reasons. In light of his family background, it is

understandable that he is interested in the American investment business. During the early years of the nineteenth century the firm of Daniel Crommelin & Sons had entered this field, and so young Claude August must have known about these activities. Several American railroads, including the Atlantic & Great Western, the Illinois Central, and the St. Paul & Pacific, were largely financed from Holland, and he is exploring other opportunities for profitable Dutch involvement. And the reverse is true; the board of the Illinois Central Railroad invites him to take part in its annual inspection tour with the intent of revealing how Dutch dollars had been spent. He probably had commissions from several Amsterdam stock brokering and banking houses to look into the affairs of some of these Dutch-financed railroads. The way Crommelin is received by many bankers and businessmen in America is significant in this respect. Apparently they knew who he was representing and what he wished to know. Apart from railroads, the nascent oil industry in northeastern Pennsylvania was another target for an on-site inspection, again to probe the possibilities for Dutch investment. In his diary he never mentions actual commissions of this nature, but it is more than probable that he had some, although he himself had no direct connection with the successors of the firm of Daniel Crommelin & Sons. His name, however, opened every door in America.

Crommelin must have been well informed about international finance, so it seems odd that he never mentions the failure in June 1866 of the London bank of Overend, Gurney & Co. During the 1860s this bank, considered a pillar of the London finance, had advanced enormous sums to English railway companies and contractors, large and small, and when the bubble burst, Overend, Gurney crashed. The subsequent nationwide panic caused a 50 percent fall in the reserves of the Bank of England and drove the bank rate up to 10 percent. Numerous contractors went bankrupt, among them Sir Morton Peto, one of the leading British and international railway contractors, who had built the Canadian Grand Trunk Railway and whom Crommelin mentions in his diary. Undoubtedly he must have heard or read about the panic, which had its repercussions in America, but he fails to note it even once.[9]

Yet the business aspects recorded were certainly not the only reason for his trip. What seems to have interested him even more in the United States were public education, prisons, religion, and the governmental structure in general, including the impact of democracy. Crommelin is also keen on visiting the South and studying the plantation system in the wake of the abolition of slavery. He appears to have taken considerable pleasure in talking with plantation owners and their families about a range of subjects. An intense interest in technology and industrial enterprises is another facet of this broad-minded young man, who is always anxious to learn so much. At one point Crommelin mentions a congress (or convention) as one of the reasons for his journey, but he does not indicate what or where. In the end he failed to attend that gathering, and so it is difficult to be certain to what he referred.

Crommelin appears to have been fascinated with religion in America. He attends services in a number of churches, sometimes two or three on a single Sunday, and his comments are often amusing. His own religious background is not quite clear, although most of the Crommelin family members were traditionally raised in the Walloon Church in the Netherlands, a fairly liberal, French speaking branch of the old-established Dutch Reformed Church. It is clear that he abhorred popery, including the more traditional aspects of the Anglican Episcopal churches. The Unitarians, strong in New England, appear to have attracted him more with their sincerity and lack of empty convention. A good, solid sermon of preachers such as Henry Ward Beecher of Brooklyn appealed to him more than outward signs and the rigmarole of rites without any real meaning.

Why Crommelin kept his diary is unclear. It may have been merely personal, a help for his memory, jotting down the names of people he met and of institutions and industries he visited. On the other hand, he may have maintained his record, as so many contemporaries did, for possible publication at a later date. After all, in those years a stay of nearly a year in the United States was exceptional, even for an affluent Dutchman. Whatever the purpose, the diary never materialized in print, apart from a small section about his visit to St. Paul, Minnesota. Other Dutch travelers, but not many, had gone before him, but generally without publishing their experiences. A market for this kind of book did not yet exist on any scale in the Netherlands.[10]

Transatlantic travel in the time of Claude August Crommelin was not something undertaken lightly. It commonly involved acute discomfort and sometimes real danger. There was no regular shipping service between Holland and America, as the Holland America Line would not be founded until 1873. Dutch travelers chiefly used British lines from Liverpool. Crommelin was fortunate that he could afford a private first-class cabin on a modern Cunard Line vessel, the *Java*. Less-well-heeled travelers had to make do with cramped and frequently overcrowded quarters in steerage. And those hundreds of Dutch emigrants who had earlier taken ships to reach their new homes in the Midwest sought only to survive, and were neither inclined nor prepared to make journal entries.

A pleasant young man such as Claude August Crommelin, well-connected and with ample funds, interested in almost everything and able to discuss aspects of household problems, religious questions, and politics, was a welcome guest almost everywhere. He must have been fluent in English too, something unusual at that time, as most well-educated Dutchmen spoke French or German, but not English. Although he complained about his shyness, he mingled easily with some of the leading families in Boston, Charleston, Newport, New York City, and Washington. And there were distant relatives in many places: the Ludlows and Verplancks, De Bruyn Kops and Huydekopers. He also met old business acquaintances of his father's firm. Armed with letters of introduction, he found that these documents opened all doors of schools and prisons, locomotive works and other large industries. This reflected his almost universal interest in *everything* American. He encountered the new social elite of the Belmonts, Jeromes, and Vanderbilts, but never really got acquainted with them or with the leading older New York City families such as the Astors and the Roosevelts. Crommelin's interests were more literary and educational and not so much in the world of the self-styled "aristocrats" of Gotham. Yet he did get invited to Newport, Rhode Island, already a fashionable coastal summer resort for the rich, and he seems to have enjoyed the easygoing style of living among the community's young men and women of the upper classes. On the other hand, Crommelin encountered literary lights such as Longfellow, Dana, and Norton and had serious discussions with them about politics and other topics. He was an astute observer and a good listener, and he possessed a sharp wit. Crommelin's descriptions of persons and situations were always well considered and occasionally amusing.

In the United States, Crommelin used nearly every available means of transportation. And he traveled widely: from Savannah in the South to Newport in the North and St. Paul in the Northwest, plus a foray into Canada. His first choice seems to have been the railroad, but when no rail service was available, he went by river steamboat or by coastal steamer, and if necessary with a rented team of horses, as into the wilds of Minnesota. In his time a unified railroad network was not yet extant. Moreover, a number of lines were laid with widths different from the standard gauge of four feet, eight and one-half inches, and on long-distance runs that necessitated a change of cars. He never mentions these inconveniences, and he is generally positive about railroad travel, especially the comforts of the sleeping cars. In the South railroad traffic had been restored after a fashion directly after the end of the Civil War, but there remained disruptions. This may explain why Crommelin traveled from New York to Charleston and to Savannah by steamboat. However, he made the return trip by train in several days, with breaks in Richmond, Baltimore, and Washington.[11]

＊ ＊ ＊

Claude August Crommelin undertook his trip to the United States at an auspicious time. The year 1866 was a pivotal time in the nation's history. Americans had only recently ended a bloody civil conflict that had symbolized the triumph of the industrial North over the agrarian South. The War between the States (or officially the War of the Rebellion) began on April 12, 1861, when shore batteries under the command of General P. G. T. Beauregard opened fire on Fort Sumter in Charleston harbor, and lasted until the surrender of General Robert E. Lee to General Ulysses S. Grant in the McLean House at the village of Appomattox Courthouse, Virginia, on April 9, 1865. This conflict brought about massive death and destruction; approximately 620,000 Americans died in uniform, roughly the same number as those lost in all the other wars from the Revolution through the Korean Conflict. The Civil War bloodbath was a private as well as a public agony. Countless families lost fathers, sons, husbands, and brothers who fell in battle or died of wounds and disease. And tens of thousands of former soldiers and sailors carried lifelong scars, both physical and mental. Vast stretches of the South were laid to waste by advancing Union forces; markets for Southern-produced commodities, most of all cotton, became disrupted or permanently altered; and huge amounts of capital disappeared with the end of slavery, which freed from bondage nearly four million people. In November 1866 a South Carolina plantation owner described the awful state of affairs:

> Considering the prostrate, and almost hopeless condition of our country; our cities, churches, farm-houses, fences burned; our banks, railroad companies, and other institutions which held the savings of the old, the helpless, the orphans, &c., made bankrupt; a large portion of our most productive lands sequestered from their owners to the freemen; we are grievously taxed without representation; we have been left without food, or the means with which to purchase that which the harvests have failed to produce.[12]

Indeed, the former Confederate States of America became an economic backwater; it would take decades before the "New South" emerged. The overall economic plight of the South at war's end was deplorable, being far worse than that of central Europe in 1919 or 1945.[13]

The North, however, generally benefited from the Civil War. While there were serious economic dislocations, the conflict enhanced the power of the business community. Republican politicians, who gained power in 1861, embraced policies that aided industrialization that Southern lawmakers had successfully resisted for years. Wartime Congresses passed such supportive measures as the Tariff of 1862, the Pacific Railway Act, the Homestead Act, and the National Banking Act. The conflict also created fertile soil for an emerging generation of resourceful entrepreneurs, including such gifted men as Philip Armour, Andrew Carnegie, Jay Gould, J. P. Morgan, Sr., John D. Rockefeller, Gustavus Swift, and Frederick Weyerhauser. Collectively they seized opportunities to advance the business sector. This period became what economic historians Charles and Mary Beard saw as the "Second

American Revolution," the start of the powerful reign of "finance-industrial capitalism."[14]

Crommelin arrived at the dawn of federal reconstruction for the defeated Confederacy. President Andrew Johnson, a Tennessee Unionist who despised "stuck-up aristocrats," lacked the political skills and compassionate worldview of his predecessor, the martyred Abraham Lincoln. The nation suffered considerably from this obtuse, impolitic states-rightist, who in time faced impeachment and came within one vote of being removed from office. A few months before Crommelin arrived from Holland, the former Confederate states had organized new governments, ratified the Thirteenth Amendment that abolished slavery, and elected senators and representatives to Congress. But there was a growing rift between Johnson and Republican Radicals, led by Thaddeus Stevens in the House of Representatives and Benjamin Wade in the Senate. These men of goodwill wished to protect ex-slaves from exploitation and to guarantee their basic civil rights. Johnson opposed the Radicals and applauded passage in Southern states of the so-called Black Codes that restricted the legal rights of people of color, including prohibitions on bearing arms and limitation of employment opportunities to only farming and domestic service. Although not all Northern Republicans embraced the Stevens-Wade perspectives, there was support for expanding the duties of the Freedmen's Bureau, a branch of the U.S. War Department that had been created in March 1865. The proposal was hoped to protect the right of blacks rather than merely caring for war refugees. Johnson vetoed the bill. Congress then responded with the Civil Rights Act, which declared specifically that people of color were citizens of the United States and denied states the power to restrict their rights to testify in court, to make contracts for their labor, and to own property. Here was a measure that put teeth in the Thirteenth Amendment. But Johnson again refused to grant his approval, and on April 9, 1866, Congress re-passed the legislation by a two-thirds majority, marking the first time that a major bill became law over the veto of a president. After this bitter fight, Congress, not the president, gained the upper hand with federal reconstruction of the South.[15]

During Crommelin's visit, more historic legislation took place in Washington, D.C. In June 1866 Congress submitted to the states a new amendment to the U.S. Constitution. This would become the famed Fourteenth Amendment. The proposal featured a broad definition of citizenship: "All persons born or naturalized in the United States and subject to the jurisdiction thereof, are citizens of the United States and of the State wherein they reside." It also struck at discriminatory laws such as the Black Codes: "No State shall make or enforce any law which shall abridge the privileges or immunities of citizens of the United States; nor shall any State deprive any person of life, liberty, or property without due process." And the amendment contained other pro-black features, including an attempt to force Southern states to permit ex-slaves to vote. After much debate the Fourteenth Amendment became part of the Constitution in 1868.[16]

Yet as Crommelin saw, a utopia for blacks was hardly developing. Stripped of their slaves, planters responded with alternative labor plans. The task system, under which workers were assigned daily tasks, the completion of which ended their responsibilities for the day, grew in importance in the rice regions of Georgia and South Carolina, and sharecropping, in which a black family worked for "shares" of the crop, was emerging rapidly throughout the Cotton Belt. This system guaranteed planters a stable resident labor force, and former slaves liked it because it allowed them to work without close white supervision and generated income that they could spend as they pleased. In time, though, sharecropping became more oppressive and severely limited opportunities for greater personal income through agricultural diversification. Blacks, like poor whites, found themselves trapped in the "crop-lien system," where the local storekeeper or "furnishing merchant" controlled their economic lives.[17]

The general impressions that Crommelin recorded mesh generally with those of a number of Northern journalists who toured the South, especially the coastal states, following the war. As Sidney Andrews, a reporter for the *Boston Advertiser* and *Chicago Tribune,* indicated, the Union may have been preserved, yet ex-rebels continued to dominate and expressed intense resentment toward former slaves, Southern unionists, and most of all Northern Yankees, especially those who lived in their midst. It also became apparent that Southerners took a new position of the conflict: the South had not fought for slavery; rather, it had fought for states' rights, constitutional government, and honor.[18]

In conversations with Americans, Crommelin detected much that annoyed, and often angered, them. Taxation was one matter that troubled the upper middle class and the well-to-do. Although everyone realized that the fight to protect the Union would be costly, some wartime tax measures caused resentment, including a 10 percent federal tax on state bank notes instituted as a provision of the National Banking Act. A center for tax discontent, especially after war's end, was the state and city of New York. "The National, State, County and City tax levies are at length spread before the people and a most suggestive sight they present," observed the *New York Times* in April 1867. "The 4,000,000 of people throughout the State are charged with a burden of $100,000,000—a formidable sum if every citizen were compelled to pay a proportion, but excessive when levied upon the comparatively few who are subject to taxation." Real-estate millage levies were already high, particularly in New York City, and increases were expected in order to prevent "ugly deficiencies" in governmental operations. And there were pressing needs for new betterments throughout the Empire state, including roads, public buildings, and the like. Here was a topic that was near and dear to Crommelin's own academic interests.[19]

While it is not a universal axiom of politics in America, there have been periods of moral breakdown following a war. The textbook example of such a situation came in the decade or so following the Civil War. Crommelin sensed correctly that ethical scruples at times were being tossed aside. His Calvinist sensibilities were bothered by some upper-class men and women being unfaithful to their marriage vows, although acts of adultery have been timeless. If he were to have remained longer in the country, he would have read or heard about the efforts of financiers Jim Fisk and Jay Gould to manipulate the stock of the Erie Railroad and to corner the nation's gold supply, Boss Tweed's reckless and dishonest ways as head of the all-powerful Tammany Hall in New York City, and the scandals associated with the Crédit Mobilier construction company of the Union Pacific Railroad that sullied the record of Western railroad financing. This was what historian Ray Ginger aptly labeled "The Age of Excess." Americans, moreover, were tired of great causes: the crusade against slavery, the crusade to maintain the federal union and the crusade to reconstruct the South. The strong feeling for reform and uplift had diminished generally, and would not return until the rise and development of the Alliance and Populist movements in the 1880s and 1890s. The post–Civil War years were very much a time of cynicism.[20]

※ ※ ※

After Claude August Crommelin returned to the Netherlands in 1867, he settled down to a career in law as a solicitor in Amsterdam. In that same year he became a member of the city council of his home town, and in 1868 he also became a member of the Provincial Government of North Holland. He was a liberal, but little is known about his duties or legislative records. He also was active in a number of cultural organizations in Amsterdam, serving on the boards of the Academy of Fine Arts, the Museum Fodor, and the literature section of Felix Meritis, the famous eighteenth-century society of arts and sciences. His compassion for the sick and the indigent found expression in his membership of the boards of the Children's Hospital and of two building societies that provided affordable housing for low-income workers. He also belonged to the founders of the Stoomvaart Maatschappij Nederland, a company organized to operate regular steam-shipping lines from Amsterdam to the Dutch East Indies. Crommelin never married, although he was certainly interested in the opposite sex, as revealed in several of his diary entries. This active Dutchman almost lost his heart, as he confessed, to an attractive teacher in one of the public schools in New York City.

Yet, although outwardly a successful young man with a bright future before him, he was known to suffer from frequent and severe depressions. After an after-

In 1865 Claude August Crommelin relaxes with his dog in front of the door to his "photographic laboratory" that he had built in the backyard of his Amsterdam house, Keizersgracht 132. The iron and glass structure was designed by a young architect, J. Gosschalk, who later became famous for his railway station at Groningen. The laboratory still stands, but it is in dilapidated condition. The reconstruction of this rare example of an early photographic studio has been proposed.   Liesbeth Crommelin Coll.

noon of vehement discussion in the Amsterdam City Council on November 4, 1874, about the future of the North Sea Canal Company, then constructing a ship canal to connect the port of Amsterdam with the North Sea, Crommelin was unhappy with the way the burgomaster and aldermen handled the complicated negotiations with the national government and canal company. With others, he advanced a motion to better protect the financial interests of the city in this respect. A majority of the council supported his motion, and after much altercation the alderman responsible stepped down. Because of the advanced hour the burgomaster then closed the session. That same night or early the next morning in the park outside the Willemspoort of Amsterdam Crommelin shot himself. A passing worker found his body the next morning, and his death was recorded officially as having occurred on November 5, 1874. A possible connection between the affairs in the city council and Crommelin's suicide, however, must remain conjectural.[21]

Crommelin had lived in an enormous, stately house on one of Amsterdam's best canals, Heerengracht 132, a structure dating to 1614 and originally named De Profeet Jonas. As an enthusiastic amateur photographer he had his own laboratory, constructed of cast iron and glass, located in his back yard, something rare at that time. He also collected watercolors, a new art form that became much *en vogue* in the nineteenth century. His collection was probably of some importance. A British art collector, Lord Ronald Gower, included Crommelin's holdings in his 1875 publication *Handbook to the Art Galleries, Public and Private, of Belgium and Holland*. Gower especially notes that Crommelin had a large number of drawings and oil paintings by Charles Rochussen, then still relatively unknown, in his collection. According to Gower, Crommelin was one of the first to recognize the outstanding quality of Rochussen's work. Even before Gower published his handbook, however, Crommelin had died and his collection had been bequeathed to his cousin Robert Daniel Crommelin (1841–1907), a naval officer later turned banker, and his wife Julie Elisabeth Tutein Nolthenius, whom we have met before. The later fate of this collection is unknown.[22]

Possibly as a way to thank their cousin posthumously, Robert Daniel and Julie Elisabeth named their son, born in 1878, Claude August Crommelin (1878–1965). This young Claude August was educated as a scientist at Leiden University, where he studied under the supervision of Professor Heike Kamerlingh Onnes (1853–1926). Kamerlingh Onnes was the one who, in 1908, for the first time ever reached absolute zero, and this triumph was greatly assisted by Crommelin, a master in the design and fabrication of the necessary complicated laboratory equipment.[23]

The fellow traveler of diary-keeper Crommelin, Meder, is difficult to place. He was not part of the English experience, but was on board ship between Liverpool and New York. In the United States Meder is mentioned occasionally as a companion, but his relationship with Crommelin remains unclear. Probably this Meder was Jacques Hessel Meder (born 1829), who immigrated to America in 1855 and is listed as a merchant. He may well have been a business contact of Daniel Crommelin & Sons or the successor firm, Tutein Nolthenius & De Haan. This would explain the relationship between the two men. However this might be, it is obvious that in America the two often went their own ways, Crommelin sometimes in the company of Hendrik de Marez Oyens, a young man from another Amsterdam business and financial family, with ample contacts in the United States.[24]

✳ ✳ ✳

The writings of the extended American visit of Claude August Crommelin did not vanish with his death. Fortunately this version of the manuscript was found in the Minnesota Historical Society in St. Paul; it consists of ninety-one typewritten pages in standard format, with a heading in ink: "Reis naar N. Amerika door Mr. Claude August Crommelin, Amsterdam geb. 1 m.ʳ 1840, † 4 nov. 1874." The provenance is uncertain, and it is not known who typed the original manuscript, as written by Crommelin himself. Of course, there were no typewriters in

Crommelin's day. The original Dutch text of Crommelin is remarkably modern, sometimes written in only key words, at other times in flowing sentences in faultless Dutch, but without the unnecessary verbiage that is so often found in mid-nineteenth-century manuscripts. Crommelin inserted many English words and expressions in his Dutch diary, and in the present translation these are reproduced between single quotation marks. Sometimes he also quotes his American friends literally, and these lines are given between double quotation marks. The person who prepared the typed text had a fairly good knowledge of Dutch, but he or she had difficulties now and then with the handwriting. Some names and words were garbled or left blank. There are emendations and additions in ink to be found in the margins, unknown by whom, but probably not made by the same individual who typed the text. The last page or pages of the original diary were already missing when the typescript was created. Yet these missing entries are minor; after all, Crommelin was preparing for his return trip.[25]

A carbon copy of the Crommelin typescript is located in the Rotterdam City Archives. And it is the same, incomplete text and the same early typescript. But there is an indication of the origin of this particular copy. With that Rotterdam document is found a letter from a Claude A. Crommelin to a Mr. Dutilh, dated February 6, 1979, and written from 750 Mount Paran Road, N.W., in Atlanta, Georgia. This third Claude August Crommelin (1919–1985), son of the Claude August Crommelin of Leiden University, mentioned earlier, writes Dutilh that he discovered the typewritten version of the diary when going through family papers after his father's death in 1965. Since no one in his family apparently cared about the typescript, the younger Crommelin sent it to Dutilh, who already had heard about it through a common relative, a Mrs. De Kanter. Who this particular Dutilh was remains unclear, but the Dutilh family is well known in Rotterdam banking and shipping circles. That Dutilh had actually read the typescript becomes clear from the small penciled crosses in the margins of the Rotterdam copy wherever Crommelin mentions the Dutilhs whom he had met in New York. With the death of the third Claude August Crommelin at Ponta Vedra Beach, Florida, in 1985, all family papers, portraits, and other documents in his possession have disappeared.[26]

Another penciled note on the first page of the Rotterdam copy, not present in the Minnesota copy, suggests an indication of the fate of the original handwritten diary. This inscription says: "compared with the original" and signed "RTN." Now the history of the Crommelin diary becomes somewhat less of a puzzle. The RTN is undoubtedly the Amsterdam engineer and financier Rudolph P. J. Tutein Noltenius, scion of the Tutein Noltenius family and related to the Crommelins. It was Tutein Nolthenius & De Haan that had taken over the assets of Daniel Crommelin & Sons when that firm was liquidated in 1859. In the Amsterdam

City Archives is also a faded carbon copy of the same typewritten text that is kept among the papers of the firm of Daniel Crommelin & Sons, and bound in a volume of other papers by this same R. P. J. Tutein Nolthenius. He was heavily involved in American railroads, foremost of all in the 1890s with Arthur Stilwell's Kansas City, Pittsburg, & Gulf Railroad (later Kansas City Southern Railway). Apparently when Rudolph Tutein Nolthenius saw the typescript, he still had access to the handwritten diary, hence his remark "compared with the original" in the Rotterdam copy. But some problems remain. In the Amsterdam carbon copy is another penciled note by this same R. P. J. Tutein Nolthenius, written at La Tour de Peilz, Vaud, Switzerland, and dated March 1930, saying that the original, consisting of six exercise books, is now in the hands of Dr. C. A. Crommelin, keeper of the Natural Science Cabinet of Leiden University, undoubtedly the same Crommelin associated with Professor Kamerlingh Onnes. How and where Rudolph Tutein Nolthenius had seen the original is nowhere mentioned by him, and so the mystery continues. It might be possible that the exercise books ended up in the hands of the C. A. Crommelin of Atlanta, son of the scientist, who wrote to Mr. Dutilh of Rotterdam in 1979, although in his letter he only refers to the carbon copy and not the original manuscript.[27]

Irrespective of the fate of the Crommelin exercise books and how exactly the typescripts came to be made, this outstanding commentary about the United States in 1866 and 1867 has survived. No other work by a bright and well-connected resident of the Netherlands, who did so much at such a critical moment in American history, has been translated, published, and edited. This diary is an authentic document. As the explanatory notes reveal, it is possible to identify most of the people, places, and events recorded by this remarkable "Young Dutchman in America."[28]

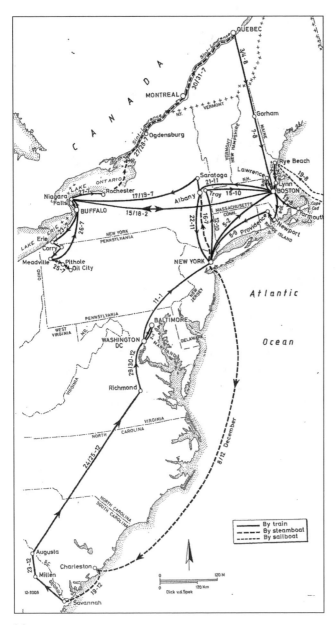

Map 1.

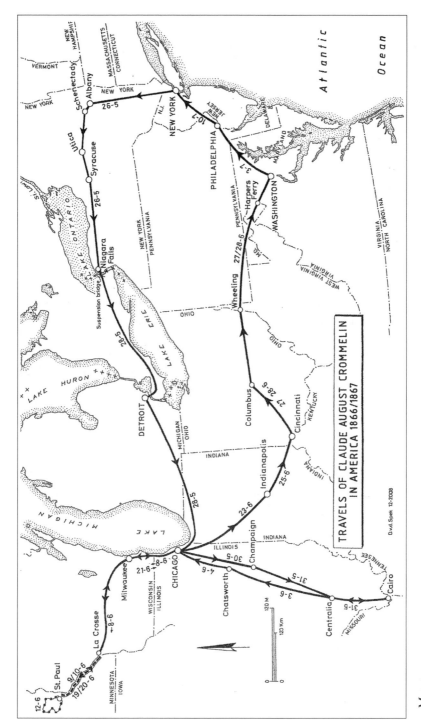

TRAVELS OF CLAUDE AUGUST CROMMELIN
IN AMERICA 1866/1867

D.v.d.Spek 12-2008

Map 2.

1

From Amsterdam through Belgium and Great Britain to New York

April–May 1866

TUESDAY 17 APRIL 1866

Amsterdam to Brussels. Stopped at Delft at 3 pm to see Adr. Huet and his drawings of machinery. Big wall spreads drawn in color, but also simple black and white drawings. His favorites, however, are big drawings in color of American steam engines, especially machinery for ships and railway locomotives, the bigger the better. Illustrated catalogs, monographs about machines, issues of journals and magazines, also photographs of machines and their details.[1]

WEDNESDAY 18 APRIL 1866

Brussels, Hotel de Flandre. City Museum; Dutch and Flemish painters well represented, the Italians less so, although they have a few good ones by Paul Veronese and Guido. Excellent Jan Steens, one a very big one, probably depicting the winning of a wager: one man is seen coming in while dancing with a herring in his hand; another is a Twelfth Day, perfect. A large Rembrandt, a beautiful Nicolaes Maes, a woman eating, with very good light effects, but darkened by age and dirt at the edges, as with most others. Two small Karl Dujardins, one, a herd of cows driven along a road, was very good. A large number of Rubenses, most very crowded with too many personages and therefore confusing. Panels by Van Eyck.[2]

Burial of Baron van der Lynden d'Hooghvorst, *général-en-chef de toutes les gardes civiques de Belgique,* former member of the provisional government of 1830. I didn't see much of it because of the crowd. Pallbearers were Rogier, Van den Peereboom, Chasal, and one other dignitary.[3]

In the afternoon a session of the Chamber of Representatives, reports and minor laws, nothing of any importance. Bara spoke, but—at least for me—unintelligible.

The interest from the side of the public seems to be greater here than with us. Even on a day such as this with few interesting things being discussed, both public galleries were packed.[4]

In the evening at the Urbans and a little excursion to the Théatre du Parc: *Le supplice d'un homme,* a parody of the play by De Girardin, a good performance, well played and most amusing.[5]

THURSDAY 19 APRIL 1866

Spent the day with the Urbans, dinner with Adam Becquet and his wife and a certain monsieur Gausset, a typical old bachelor.[6]

FRIDAY 20 APRIL 1866

Started for London at 7.15 am. Calais-Dover in two hours, with a lot of movement of the ship. Traveled Dover-London in the company of an American, an Englishman, and a regular braggart. [The latter] came from the races, and boasted about his acquaintance with Lord Stamford. He talked like this: "Jim, Lord Stamford said to me, for he knows me well, I say do this or that" etc. He then produced a deck of cards and immediately cheated our American companion out of 20 or 25 shillings. After that and until our arrival in London my three companions played a game of shortwhist, but I was wise enough to keep out of that. I couldn't get a room in Charing Cross Hotel, so I went to De Keyzer's Royal Hotel, Blackfriars.[7]

SATURDAY 21 APRIL 1866

To Morris, Prevost & Co., and fairly well received by one of the younger partners. The others were all out. Saw the Houses of Parliament, and they made the same impression on me as ten years ago. The St. Stephen's Crypt under the old St. Stephen's Chapel has been restored magnificently. Dinner at Simpson's, Hyde Park. To Her Majesty's, £1—1 sh. for an orchestra stall. *Fidelio* performed by Titien and Gardoni. The first named I liked much but didn't think she is a real great star of the first rank. The second still had a very lovely voice and is clearly a most experienced singer, but without any power left; in one word he is old. Her Majesty's is built with boxes all around, in places six stories over each other, and provided with yellow curtains. They are all counted as most fashionable. Hardly any lovely face among the audience, wherever I looked, and not that freshness that is so often mentioned. Many scarlet 'sorties' with blue gowns, after the latest fashion.[8]

SUNDAY 22 APRIL 1866

To Hampton Court, by the 10:30 am from Waterloo station. Arrived around 11:15 and was pleasantly surprised by a notice: "The rooms are opened at two. You may take a walk in the park first." In the park no smoking allowed. Beautiful lanes with elms leading through vast lawns, but everything fenced off with a very long and expensive iron railing. All accessible grounds are well kept and neat. Pretty yew trees, some old ones changed into ivy trees that have killed off the original tree. The views of the Thames from the long terrace are lovely, especially on a day as this, with real English Spring weather, a bit hazy. The river full of gigs, typically English, willows, glassy pools, beautiful meadows, etc. Vinery, but prettier glyditzia, pert girls behind a fence, stroll in Bushy Park with its beautiful chestnut lanes. At two the rooms opened at long last, but a new deception. Awful lighting, horribly neglected paintings, and the cartoons gone to South Kensington Museum, I was told by a guard. There were a few good pieces, however, a couple of Denners (*Age and Youth*), Murillo, a fine Rembrandt, but the large number of older Italians, Pordenone, Palma, etc., hardly ever arouse my admiration. Dinner at the King's Arms: "Notice the seven splendid elms before the gate." Back by train: "No smoking on the platform, Sir."[9]

MONDAY 23 APRIL 1866

To Morris, Prevost & Co., who told me laconically that it would be impossible this week to obtain a pass for Parliament and that they were not going to try to get me one. I hope that they will get me passes for the bank and the docks, but they are slow and not very cooperative. At their place I also understood that Buckingham Palace is not open to the public at the moment. Always these disappointments! Bridgewater Gallery closed too, "the countess being dead in the house." They are stricter anyhow, because a Van der Velde was stolen there last year. Buckingham Palace is always open to the public when the queen is out of town, only not now. The same happened to me twice in Brussels with the Musée Wiertz and Arenberg [Galeries], out of luck every time. The other galleries in London are open only with permission of the owners, and these permissions are hard to get, of course.[10]

From there to the South Kensington Museum, only partly open because of a major rebuilding and everything only on view in temporary locations. There are several sections, and the chief aim of the museum is the development of the artistic sense of the people, and to apply this sense first of all in the field of industry. The same intentions as those of the *Société des Beaux Arts appliqués à l'Industrie* in Paris. Many art classes have been set up by the South Kensington Museum all over the country and with good results.

What interested me most was the painting gallery, with one exception all of English artists. One is able to get a good understanding of painters like Sir Joshua Reynolds, West, Sir Thomas Lawrence, Sir David Wilkie, Landseer, and others with many different works of them. I liked Sir Joshua Reynolds very much; his well-known young *Samuel* is a pretty piece of work, as are others such as *The Age of Innocence.* But most of them are in a terrible condition, yellowed and cracked and badly preserved; a couple by Sir Lawrence are in the same condition. *Study of Lady Hamilton as a Bacchante* by Romney. Lee's landscapes are very good and many portraits by Lawrence excellent. I liked Wilkie too, especially his *Parish Beadle.* But generally these genre paintings give me little satisfaction, although the English seem to be mad about them. Moreover, many are hard to see as they are behind glass. Apparently someone is trying with an excess of care to make good the many years of neglect.[11]

The greatest treasures of the museum, however, are the cartoons by Raphael, transferred here from Hampton Court last year to get them out of the bad lighting there. They are too well known to describe them here, and too beautiful to dwell long upon them. Only this: the drawing is here very broad and powerful as with Michelangelo, while Raphael, as far as I have seen his works, usually excels in softness and round shapes. The same is visible in his *Transfiguration.* Does this show the characteristics of his third style?[12]

Walked around a bit in Pall Mall and St. James Park, bought some photographs of Mrs. Cameron at Colnaghi's, dined at Simpson's, and then home.[13]

TUESDAY 24 APRIL 1866

Visited with Dalmeyer, chiefly to see the beautiful photographs by Robinson that he has in his possession. *Bringing Home the May,* a composition by Robinson, is a real work of art, not only from the photographic point of view, but also as a composition, really worth a painter! I saw so many good examples of the work of the New Group Lens that I think that I will bring some of their products home on my way back.[14]

After that I went to Thomas Baring's Picture Gallery. I had obtained a very friendly worded permission from him and I was amazed that, contrary to what I had expected, I was left alone in most of the rooms, something that surprised me in London. Did I have to thank my name for this? The mansion is lovely, particularly a back room with a view of a conservatory with nice statues. The paintings were a bit disappointing, but a Both over the fireplace in the back room, two Jan Steens, one a guitar playing man and the other a sick woman in bed with the doctor prescribing his drugs, while a child is playing with the symbol of the apothecaries, are very good. A beautiful Metsu, a bride just getting into bed while her husband is entering the room. But best of all were three Greuzes, especially one, a girl's head, a thing to steal.[15]

Zoological Gardens; the refreshment room pleased me most. To H. P. Robinson, the famous photographer, 68 Winwood House, Canonbury Park South. He received me very friendly, had been in business in Leamington in the old days, but was now retired. I saw a lot of beautiful things at his place.[16]

WEDNESDAY 25 APRIL 1866

British Museum. The Elgin Marbles and the Assyrian monuments are the most interesting.

THURSDAY 26 APRIL 1866

Visited the bank. The exterior of such an institution has little character of its own, but impresses the passerby nevertheless, a nice thought.

Dulwich Gallery in Dulwich. The situation of Dulwich, in the midst of parks and beautiful country houses, is most pleasant. The gallery of paintings, collected for the last king of Poland, but never delivered because of the partition of that country and left in the hands of the collector and later donated to Dulwich College, contains a large number of excellent works. I thought the best piece to be *Saint John the Baptist* by Guido Reni, an excellent work in every respect. Power, truth, the expression in the eyes of the subject, superb drawing, everything is there. I was especially struck by the freshness of the colors, a thing most unusual for Guido Reni. In all his other works the coloring of human flesh resembles a deadly pallor, something I have always thought to be discoloration caused by age, but this Saint John has given me food for doubt. The *S. Sabastiano* after his usual manner, is as far as I know, a copy of the one in the Louvre. Two Murillos, one a flower girl, the other two Spanish boys, both excellent, well conceived, graciously executed, with a fine tone and pleasant lighting. Also a very pretty waterfall by Ruysdael, fine Van der Veldes, and last but not least a servant girl by Rembrandt himself, certainly one of his best works.[17]

Walked to the Crystal Palace, but was disappointed; it didn't impress me as much as it had done in 1856. The lack of height in the building is something I don't like. Home by train.[18]

FRIDAY 27 APRIL 1866

I had planned to visit the National Gallery as the last item on my sightseeing list for London, but to my great disappointment it turned out that today it was open only to artists. I had to find something else to do in the oppressive spring heat, so I walked to Westminster Abbey. Here I was not disappointed; it is a beautiful gothic edifice, very imposing because of its sheer height when compared to its width. Henry VII's chapel, built in perpendicular style according to my Baedeker, struck me most. The walls are vertical and carry a heavy stone roof, which lies flat and square on the top without any supporting arch to speak of. The roof itself is made up completely of finely chiseled rosettes, most of them with a central pendant. How such a weight can be carried in this way is incomprehensible. A very bold style, but yet it gives an impression of lightness and grace. The monuments didn't strike me much. Curiosities such as these may look nice from a distance, but close by I don't feel anything or hardly anything for them. In the past I liked them better, maybe too much at an early age, and that may be the cause that they don't move me anymore. Or is it that I don't know enough of the persons or places depicted? Who knows?

In the evening to the Lyceum, where I saw Fechter as Hamlet, that is, in the first three parts, because I had to leave early. I don't believe that Hamlet can ever be performed better and more dignified. Here the figure of Hamlet is very different from the usual personality. Fechter is heavily built, with long blonde, almost reddish, hair, and he has nothing of the gushing, almost ecstatic character that is so often seen in Hamlet. Generally, I am inclined to say, he is more simple, less histrionic than most others who venture to impersonate Hamlet. In masterly style he manages to avoid the stressing of those universally known lines that always arouse so many bravos in the audience. His emphasis is always different, and by that he even changes the sentence now and then. I would compare him to Ristori, and the others whom I saw, for instance Davison and Devrient, can be put together in league with Rachel. It has been said of her that her real art was visible in a few lines only, and that she treated the rest of her text lightly, but that Ristori paid attention to every small detail and thereby achieved a more complete work of art, close to the essential elements of a play. Fechter changed and rearranged a lot in his Hamlet, and I can't explain why an English audience has approved of that. The entry of Hamlet, for instance, when the king lies on his knees in prayer, was completely left out. The settings were very well done and beautiful, but the other actors less so. Ophelia was too fat and not very pleasing.[19]

SATURDAY 28 APRIL 1866

While I had been looking forward to enjoying the fine spring weather outside the London hustle and smoke, I was very disappointed to see the dark skies and feel the first few raindrops coming down on the day of my departure. Shortly after leaving Paddington Station it really started to rain in earnest, it got colder and colder, and I had the doubtful pleasure to understand that all my ideas of spending some beautiful spring days in the lush English countryside of Derbyshire and Warwickshire had just been illusions. In driving rain I got out of the train at Oxford, and under heavy showers I crisscrossed through that old university town, "very disconsolately." As my visit was on a Saturday afternoon, I had entertained visions of young men rowing or playing cricket, but today everybody was inside, and only now and then I had a glimpse of some tutor or undergraduate crossing a quadrangle. Everything was grey and gloomy, with only a six-man gig and a lone rower in a wherry on the river. I admired the latter, for braving the rain with seven men is something, but all alone, brrr![20]

With nothing better to do, but also moved by some interest, I went to the Cathedral at 4 pm. This is also the chapel of Christchurch College and it was a real High Church service. Dr. Pusey is one of the deans of Christchurch. Everything was being sung by a choir; even the parts read were set to the tune of psalms and chanted with vigor, with the result that I couldn't understand a single word. Continuous kneeling and standing up, much more so than I remembered from earlier services I attended. With the Credo the congregation turned to the right making all to face the altar, bowing deep at some stages in the prayer. Isn't that popery in its most complete form?[21]

Cold and in a bad mood I arrived in Warwick, but was consoled by my stay in a typical old English inn. In the evening I had a long talk with my host in front of the fire in the barroom.[22]

Sunday 29 April 1866

Warwick Castle and Kenilworth are closed to the public, as it is Sunday. To cheer up I am driven to Stratford on Avon through the Siberian cold in an open carriage, less so for the lions, which are not worth the trouble, but to see the countryside. I don't see the country at its best because of the gloomy and cold weather, but it seems to be lovely. Lucy's Park is very beautiful and interesting because of its connection with Shakespeare, even more so as it is still in the possession of the Lucys. How important those entails are! It should be very interesting to rummage about in such a house, for three or four centuries in one and the same family. In snow and rain I am driven back. The best part of the afternoon I stay in the hotel and write letters.[23]

Monday 30 April 1866

Luckily Warwick Castle is open today, although the doorman frightens me by saying, "They don't fancy to take single gentlemen over the house, only take parties." But I do get in nevertheless. Through the ages the title and the castle have been in the hands of many families. The title has been in the Beauchamp, Neville, Plantagenet, Dudley, Rich, and Greville families. The last but one never had possession of the house, which had been owned by the Grevilles since the days of James II. They got the title too when the Rich family died out in 1759. Moreover they are also earls Brooke. It is most curious to see how such a collection of curiosities and valuables has been brought together by the several families, all after the fashions and tastes of the times and the owners. The monetary value of all these things together is impossible to express in present-day money. Nowhere in the world, not even in royal palaces, did I see such a collection of really valuable things together. A vast collection of Van Dycks is gracing the walls all around, and his portrait of Charles I on horseback is without any doubt one of the best of the master. A table inlaid with mosaics was said to be worth £10,000. Guy's Cliff not visible. St. Mary's Church. To Matlock.[24]

TUESDAY 1 MAY 1866

It is May today, but the weather doesn't look like it. It is penetrating cold and snowing continuously. They even say that this night it was 11 degrees below zero, but I take the liberty to doubt that. Despite this bad weather I travel to Chatsworth, although with many misgivings about the sensibility of this plan. The snow keeps falling, and the idea of visiting a country house under those circumstances is not very cheerful. At Rowsley—the railway station—I meet a lady and gentleman with the same expedition in mind, and together we are driven in an omnibus to Chatsworth. We are received by the porter, an archetypical servant of a great English family. After a short wait we are admitted and allowed to walk through the whole building, almost a royal residence in its splendor. The treasures of art that have been accumulated by the different dukes of Devonshire are stunning indeed. Best of all, however, is the collection of several hundreds of drawings of old masters, all hung behind glass in a well-lit gallery. The statuary in another gallery is also worth being seen and contains many good pieces. The orangery, greenhouses, and conservatory, constructed by Sir Joseph Paxton, make a big impression on me, despite the horrible weather today. All through the year some 50 men are being kept busy in the grounds. The present duke is a widower and still young, but he hardly ever resides here.[25]

Back to Matlock in the afternoon and to Manchester in the evening, where I met Th. Huet, who took me first to Alexandra Hall, a kind of *café chantant,* where we saw the end of a ballet, and later to a *divan.* I met Barge and the brother of Bake.[26]

WEDNESDAY 2 MAY 1866

Walked around a bit, but the downpour made that definitely unpleasant. In the afternoon to Rochdale to see the Cooperative Spinning Mill. I had obtained an introduction for Mr. Gord, whom I found at the station. He drove me to the mill and was my guide all through that enormous factory, one of the biggest and most profitable of the whole kingdom. To what extent the cooperative principle is being applied here was not quite clear to me. The work was definitely not being executed along those lines, and what would remain is an ordinary limited company of which the shares may be in the hands of the workers. More probable, however, is this: my guide told me that the board of the factory is made up of the same people as that of the Equitable Pioneers. This, with other facts that I heard, makes me think that the cotton mill is simply an investment of the enormous capital of the

Equitable Pioneers, and that the profits of the mill are just passed on to the members of that association. Although for administrative reasons the business is being conducted under the name Cooperative Manufactories Society Ltd., this seems to me the most logical explanation. Despite my taciturn guide, I could obtain a fairly good idea of how the spinning was done here. If I understood him correctly every thread is being handled seven times in different operations, but these are repeated over and over again, altogether 430 times, before the thread is ready for weaving.[27]

In the evening in the Theatre Royal: *Family Jars* was not badly performed and was worth being seen as an example of a real good English farce.[28]

THURSDAY 3 MAY 1866

By express train to Liverpool in one hour. Brown, Van Santen & Co.[29]

FRIDAY 4 MAY 1866

Been on board the *Java* and inspected my cabin. Birkenhead Park, concert in St. George's Hall, Parssa and the Chatham's Engineers Band.[30]

SATURDAY 5 MAY 1866

On board.

SUNDAY 6 MAY 1866

At sea. Over a glassy sea, in full view of the snow-capped mountains of Wales, we float over the Irish Sea and arrive early in the morning before Queenstown. After some cruising out at sea we enter the harbor to pick up the last mail for America, which arrives only at 4 pm, and so gives us a quiet afternoon. Some of the passengers go to Cork; I remain in my cabin to write letters that will be mailed in the afternoon. Not far from our moorings two of the biggest ironclads of the Royal Navy are anchored, the *Warrior* and the *Black Prince,* probably because of the Fenians. Around 4 pm the tender comes along with the last mail, and as soon as this is transferred we put on steam and soon the European coast is disappearing from view. I am not unduly worried by that, but the fear of seasickness weighs heavily on my mind. And, of course, I think about my journey. Is it prudent, and am I not sacrificing too much in the hope of acquiring some imaginary benefits? But it is too late now for such thoughts, and the only thing I can do is to follow my fate, execute my plans, and hope for the best. I am still young enough to reform some traits of my character and overcome, at least partly, my shyness and customary silence in the presence of others. *Utinam ita sit!*[31]

On leaving the harbor of Queenstown we soon feel the waves of the ocean, although the first night is still fairly smooth. The next day—Monday—the movement really starts and continues all through the journey until Friday. Then the conversation of the passengers chiefly concerns the rolling and pitching of the vessel and which one of the two is worse. On deck I don't care and I even like to see a big wave coming on and rolling away under the ship. But in the cabin, stupidly enough placed at the stern of the ship over the screw, both movements are a real nuisance, chiefly because of the impossibility of eating soup and drinking tea and coffee decently. Fortunately I am not troubled at all by seasickness and suffer this little unpleasantness gladly and enjoy the voyage. One morning with heavy seas I liked best, as I could get a true idea of being at sea. The head wind we had was the chief cause of the movement of the ship, and a screw steamer is always worse than a paddle steamer in this respect. We didn't see much of the wonders of the ocean, a lone dolphin at a distance perhaps, but no whales, no icebergs, nothing. Few ships too, only one now and then, maybe altogether not more than five or six. The last days the sea was smooth, and Saturday and Sunday were beautiful pleasant days. Fog on Monday, which lifted only toward the evening.[32]

I didn't get to know my fellow passengers very well, thanks to my nature. Sometimes small talk here and there, that was about all. Only one young man, who had studied at German academies for a year, did attract me. I don't even know his name, but he had a very intelligent face and was the first American who spoke with some common sense about America and American society, without straightaway breaking into praise for his country. On the contrary, he is somber about the future, largely due to the enormous corruption everywhere. I met also a New Yorker, who had traveled a year in Europe, and with whom I was on speaking terms. He was a good little man, who befriended my companion Meder chiefly, but who made himself useful by telling us a lot about New York.

WEDNESDAY 16 MAY 1866

In the morning at six everybody was on deck to see land for the first time after ten days. The coast of New Jersey was the first to come into view, with the contours of the Nevisink Hills giving some shape to the otherwise very flat and monotonous coast. Long Island appears as a low line, and on coming closer Staten Island is raised and offers a pretty sight.[33]

The fear of a possible quarantine is alive among the passengers as the cholera has been brought to America by several ships from Europe, but it seems to be under control now. We are anxiously waiting for the arrival of the health officer. After a long wait he turns up, "in a most undignified way," steering his own launch, in civilian clothes without any marks of his office, and with a large cigar in his mouth. Fortunately our health on board is in order, and he at once gives us permission to proceed. While we were lying by waiting for him, we had plenty of time to observe an emigrant ship and a large French steam frigate of war, that had come in just after us. In the North River we were kept anchored on stream because for some reason or other the *Java* could not enter the piers. A tender came alongside to transfer passengers and baggage, which took a long time, and we did not arrive at the Custom House but after noon. The inspection of the baggage was somewhat cursory, and after a short wait we were allowed to leave by omnibus or hotel hack to our Fifth Avenue Hotel (fare $2 each passenger [$29 in 2009 dollars]). Early to bed, as I was tired of all this activity.[34]

2

In New York City and Westward to Chicago

May 1866

THURSDAY 17 MAY 1866

Coming down in the morning I met young Oyens at once, who had come to meet Meder. Had breakfast together and after that walked through the city, along Broadway to Castle Garden, where all emigrants are landed, and visited several persons for whom we had brought letters of recommendation, like Schushardt and Dulman. I just looked in at Morgan's but found him leaving at that moment and promised him to come back tomorrow.[1]

FRIDAY 18 MAY 1866

Handed out still more letters, among others at Osborn's, who received me most friendly and, without asking if it would be convenient at all, at once decided that Oyens and I will depart for Chicago this coming Thursday to inspect the Illinois Central. In God's name we accept, and will adjust our itinerary accordingly, although it means that I will be unable to attend the congress. But because of what I have heard of it, I am not too much disappointed to have to miss it. Moreover, the opportunity to accompany Osborn is too good to refuse and after all, best of all, we are just wrapped up and taken. *Enfin vogue la galère.*[2]

Letters delivered to Cousinery, represented by the Thorons, and visited with Blake. He receives me most friendly and I am looking forward to a lot of pleasure with him and profiting from his vast knowledge.[3]

In the evening to a reception at the Dutilhs' with Oyens and Meder. Mr. Schermerhorn, one of the Knickerbockers, with two daughters. Mrs. Wilkinson with two daughters, "one of whom is engaged to be married to Mr. Casimir Thoron.

The engagement is first known today." We danced a lancer and talked all evening, I especially with the engaged Miss Wilkinson, who did not neck much with Mr. Thoron. The Wilkinsons lived in Charleston and went through the bombardment of Fort Sumter and the siege of Charleston. They left before the bombardment of the city, but they survived all horrors of the war. Six months ago they had come to stay with the Dutilhs. Fiercely Southern in their views, I heard the girl of sixteen say: "I wouldn't care for all the misery and all the sorrow over again and to have as many deaths again, if we could only whip them once." I am not quite sure that I heard the word "whip" coming from her sweet lips, but I do think so. "We ought to fan the hatred." What a situation! Mrs. Dutilh is a charming woman who knows to perfection how to organize receptions.[4]

Saturday 19 May 1866

To the Morgans' in the morning, where I had a conversation with one of the partners. I liked none of the two I met. One is a fop and has a most ridiculous appearance; the other looks more caddish. His speech didn't make a favorable impression on me either. He has some superficiality and he lets his tongue run away with him, or so it seems. But I don't want to judge him yet. With Americans this is always hard to do; often the crust is so different from the inside. In many respects he is showing some composure, something that works in his favor. He doesn't think much of the present situation of the country and is not so much in favor of paying off the national debt, as so many other bankers seem to advocate so vehemently.[5]

He couldn't tell me much good of the Atlantic & Western. The construction costs have been much too high and are a drain on the coffers of the company, caused chiefly by the stealing by the contractors. He named three or four persons who are most culpable, who have made their fortunes out of the business. In one word, his opinion was definitely in the negative.[6]

In the afternoon with Oyens and Meder to Newark to see the Scharff family. Their abode is lovely situated, but the whole doesn't show much prosperity; on the contrary it is more decent poverty. He was full of complaints, and although he tried hard to show things in a positive way, it was clear that he would welcome more income. Statistics are clear: a barrel of flour twenty years ago bought—too expensive—for $5, is now $20; cloth before the war $1.25 the yard, now $3.50 or $4, etc. Taxes have been raised twenty times; Scharff paid $60 before the war, now $1,100, a third of his total income, as he said. Day labor was [. . .], now $3.50 or $4 for skilled labor, spade labor $1.50. Scharff himself looks old and is making heavy weather of almost everything. Mrs. Scharff is much more pleasant. Their only unmarried daughter, Annie, is engaged to Abrahams. Too bad that he had just left for Holland, because I would have liked to make his acquaintance and had expected a positive result from a very warm letter of recommendation to him from Klaas Pierson. He is expected to return in July, and I hope to have the opportunity to meet him upon my return here.[7]

My first encounter with the American railroad cars wasn't as bad as I had expected. Everyone was most civil and the seats were comfortable. But is strange to see that there are no fences or other barriers at the depots or along the tracks, only boards with the text "look out for the locomotive," and they make a somewhat unusual impression. Also unusual in my eyes were the conductors in civilian clothes, with only a small and almost invisible button as a mark of their office.[8]

SUNDAY 20 MAY 1866

By steamer *Chicopee* in 1.5 hour from the foot of Dey Street to Yonkers, where I found Thomas W. Ludlow waiting for me at the steamboat landing. He drove me to Cottage Lawn, where I had breakfast and talked with him; later we strolled about a bit. His views of the future are not as somber as those of the others, but not very positive either. He is also pointing at the high prices for everything now. Alcohol, four years ago $0.40 per gallon, is now $5, and other examples. He is paying more than half of his income in taxes, federal tax, state tax, county tax, town tax, and school tax. Business people don't care much about this for they are making money, but for persons of independent means living off their capital it is terrible. Moreover, with every little thing he buys, he is paying indirect taxes, and because of the enormous rise of all prices their buying power is already reduced by at least a third when compared to the pre-war situation. How this race between high prices for necessities and high wages is going to end, he couldn't tell. This race is a serious thing, but import of all kinds of goods and immigration will undoubtedly do their work, the first probably the quickest. Already now imports are up from 16 million in 1865 to 95 million this year, if I am correct.[9]

How the financial future will be is very hard to say. Will the people be able and willing to bear this burden of taxation for a long time? The commercial and manufacturing circles have made enormous profits until now, and they don't complain. But as soon as the profits will be diminishing, as they have started doing already, and a crisis will develop, how will they react then? And such a crisis may easily come, caused either by large foreign imports, by disappointing cotton crops, by unexpected slow growth of the petroleum industry, or by the return of American bonds from Europe when the markets there will dry up. In such a case not only the will to pay taxes, but also the ability to do so, will suffer. For the mass of rich people live off their profits, not off their investments. If they will be able to bear the tax burden for three or four more years, and if the West remains faithful, then there is a good chance that the growth of the Far West and the development of the South will change the picture for good and will enable the people to shoulder the burden. Now, however, the situation is dangerous. Today I read in the *Herald* that the total amount of real property in South Carolina, in pre-war days estimated at $400,000,000, is now down to $50,000,000. It is clear that they cannot bear the same burden as in the North, not to speak of the accumulated charges of the last four years. It is often forgotten that on top of the $3,000 million federal debt, there are the debts of the states, counties, and towns, often very considerable. And as apart from the exceedingly high import tariff, such a very high direct taxation is being imposed that some people have to pay more than half their income, the situation is not free of worries, and the outlook not very bright. Sometimes I see all this as a house of cards, which is still standing, but the first little breeze will blow it down. One should read Sir Morton Peto on this![10]

Ludlow has found a way to set off against these taxes. His estate of 150 acres, bought at $150 per acre, is now worth $2,000 to 3,000 per acre, and he is slowly cashing in by selling in small parcels. Roads have been built through, and this is done here in the following manner: within the limits of the village, the corporation has the right to decide if and where a road will be constructed. The owner of the land not only has to donate the land, but he also has to pay for the actual construction of the road being made for him. Ludlow had paid $4,600 for a road of 2,300 feet. The corporation, however, cannot do anything without being petitioned by the majority of the landowners of the area in question. As land prices always shoot up after the construction of a road, few landowners grumble or refuse to cooperate.

Ludlow is still hale and hearty, but not really pleasant. The way he talked about my father was not as I would have liked, and I cannot fail to think that he was more of a pleasant acquaintance and a good correspondent than a close friend of my father's. He has some egoistic traits, more like "hard-heartedness." His wife is lovely and friendly. His nephews are queer fish, always helping him in his favorite pastime of "dollar-hunting" and to "coin money out of everything." From a couple of little ponds they get a harvest of ice that brings one of the nephews $2,800 a year [$40,500 in 2009 dollars].

The situation of Cottage Lawn is lovely, with a very pretty view of the Hudson River. The beautiful spring day made my spirits rise, and I enjoyed the day. Toward 4 pm I departed by boat to New York. On 34th Street a boiler shop caught my eye, a store for steam boilers. All kinds of boilers were lying around.

NB This morning I couldn't have breakfast in the hotel, as on Sundays they start serving only at 8 am. I was lucky to buy some bread in a confectionary, as in the hotel they absolutely refused to give me anything. O, American hotels, so highly praised by many!

MONDAY 21 MAY 1866

Mr. Boese, clerk of the Board of Education of the City of New York, for whom Oyens and I had an introduction from Osborn, came to pick us up at 9 am to see one of the schools. School no. 50, 20th Street near 3rd Avenue. There are two schools in the building, one grammar and one primary school, both for girls only. Miss Susan Wright is the headmistress. Girls between the ages of 4 and 11. When we arrived the school day was just being opened, and we had to wait until that was done, so we missed the reading from the bible and the prayers, etc. After our entry we were honored with a special calisthenic exercise, consisting of indoor gymnastics by some 300 or 400 girls. It was done in a big hall, which could be divided into several rooms for different classes. All accompanied by music played on a very good piano and executed with great pleasure and enthusiasm and with all movements well regulated. I could see no one who did not do her best as much as possible, with great swiftness and elegance, but tiring to the eyes. We also saw the youngest ones at play in a downstairs classroom, everything on a much higher level than in our kindergartens at home. All these games and gymnastics are being practiced daily. Of the actual instruction we saw little through lack of time. Only a little bit of arithmetic, not so perfect to my eyes. I liked one feature particularly: every week one of the teachers is giving the lessons not in her own classroom but in the big hall under the eye of the principal. There was a system of prizes and medals, which are worn for two weeks. The principal, Miss Susan Wright, is an excellent woman. The classrooms were tidy and clean, with flowers in the windows and on the platform, but the ventilation only mediocre. The pupils neat and clean, as were the teachers.[11]

From there to the colored school in the 114th Ward, where Reception Day was being held. The care of all colored schools has been transferred to a special commission of the Board of Education from the several sub-commissions of the different wards where they are situated. Today the former trustees were treated to a farewell performance: singing, both by soloists and choirs, recitals, dialogues and little plays, etc. It was a pleasure to see all those little Negroes, from coal black— very few only—to white and blonde, all well dressed, many from the audience and a few of the children even elegant, and all excited and merry. Everything was executed with great enthusiasm and pleasure, without false modesty or timidity. The speech, however, was hampered by the thick lips. Afterward addresses delivered by Mr. Randall, Mr. Hartley—a parson—Mr. Peterson, the principal of the school, Prof. Day—a black professor from somewhere in Ohio—and "Mr. C. A. Crommelin, the distinguished foreigner who came over in an official capacity to visit the schools, etc." The whole was a bit too long and tiring, but in general I had a very favorable impression. I hadn't thought that so much had already been done for the Negro race, and on seeing so many almost white faces I couldn't help but think that the day wouldn't be far off when the dividing wall between the two races would fall, maybe with slow transitional stages, and that white and black will truly mix, not only in the schools, but everywhere. The girls were singing *Ich kann spielen auf einer Geige.*[12]

Later to the Kopses, who received me most hospitably. Paid a short visit to the Academy of Design, where an exhibition was being held. At Oyens's invitation we had dinner at Delmonico's, with him and Meder, Ralli, and Casimir Thoron. I liked Ralli and Thoron very much. Café Louvre.[13]

TUESDAY 22 MAY 1866

Had rendezvous at 8:45 am with Mr. Richard Warren, one of the other members of the Board of Education, at School no. 35 in 39th Street. Assisted at the opening of the day and I had to give another speech and after that walked with him through all classrooms. Ventilation is perfect everywhere, with fresh air being supplied at ground level and the exhaust by high chimneys only, without gas. Classes of fifty children, 16 classrooms each for one grade only. The same system of rotation, as seen earlier, with one class a whole week in the reception room under the eye of the principal. Female teachers until age 13 or 14, male teachers after that. One lesson pleased me most: reading with analysis, done with vivacity and pleasure. Both the teacher and the boys were full of enthusiasm and fun, and the boys responded very well. She asked questions left and right unexpectedly, and it was plain to see that this was the usual way of teaching, not "got up for the occasion." Downstairs was the primary school of Miss Agnes Turnbull. Again I was much impressed by the order, the neatness, and the smartness, in one word the whole is striking. Not in the least the teachers, all very nice ladies, and all well dressed and smart that it is a pleasure to see them. Most surprising to see the great number of pretty faces among them.[14]

Miss Agnes Turnbull made me almost lose my head, and I simply fail to understand why so many women are still unmarried and have to make their living as teachers. Most remarkable, however, is the perfect discipline at all schools and the cheerful acquiescence of the young Americans to that regime. One never hears the least sound, no fidgeting, no whispering, and no cracking of jokes. They look more like automatons than boys when they enter school and sit down, often with hundreds together. I don't understand how they are trained to do this. For instance, in this last school, at the end of fifteen minutes of free playtime, the bell was rung and everybody at once stood still and in his appointed position, without anybody still trying to continue the playing and romping. One of the schoolmistresses stood on the platform with the bell in her hand and ordered the boys around, everything with an almost military precision. That perfect order and discipline is surely one of the most remarkable features of the American school system.

Saw the ruins of the Academy of Music that burned down this past night. To the Morgans', Ludlow at the Trust Company, J. Kearny Warren, etc. Had dinner with the eldest Thoron and then to the Dutilhs'; had a very pleasant time with both.[15]

Wednesday 23 May 1866

Wrote letters. Tried to see Gulian C. Verplanck, but he was out. As oldest and closest relative in this country I would have liked to see him, but I will have to postpone it until my return here. Kruseman van Elten. Had dinner with the Kopsjes at the public table in their boarding house, so the conversation was a bit difficult. After dinner most guests left, and I stayed on with them and Jan Kops and wife, and the company became more pleasant. When I get to know them better, I expect that we will get along even better. Lena looked very pretty.[16]

Thursday 24 May 1866

To the city in the morning to discuss a few things with Morgan before my departure. At 3:30 pm with Osborn and Oyens [by train] along the Hudson, on our way to Chicago. First stop was his country estate at Garrison's Station near Cold Spring, opposite West Point. We arrive at 6:30 pm and meet his wife and her brother Arthur Sturges and Miss Davison, his fiancée.[17]

Friday 25 May 1866

Toured to Cold Spring in the morning, in the afternoon with Mrs. Osborn and Miss Davison to West Point Military Academy, parade.

Saturday 26 May 1866

In the morning from Garrison's Station at 9:10 along the Hudson by way of Albany, Schenectady, Utica, Syracuse, etc., to Niagara Falls, arrival there 12:30 pm. Syracuse looks different, with many timber houses. Everywhere the trains run through the streets, with the bell on the locomotive ringing. Many primeval forests, with clearings in places only here and there. It seems that the population in these regions is decreasing instead of growing. Since the prairie lands have become known, the full flow of immigration is being directed to Illinois and Minnesota and beyond, and no one is staying in these less fertile regions. Moreover, cultivation of this land is much harder to do because of the many trees that have to be cleared away first with great trouble and much hard work. On the prairies it will suffice to plough up the land, that's all.[18]

SUNDAY 27 MAY 1866

At the Niagara, rainy weather.

MONDAY 28 MAY 1866

In the morning at 6:30 from Niagara Falls to Suspension Bridge, across the bridge, that looks fine to me. Through Canada to Detroit per Great Western. Clearings in the forests everywhere, with the half-burnt trunks still standing. This is the first step in cultivation; the second is the cutting of the trunks, with only the tree-stumps left. In almost every field, even in the better cultivated ones, one sees the stumps still among the plants. After nine or ten years, when they have almost completely rotted away, they are finally cleared away. Really well cleared land is still very rare.[19]

In Detroit the ferry brings us across the St. Clair River and from there per Michigan Central in the most beautiful sleeping car, Pullman's *Atlantic,* to Chicago. In the morning at 7 am arrival there, Fremont House.[20]

3

From Chicago through Illinois and Northward to Minnesota

May–June 1866

Toured Chicago in a nice buggy with one of the clerks of the Illinois Central. Stockyards (cattle market) enormous, clean, and well-equipped, but dirt and dung everywhere on the streets. (Trollope) Visited with Mrs. McLane *née* Scharff in the afternoon; she was out but came home later after some waiting. She received us most friendly and we had tea with her. I liked Captain McLane very much, a robust, rotund seaman with a lot of common sense and a most engaging natural pleasantness.[1]

WEDNESDAY 30 MAY 1866

Spent the morning with packing, shopping, and writing letters, and at 3 pm we were only just ready to begin our trip over the Illinois Central. At the depot we found a special train, which we boarded together with Osborn, Douglas, the present president, Hughitt, general superintendent, Joseph F. Tucker, general freight agent, and Remmer, secretary to the president. The purpose of the trip was the annual inspection of the road by the directors, and thanks to Osborn's kindness we were allowed to participate in this most interesting journey. The 30th we rode as far as Champaign, the 31st from there to Cairo and back to Centralia; on the first of June to Chatsworth on the Peoria & Oquawka RR, where we saw Osborn's farm on June 3rd; departed from there on June 4th, and arrived back in Chicago that same evening. Made a tour in the rain with Frank Osborn to Onarga.[2]

As is well known, Illinois is the delta between the Mississippi and Ohio Rivers and consists completely of alluvial soil of the most fertile kind, just like the area between the great rivers in the Netherlands. Originally this delta, like most of the rest of the continent, was heavily wooded, but in the course of many centuries most of these forests have been destroyed by fires, sometimes caused by lightning but also deliberately set by the Indians. Only the parts protected by some river against the prevailing southwesterly winds have been preserved. Fires can jump the vast stretches of rivers only under the most favorable circumstances, and because the forests have such remarkable powers of recovery and start growing again after every disaster, only repeated fires are able to destroy a forest forever. Being in the lee of a river has been enough to protect against fires in such cases. The southern part from Cairo to Centralia is still wholly covered in woods, hardly accessible because of the marshy soil. North from Centralia the forests give way to prairie land, and the farther north one goes the more prevalent the prairies become. Only along the Mississippi River some forests have been spared. South of Chicago, between that city and Mattoon, the prairies extend for hours on end, with only here and there small copses. This is the great advantage of Illinois, with a soil without par in the world. Formed by many thousands of generations of plants, trees at first, grasses later, a layer of the most fertile black soil, 1.5 to 2 feet thick, stretches into the vast distance. This layer is just plain leaf mold, and needs only to be plowed up to produce the most excellent crops. Since 1854 this region now has been opened up from north to south by the Illinois Central. Only a railroad could make these lands accessible and suitable for the influx of immigrants. That the visions of the early railroad planners have become realities is proven by the fact that since 1854 the population of Illinois has grown from 800,000 to 2,500,000. The wealth created here is plainly visible everywhere in the flourishing little villages and towns along the lines of the Illinois Central.[3]

Working the soil cannot be simpler. The first year only the top soil is plowed and corn sowed, yielding what is called the 'sod crop,' a lesser sort of crop. However the next year, after deeper plowing, the harvests are excellent and rich. If the top soil will ever be exhausted, 'sub soiling' can be resorted to with success. At present the soil is still so rich that most farmers do not use fertilizer, and in Chicago people have to pay for the removal of manure there. The chief crop is corn, 120,000,000 bushels annually, wheat only 30,000,000 bushels. A bushel varies between 60 pounds for wheat, 56 for corn, and 33 for oats. The corn is transported in bulk or fed to the animals, cattle and hogs, to make it easier to transport. Beet sugar has also been produced for some time, and coal mines are being developed everywhere. Generally the prosperity of the farmers is great, and with diligence and economy they will advance even more.

Prices vary between $6 and $18 per acre for the company's land. Land sold some time ago has reached fabulous prices now. Without taking the town lots in consideration, prices of between $40 and $50 per acre are being paid sometimes. Paying off the land purchased by the farmers does not mean anything for the mea-

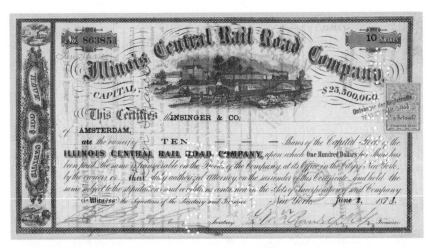

The Illinois Central Railroad was one of the American railroad companies that raised a large amount of its construction capital in Amsterdam and London. Here is a certificate for ten shares of the Illinois Central common stock made out to Insinger & Company, an Amsterdam stock brokerage firm.   Veenendaal Coll.

sure of their prosperity. As they only start paying taxes after the last installment has been paid, most farmers postpone the last payment as long as they can. Chief problem here is the high wage of workmen. A common workman makes $1.50 to $2, engineers and conductors $3, firemen $1.50 per day, a farmhand with board and lodging $20 per month. Handwork is being replaced by machinery as much as possible, with positive results, such as with the ditch plow of Mr. Danforth. The steam plow is not being used here, as it is cheaper to buy lean oxen in the spring for $100–$120, which, despite the heavy work, are being fattened with the good fodder, and sold in the fall for about $150. An example of the growth in value: eight years ago Osborn bought 8,000 acres for $6 per acre, sold some 6,000 acres, and now has 2,000 left, developed and improved and with 1,500 sheep, without any debt. Common opinion here is that a person without any capital at all will have a hard time before being on his feet, but that someone with, say $2,000, has every chance of succeeding on a farm of 80 acres. Usually they can pay off the debt in four or five years, have been able to live there, and have developed their farm and equipped it with machinery. Messrs. Kinnard, Schot, Pickering, and Roberts are farmers of Osborn. Usually the tenants pay one-third of the crops to the owner, and keep the other two-thirds for themselves.[4]

Had dinner with Frank Osborn at Chatsworth. Chief drawbacks here are the bad roads and lack of timber; roads are difficult to improve.

TUESDAY 5 JUNE 1866

In Chicago. I was sick between 12 and 6, Oyens between 8 and 12 pm.

WEDNESDAY 6 JUNE 1866

After some walking around and sampling the view over the city from the lighthouse, we went to one of the elevators where grain is being shipped. These elevators are enormous structures equipped with all kinds of machinery to get the grain from the railroad cars up to the several floors, where it is weighed and then stored in immense bins 50 feet deep, to be subsequently loaded into ships by means of other pipes. Each one of the two elevators that we visited holds 750,000 bushels. Upon arrival the grain is classified by an expert of the Board of Trade in several classes, nrs. 1, 2, and 3, etc., and then stored in bins with other grain of the same quality irrespective of ownership. In return the owner gets a check, which can be sold or traded. The fungibility of the grain is an important consideration in this trade. For loading and storage for 20 days two cents per bushel are charged, so it is in the interest of the elevator owner to get rid of the grain as soon as possible to gain on these 20 days. The speed of everything connected with this business is amazing. A railroad car of 500–600 bushels is unloaded in five minutes, and a ship can be loaded with 25,000 bushels in an hour or so. About 200 million bushels pass through the twenty elevators of Chicago annually, so every one of them handles some 10 million bushels. A single elevator can handle about 3,500 bushels in an hour, which makes 350,000 per working day.

Later that same day to the engine shops of the company. Mr. Hayes. We had little time left, so we inspected the whole somewhat superficially. I didn't see anything that I hadn't seen before. The roundhouse for eighteen locomotives to be cleaned and readied was impressive.[5]

In the evening with Osborn to a family named Newbury, good friends of the Osborns who had invited us graciously, although they were mourning a sister-in-law and were not really receiving guests. Mr. Newbury was sick and we didn't see him, but Mrs. Newbury and two daughters made us a friendly welcome in a lovely pleasant room, with good furniture, and we were served excellent refreshments. The daughters, however, turned out to be "pretty pert."[6]

THURSDAY 7 JUNE 1866

Rode with Mr. Kelloch, chief engineer and superintendent of the track of the Illinois Central, a couple of miles outside Chicago to a pumping engine. This machine pumps water from the Chicago River into the Illinois and Michigan Canal, which runs from here to La Salle, and connects the Chicago River with the

Illinois River, or to be more precise, Lake Michigan with the Mississippi River. The difference in level between the rivers and the canal is between eight and nine feet, and this engine has been erected to keep the canal full of water. A most interesting machine: the water is being raised by an enormous waterwheel, 36 ft. in diameter and 10 ft. wide, which runs in a wooden enclosure, and is equipped with wooden buckets to carry the water. Every turn of the machine hauls up 1,000 barrels (of 40 gallons each), and its speed is between three and five revolutions per minute. The steam engine delivers about 400 horsepower, and has two sets of cylinders, one high- and one low-pressure. The power is transferred to the waterwheel by means of cogwheels on the outside of the large wheel. At the point where the water that has been raised is being thrown out into the canal, a heavy gate is installed, which rotates on hinges at the bottom. Water is let out, but any backwash that would hinder the movement of the wheel is prevented by the automatic closure of the gate. When built in 1848 this installation cost $55,000, the renewal in 1860 $45,000. Ten pounds of—bad—Illinois coal are needed for every revolution of the wheel, and in the days when coal was $2.5 per ton it was possible to raise a body of water one mile long, ten ft. high, and five ft. wide for $1.50.[7]

Soon this arrangement will become superfluous. The level of the canal is eight feet above that of the Chicago River for its first 30 miles, and 90 feet above that of the Illinois River. To obtain a natural current of fresh water from Lake Michigan and get rid of the foul stagnant water in the river inside the city, the municipality has decided to cut away the dam of eight feet high and 30 miles long. Instead of a river flowing into Lake Michigan, a reverse flow from Lake Michigan into the Mississippi will result. Even now the lake water gets that far when the pumping machine has worked for eight days continuously. The stupendous work of deepening the canal has already been started. Enormous steam powered dredges, with an iron bucket holding some 1.5 cubic yards, scoop up masses of beautiful rich clay that is dumped along the banks of the canal and smoothed out with a crane. Every cubic yard costs $0.33, the complete work $3,000,000. The bottom of the canal is lowered by ten feet.[8]

Dinner at Kinsley; to Crosby's Opera House and saw one act of the *Streets of New York;* handsome and well-appointed hall.[9]

Friday 8 June 1866

Left Chicago by train at 9 am, arrived 1 pm at Milwaukee, and driven around. A city of 80,000, half of them Germans, who still live in their own part of town. At the moment there is little visible growth, and although the city is older than Chicago, it has been completely overshadowed by its neighbor. Newhall House is our hotel. At the moment of our departure at 8 pm we saw one of the most beau-

In 1859 the Mississippi River steamboats *Grey Eagle, Frank Steel, Jeannette Roberts,* and *Time and Tide* stand at the lower levee in St. Paul, Minnesota. When Crommelin arrived here seven years later, the levee had changed little.   Minnesota Historical Society

tiful sunsets I have ever witnessed. Thunderstorms on all sides and a lot of heavy weather apparently coming on, but shortly after our departure on the Milwaukee & La Crosse Railway it dissolved. Traveled all through the night in a sleeping car.[10]

Saturday 9 June 1866

Arrived at 8 in the morning at La Crosse, where we had to wait for the up-river boat, the *Key City,* until 1 pm. At long last she arrives and puts an end to our impatience. The first section of our journey is pretty, mountains on both sides heavily wooded, with the river wriggling through a large number of small and bigger islands. Although our draft is only 33 inches, our passage is slow and difficult, the more so because of the two loaded barges tied on each side of the boat.[11]

Sunday 10 June 1866

Instead of 8 am we arrive only at 7 pm in St. Paul. Now a town of some 15,000, St. Paul has existed only since 1848. Before that year there was nothing more than a little chapel dedicated to Saint Paul and founded some forty years ago. But settlers soon found the way to Minnesota and began to develop the great riches of Minnesota's prairies and woods.[12]

MONDAY 11 JUNE 1866

Handed a letter of recommendation to Mr. E. S. Edgerton, president of the Second National Bank, and looked in at the offices of the St. Paul & Pacific and asked for young Mr. Kloos, who is acting as engineer—without pay—for that company. He has been sent out by Kerkhoven & Co. to keep them informed about the present and future situation of that railroad.[13]

We meet the president, Mr. George L. Becker, and the head of the land department, Hermann Trott, who receive us very friendly and tell us that Kloos is surveying the line in the middle of the woods and will not be back in St. Paul for a time. After some discussion they understand that we have an interest in the company and that we may be able to influence the sale of the bonds now on the market in Amsterdam, so Mr. Becker proposes to send us out, in the company of Trott, to view the line as far as Big Lake, the present terminus. However, after dinner Trott returns and proposes to extend our plan. Instead of going as far as Big Lake, we will journey into the woods with a team and see the camp of the survey party, where Kloos is presently staying, and return by way of Lake Minnetonka to Minneapolis and St. Paul. As this seems to be the only way to see some of the backwoods and sample the way of life there, we accept eagerly. We agree to leave early next morning.[14]

TUESDAY 12 JUNE 1866

We meet Mr. Hermann Trott at the depot and he provides us, as guests of the company (First Division of the St. Paul & Pacific Railroad), with free travel over the road. He also pays all our other expenses later. In three hours we travel to Big Lake, where the road ends for the time being. The roadbed is ready as far as St. Cloud and only the rails are lacking, and as these are on their way from Europe, the road will soon be extended that far. From St. Cloud to Watab, the end of the First Division of the St. Paul & Pacific Railroad proper is about ten more miles, which will be finished soon. When the original plan was conceived by Edmond Rice, he envisaged a line all the way to the Pacific plus a connection with Lake Superior. However, Rice's resources did not measure up to the requirements for this undertaking, and about two years ago he sold a large part of the company, viz., the road from St. Paul to Watab then under construction, the line from St. Paul to Big Stone Lake, then not even begun but now just started, to Mr. Litchfield and party. Also included in the sale, if my information is correct, was the right to build on from Watab all the way to the Pacific, a project in the distant future at best. Rice kept for himself the right to build the northern extension from Watab

The first steam locomotive of the St. Paul & Pacific Railroad was the *William Crooks,*
No. 1, built in 1861 by the New Jersey Locomotive and Machinery Company of Paterson,
New Jersey. Crooks was the engineer in charge of construction for the StP&P. Although
Crommelin does not mention him in his diary, he must have met him in Minnesota.
Later during his travels Crommelin visited the New Jersey Locomotive factory in Pater-
son. The *William Crooks* has been preserved and is on display in the Museum of Trans-
portation in Duluth, Minnesota.   Jannie W. Veenendaal photo

to Crow Wing and the British Possessions and from some point on that line to the
western corner of Lake Superior. These rights include the land grant of the State of
Minnesota for these lines. Also kept was the right to the line from St. Paul to Winona, now under construction, and all the way to La Crosse, I believe. This latter
line will provide the necessary connection between St. Paul and the railroad network of the East. At the moment the connection between St. Paul and the rest of
the country is almost impossible whenever the river navigation is suspended. The
only possible way in that case is by rail to Faribault, by stage—some 40 miles—
to a place called Crescent or some similar name, then by rail to Winona and from
there by stage to La Crosse. It will be readily understood that traveling by stage on
those bad roads and crossing the frozen Mississippi is not a lot of fun.[15]

Originally Litchfield was one of the contractors, who, when Rice's resources were
exhausted, took over the business and incorporated the new First Division of the

St. P. & Pac. RR.C. instead of the old St. P. & Pac. RR.C. This new company, however, has no share capital of its own but rests completely on Litchfield's means and credit. The road is being built as far as possible from the revenues of the sale of its bonds on the Amsterdam Bourse and constitutes a mortgage partly on the road, partly on the land grant. Together both mortgages amount to $2,020,000. There is a plan, and it is already being executed, to replace those two loans with a single new one, amounting to $2,800,000, and mortgage both the road and the land grant to that sum. All these loans and mortgages apply only to the branch line St. Paul–Watab, while the lands along the mainline St. Paul–Big Stone Lake are still unencumbered.[16]

The land grant consists in ten sections (square mile = 640 acres) for every mile constructed. According to the gentlemen present, this company was in the favorable position to be established here early so that it could choose its lands while almost nothing had been sold to or claimed by settlers. In Illinois a lot of the land had already been claimed or sold when the Illinois Central RR started its operations, so that the land obtained finally was not always of the very best. The maps we saw here seemed to confirm this, as the railroad lands are spread out along the line in a most regular way, without the open blocks as often seen along the Illinois line. On the other hand this indicates that the country is not yet as far advanced as was the case in Illinois, but the immigration that is growing daily will soon offset this. On average the price today is between $5 and $6 per acre, but it is the policy of the directors to sell as little as possible and wait for better prices in the future. The Illinois Central followed the opposite policy in selling as much as possible to foster the rapid growth of the population—and hence the traffic—as soon as possible. This seems to be the most natural way of doing, as the first mentioned policy easily leads to a lot of speculation.

The new bonds seem to be issued with the stipulation that possible future profits will not be distributed as dividends but first used for the forming of a reserve fund as large as the sum of the outstanding bonds, which will then be secured not only by the mortgage on the road and the unsold lands, but also by this safely invested fund.

The road from St. Paul to Big Lake runs close to the Mississippi, but on the high tableland scoured out by the river so that one hardly sees anything of the water at all. Most of the country is prairie, that did not look very fertile, with only little growth, more weeds than grass. However, Trott claims that this one of the least fertile regions and that other areas are infinitely better. There are very few settlements to be seen.

People here have high hopes of the prospects of this railroad because of the vicinity of the British Possessions. A lively trade is already being conducted with that country by means of the so-called Red River carts, which are made of wood

The strange but effective Red River carts are pictured in an immigrant camp where travelers are on their way from St. Paul to Pembina, a distance of approximately 600 miles. Photographer Benjamin Franklin Upton made this image ca. 1858.   Minnesota Historical Society

without any iron, drawn by one ox. They come in large numbers, mostly loaded with furs from Fort Abercrombie and the Red River, and they are considered to be one of the most remarkable sights of the country. To our regret there was not a single one to be seen at our arrival in Big Lake. St. Cloud is also seen as a most promising place for the growing trade as soon as the road will have been extended that far. People say that Minnesota, and especially the western part, is the best wheat-growing country in the whole Union.[17]

Even now fabulous crops are being harvested. I heard that in New York Minnesota wheat is being quoted separately and higher than any other, and that in the Milwaukee elevators Minnesota wheat is being kept separate, where generally all other wheat is just stored according to its quality as nr. 1, 2, or 3. Minnesota wheat seems to be even higher qualified than the ordinary first quality. That this will open up a bright future for the country and the railroad is plain to see, for wheat is much higher priced than Indian corn, nowadays $1.77 against $0.57 per bushel, and can easily bear higher transportation costs. On the other hand, one acre produces about 60 bushels of corn against 20 bushels of wheat, although I heard about crops of 40 bushels per acre in Minnesota. The main reason why Illinois is producing so little wheat is said to be that the soil is too rich. Whenever it will be somewhat exhausted it will be more suitable for wheat growing, at least that is what I have been told.

At Big Lake we rented a team, crossed the Mississippi River, and drove to Monticello. As far as this place, and even a little farther, the country is mostly prairie, with big or small groves of trees here and there. Only still farther out the real backwoods begin, commonly called bush here. We passed by Buffalo, where we met Captain Overton, and drove on to Rockford, a most lovely little town in the midst of extensive woods and chiefly consisting of sawmills. It was the first place in the West that could be reasonably called a town, not a settlement *in statu nascendi*. It reminded us of a pretty Alpine village, and to make this illusion even stronger it boasted no hotel and we spent the night with well-to-do farmers, Mr. Hayford, with a lovely little daughter, May, in a pink dress.[18]

My first introduction to the Minnesota woods made a very positive impression on me. The countryside is beautiful, with many large and small lakes, hilly and picturesque. The woods consist of white oak, elm, hickory, hard and soft maple, ironwood, etc. The soil is sandy, but the enormous amount of leaves that have fallen over the centuries has created a layer of pure leaf mold, some two feet thick, and eminently fertile. Generally this top soil is lighter than in Illinois and consequently warmer and also dryer, because the land is better drained. In the beginning the land here may even be better than in Illinois. A great advantage here is that roads are easier to construct and maintain, so that the railroads will be able to cover a larger area.

WEDNESDAY 13 JUNE 1866

Up early at 7 am and after some searching around found the engineers' camp. Sam prepared us a good lunch and we set out for the engineers, who are out surveying the line some distance from the camp. After a couple of miles through the woods we find Mr. Place and Kloos, who agree to accompany us to the camp. Dinner, and the evening under the tent, big fire, yarn by Trott of his adventures in Austria back in 1848, where he participated in the revolution, was taken prisoner but got out through intercession. Slept with Trott between two buffalo hides, but spent a terrible cold night.[19]

THURSDAY 14 JUNE 1866

Departed at 7 am, and rode some 30 miles along Lake Minnetonka. In the evening in Minneapolis, we watched a performance of some Indians, song and dance, terribly monotonous and boring, but yet entertaining and remarkable because of the colorful costumes. People said that Other Day, who saved sixty whites during the Sioux Massacres some time ago, was present. The gratitude of those saved does not seem to have been very great. Falls of St. Anthony, suspension bridge at Minneapolis.[20]

FRIDAY 15 JUNE 1866

Lake Minnehaha lovely, back to St. Paul. Had tea with Trott, pretty wife and nice little daughter. In the evening I found Jakob and Karel de Bruyn Kops.[21]

SATURDAY 16 JUNE 1866

Trott took us to the office of the Lake Superior Company, which is planning to construct a railroad from St. Paul to Superior City. They profit by the occasion of the visit of the two Dutch railroad men and capitalists to recommend the bonds of the company for sale in Amsterdam. With the Kopses by train by way of Mendota along the Minnesota Valley RR to Shakopee.[22]

SUNDAY 17 JUNE 1866

With them in a buggy by way of Carver to Benton Post Office, where we had heard that a colony of Dutchmen was established. We find them at the inn and they turn out to be from Limburg. They are well-to-do, and had come out with some capital and greatly prospered. Lake Waikonia and back. A most beautiful tour and we have a great time. Slept at Shakopee.[23]

MONDAY 18 JUNE 1866

Return to St. Paul. Said farewell to the Kopses at Mendota. Saw some people and did some business with Trott. Toured with Becker in the evening and ate strawberries at his house; his wife is lovely. A certain Mr. . . . helped us pass the time.[24]

TUESDAY 19 JUNE 1866

Departed St. Paul per steamboat *Phil. Sheridan* down river.[25]

WEDNESDAY 20 JUNE 1866

Arrive next morning about 5 am at La Crosse. Left at 6 am by train, hoping to arrive at 4 pm in Milwaukee. But around 3 pm we are held up by a derailed train, and only after four hours of hard work are we able to proceed to arrive at 9 pm in Milwaukee.

4

In Chicago and by way of Cincinnati and Washington, D.C., to Philadelphia

June–July 1866

THURSDAY 21 JUNE 1866

Returned to Chicago. Visited with Mr. Moring, vice-president of the Chicago & Great Eastern Railway. Had dinner with Joe Tucker, and wrote letters in the evening.[1]

FRIDAY 22 JUNE 1866

Mr. Kelloch, one of the shareholders of the Illinois Central RR. invited us to visit the Chicago waterworks now being built. Until now the water for the city has been taken from Lake Michigan close by the shore, which makes it less clean than desirable now and then because of the enormous growth of the city. To obviate this drawback, the idea has been conceived to take the water from the middle of the lake far from the shore, transport it by means of a tunnel under the bottom of the lake to the reservoirs on the shore, and distribute it from there all through the city. This stupendous work is being executed by Mr. Cheesborough, and as he had invited us to see the works, we go around 1 pm to the building where the enormous steam pumping engine is located. Close by is the hole where the tunnel begins. We are pushed along on a trolley by one man as far as the very end, 1.25 miles from the shore. The tunnel is situated between 67 and 70 feet under the surface of the lake, with three-feet inclination from the lake end toward the shore to be able to drain it easily. Its diameter is 5 feet 2 inches, and it will be two miles long. Distance between tunnel and lake bottom is at least 27 feet. It is being excavated in a layer of clay and does not have to be reinforced with planks or shored up. Of course, it will be lined with masonry afterward. It is being hoped that the water can be let in on January 1st, 1867. The work was let for $350,000, but total cost will be somewhat higher. The work is being done by three shifts of laborers, working eight hours each. Two shifts are miners, one are masons, who line the excavated portions. Miners make $2.25 per day, but they are complaining.

Visited with Mrs. McLane; dinner with Joe Tucker, Mr. Phillips, chief of the land department of the Illinois RR., and Mr. Johnson, a gentleman of independent means. The three of them keep house together, nice situation, good food, and lots of fun.[2]

Saturday 23 June 1866

Per Chicago & Great Eastern to Indianapolis. My impression of this railroad is not very favorable. It runs through the forests almost everywhere and no human dwellings are visible, and the depots are inconspicuous. In one word, I cannot see that this road will ever be profitable. Strolled around with young Morton in the evening, terribly hot weather.[3]

Sunday 24 June 1866

Sunday. Waited all day for young Morton, who had promised to come and see us in the morning. Saw him calmly strolling around with three friends at 3 pm! Terrible heat. Drove around in the evening; Asylum for the Blind, beautifully situated. Pleasant evening, thermometer everywhere 90–100.[4]

Monday 25 June 1866

To Cincinnati in the morning. Weather still hot. Walked around in the evening in the pleasant "Über den Rhein," the German quarter, full of cafés and *bierkellers*. In many places one sees only saloons from door to door. Heard a most miserable performance of *Fra Diavolo* in a small opera house.[5]

Tuesday 26 June 1866

Visited Gilmore, Dunlop & Co., my bankers. A young Gilmore introduced us at the Merchants Reading Rooms, a nice reading museum. This young man, who was at Sillig's school at Vevey for four years, persists in introducing us everywhere as German gentlemen, although he knows very well that we are from Amsterdam.[6]

Saw Mr. Sargent, a sea companion of Oyens, who invites us to visit with him outside the town. Saw Bohlander off to Holland. Drove to Clifton, where one is supposed to have a pretty view over the city, but a sudden thunderstorm turned everything dark and somber and we hardly see anything. Violent rain and we seek shelter under a couple of trees. From there to Mr. Sargent at Avondale. He is not yet home, and we have to wait for some time before being admitted, but we do spend a pleasurable evening with him after he returns. His daughters, Miss Molly, Alice, and some younger girls, with a governess from Paris, who seems to have lost most of her French, and who has not yet taught Miss Molly enough to enable her to follow a common discourse between the governess and myself.[7]

WEDNESDAY 27 JUNE 1866

By train to Washington by way of Columbus, Bellaire, Wheeling, and Harpers Ferry.[8]

THURSDAY 28 JUNE 1866

Arrived in Washington around 5 pm, suffering from a terrible cold.

FRIDAY 29 JUNE 1866

Visited with Mr. Riggs. In Congress, tariff bill, but heard not a single speech.

SATURDAY 30 JUNE 1866

Tour to Georgetown and Alexandria, both small unassuming towns. Saw Arlington House, formerly belonging to Mr. George Washington Parke Custis, the adopted son of General Washington, where Lafayette often stayed. Mr. Custis's daughter married General Lee, and hence Arlington House was confiscated at the outbreak of the rebellion and converted into an immense military cemetery. The view from the house is beautiful, the house itself heavy with enormous pillars in front.[9]

SUNDAY 1 JULY 1866

Sunday. Wrote letters in the morning. In the evening around 8 pm visited with Mr. George Riggs, for whom I had an introduction from Stanton Blake of New York. I had already seen him at his office but never at his home. They live at 280 I Street, behind President's Park, in a fine new house. We were graciously received by Mrs. Riggs and two daughters. Riggs himself did not show up. A couple of elderly gentlemen were present, among them baron [. . .], the Prussian ambassador, and Mr. Corcoran, former partner of Mr. Riggs, who remembered Daniel Crommelin & Son very well and also the affair of the Three Cities. He told me that the company of W. Wilson & Sons of Baltimore was still in existence and even in the same house where they had been for 100 years. He was very warm and friendly. The two daughters pleased me very well; they were "neither very young nor exceedingly good looking," but well educated, and their conversation was most pleasant.[10]

Monday 2 July 1866

In the morning obtained permission through Mr. Riggs to visit the Greenback Manufactory. We were received by Mr. Clarke, chief of that department. He knew my name very well and was full of pleasantries about the fear that back in those years the 'Three Cities' were about to be bought up by the Dutch. It seems that the loan in question became too difficult to be serviced by the parties involved and that Congress, to avert the danger, had stepped in and paid off the debt.[11]

The Greenback Manufactory is very interesting. It produces all bonds and paper money of the United States. We saw some of the several operations, executed by most ingenious machines. Most if not all of the work is done by young girls, most of them very well dressed. Later I heard that many of them were indeed ladies, who preferred this kind of work over being governess to make their own living; they make about $60 per month. This all started as a kind of experiment, and it succeeded quite well. The printing itself is done with hydraulic presses of some 800 tons pressure, and is done mostly dry, which is seen as something extraordinary.

The State Office, Department of the Interior, also houses the Patent Office, where models of all patented inventions are being exhibited. The heat did not allow me to stay there long, although among the many ideas that have never been used, and that would undoubtedly have failed any test of practicability, there should possibly lurk some excellent ones that have never been tested but might have advanced the progress of mankind.

Also exhibited are some cases full of presents from foreign princes to the government of the United States or its servants. Many relics of George Washington, looking dull and dusty, the printing press operated by Dr. Benjamin Franklin in his youth in London, and finally the original Declaration of Independence and Washington's commission. They are hanging in the dark, which is probably done on purpose, to preserve what has not already been destroyed. The long exposure to bright daylight of the Declaration of Independence in earlier times has caused the fading of most of the signatures, except a very few. I don't have to stress how sorry we should be for this. Taken all together this Declaration of Independence is certainly one of the most remarkable documents ever wrought by man. The unselfishness of those members of Congress, the noble thoughts that make up the contents from the beginning to the end, and the beautiful classical form of Jefferson's hand, all combine to present a document that will not easily find its peer anywhere.

NB Mr. Riggs's father has educated George Peabody and was later associated with him. Dined with Mr. Riggs, Mrs. Riggs, and the two misses, and Mr. Chilton. Fine dinner and pleasant conversation.[12]

TUESDAY 3 JULY 1866

In the evening to Philadelphia by rail. At Havre de Grace the Susquehanna River is crossed by means of a steam ferry, an immense steamer that carries ten American railroad cars, plus the locomotive and tender in one trip, and it could easily have taken one more car.[13]

In Philadelphia everything is in confusion for tomorrow. Everywhere big and small flags are flying. In our hotel, the Continental, and the Girard House opposite, every window is adorned with a small flag and bunting in the three national colors, which remind me strongly of home. Everybody is out on the streets and prepares for tomorrow. For me the news from Europe of the outbreak of war and the Prussian occupation of Saxony, Hanover, and Hesse casts a pall over the festivities.[14]

WEDNESDAY 4 JULY 1866

Independence Day. All windows and balconies full of ladies, the streets thronged with people, the air poisoned with powder-smoke from the enormous number of firecrackers. At 10 am beneath our windows the march of the several regiments of Pennsylvania volunteers started, who are going to hand their "colors" received during the war to Governor Curtin for preservation in the State Archives. Generals Hancock, Meade, and Geary, and all those old comrades have assembled again under their ancient flags, and they march together once more under the command of their own officers. Many old uniforms are in tatters—and the original uniforms were already very plain—and some men have not even donned theirs and march in civilian clothes, making this parade not really resplendent. Yet seeing all these men, who, leaving home and family for a lofty ideal, had taken up arms and had suffered uncounted hardships to fight for this ideal, did impress me much. The enthusiasm of all here was great and made a deep impression on me. On the other hand it is sad to think that this was a civil war and that all this enthusiasm was for a bloody war against those who are now once again brothers and fellow citizens. What feelings the South has at these occasions is better not asked. With us were Mr. Chilton and Mr. Griffiths, both with their mother and sister. The first is a friend of Oyens. Strolled around in the afternoon, people everywhere but only ladies and gentlemen, no common people anywhere.[15]

THURSDAY 5 JULY 1866

Visited with Mr. Parkman Blake. Warm weather. In the evening we rode in Fairmount Park, well laid out on hilly terrain, with the Schuylkill River flowing past.[16]

FRIDAY 6 JULY 1866

In the evening to Holmesburgh with Mr. Chilton to visit with his mother and sister. Slept there.[17]

SATURDAY/SUNDAY 7/8 JULY 1866

Broiling heat, stayed home most of the time.

MONDAY 9 JULY 1866

Penitentiary; if I am correctly informed the first cellular prison. The cells are almost dark, with narrow slits in the walls that let in some light on a clear day, but only on the upper floors. For ventilation they are absolutely insufficient. The cells directly under the roof, although vaulted, must be very hot. The lower cells are even more somber, but have a little garden each, where the inmates may spend an hour every day. Those in the uppermost cells often do not get out once in six months. And yet the man who took us around told us that the health of those in the higher cells is generally better than of those in the lower cells. These latter must be damp indeed. And some have been sentenced to 26 years![18]

Girard College, but everything was closed so we had to be content with seeing the outside and the staircases. House of Refuge for children to 21 years of age; nothing special.[19]

TUESDAY 10 JULY 1866

Through Mr. Etting, friend of Mr. Blake, we obtained a pass for seeing the many ironclads lying about here. At the special request of Mr. Etting, Commodore Turner had favored us with this special treatment, which apparently is distinctly uncommon. All ships are moored near League Island, some in a canal that runs from the Schuylkill to the Delaware, and that, together with those rivers, forms League Island.[20]

We saw three ships, one each of the three more common classes of ironclads of the moment. The first was a kind of floating battery, of the type the British had built during the Crimean War. She had a wooden bow and stern, and only the center part was armored with six-inch iron plates. Her sides were fairly steep, and she carried sixteen guns of 10 or 11 inches. She had been built in 1862, before people had thought of *Merrimacks* or *Monitors*, and was already a thing of the past. But she had behaved well, and although she had been under heavy fire a couple of times, her armor had never been pierced by enemy bullets, although one could see the impressions made by heavy projectiles everywhere.[21]

The second was a ship taken from the rebels. It had the shape of the famous

Merrimack, and her sides were formed at an inclination of 40 degrees and therefore less heavily armored. Plates of only two inches had been deemed sufficient.
She carried two pieces, one fore and one aft under the steeply inclined deck. The
gun ports were opened by means of chains running outside, a great mistake in my
opinion. The pilothouse was elevated only a few inches above the deck, just enough
to provide the captain with a view through narrow slits of two or three inches high.
This had been a weak point: a bullet had pierced the pilothouse, killed the helms-
man, and damaged the steering gear, and made the surrender of the ship inevi-
table.[22]

The third was the *Dictator,* a real monitor and the biggest ever built, 330 feet
long. Made of iron only, the sides of T-iron with plates riveted on. The hull, as
is well known, is almost completely submerged, the deck only about 2.5 feet above
the waterline when fully loaded. Counting from the deck, the sides are armored
with 6.5-inch iron plates for some 6 or 7 feet down, the lower part with 1- or 2-inch
plates only. Engines of 4,500 hp, crew 350 men, 1,000 tons of coal, speed six knots,
which is a failure according to our guide. The turret is the most interesting part,
with walls made up of fifteen 1-inch plates, and two 15-inch guns that fire 450-
pound solid shot over a distance of five miles. Each of the guns can be positioned
by one man. The closure mechanism was most remarkable, and I hope to make it
clear with the accompanying drawing. Even the smokestack was built up of 3-inch
plates to protect it against enemy fire. This monitor was originally to be armed
with two turrets, but the badly located center of gravity has made this impossible.
Generally the whole ship seems to be a kind of failure, although it is hard to judge
properly as she has never been under fire. Total cost was $2,000,000.[23]

In the evening to New York by train.

5

New York City, Albany, Niagara Falls, Pennsylvania Oil, and Canada

July–August 1866

WEDNESDAY 11 JULY 1866

Visited with some friends in New York.

THURSDAY 12 JULY 1866

Ditto ditto. In the evening with Casimir Thoron to Staten Island; tea at the Dutilhs.

FRIDAY 13 JULY 1866

Dinner with Blake in the New York Club. Two brothers of Blake's, two gentlemen Mackay and Mr. Chapman.[1]

SATURDAY 14 JULY 1866

In the City in the morning, in Central Park in the afternoon.

SUNDAY 15 JULY 1866

Sunday, wrote letters.

MONDAY 16 JULY 1866

By boat on the Hudson to Albany. Drove around Albany in the evening. Street names: Colonie, Van Tromp, De Witt, Orange, Van Woerdt, Ten Broeck Street.[2]

TUESDAY 17 JULY 1866

Saratoga.

WEDNESDAY 18 JULY 1866

Trenton Falls; man run over.[3]

THURSDAY 19–SATURDAY 21 JULY 1866

Niagara, Clifton House. Been under Central Falls.[4]

SUNDAY 22 JULY 1866

Sunday, wrote letters.

MONDAY 23 JULY 1866

By way of Buffalo, Erie, and Corry to Meadville. Arrived late at night.[5]

TUESDAY 24 JULY 1866

Visited with the Huidekoper family. Alfred and Frederick were at home, also the children and widow of their deceased brother Edgar. Dinner at Frederick's, tea at Alfred's. Children of Frederick: Nelly, Annie, and Willie. Children of Alfred: Mrs. Bond in Boston, Emma in Europe, Annette, and a son, Arthur, who is now at Harvard College. He was already in the army at 16 and promoted to captain on his 18th! Frederick was the only son of Edgar whom we met there.[6]

WEDNESDAY 25 JULY 1866

In the morning by train to the oil region. At Reno Station we meet John Huidekoper, a cousin of the others who came over later. He will accompany us, and together we arrive around 11 am in Pithole. Although the real excitement and rush is over here, Pithole is still much more alive than Oil City and other places where the wells have dried up. Here in Pithole and some other places most wells still produce oil, but it has to be pumped up now. At many of them, which were still flowing at the time of an earlier visit by John Huidekoper, the pressure had dropped off, and only after a long search could we find a single well that was still flowing. For the visitor there is little distinction between the two systems, as one sees only the petroleum flow from a pipe into a tank, fed by pumping or natural pressure. But in the case of natural pressure, the fluid is flowing stronger and because of the gas that is still carried along it looks more clear and whitish. The quantities produced by the several wells differ from four or five to two hundred barrels a day. Only a few have produced more than that, and then only temporarily. Of course, all wells are only temporary and are destined to die after a longer or shorter time. The petroleum seems to gather in underground cavities, and when these are pumped out, it does not flow fast enough to fill these cavities again. It is

Edwin L. Drake first struck oil in 1859 in Titusville, Pennsylvania. At the time of Crom-melin's visit to the oil region, the greatest excitement had subsided, but primitive rigs like this one remained. The rig pictured here is a replica of Drake's initial installation, and now graces a park in Titusville.   Jannie W. Veenendaal photo

possible that these dried-up wells will produce again in the future. The depth var-ies between 700 and 800 feet; the size of the drill hole is usually 4 inches.[7]

Nowadays all excitement here is over. The price of the oil is now only $3 per bar-rel, against $10 and even $16 earlier, and the steadily declining production seems to discourage everybody. Pithole—founded only one year ago—once had a popula-tion of about 14,000, but now much less. Nobody wants to buy a lot for well drill-ing, where earlier gigantic sums were being paid for that purpose. First owners have made a lot of money out of that. Lots are generally being leased now, which means that the owner of the land will get half of the oil found. If a well turns out to be productive, this may be very profitable. It should be borne in mind that early wells of two hundred or three hundred barrels per day were not rare in those days. Now the oil business is more centered on the oil as a product, no longer as a matter of reckless speculation and a way to get rich quickly. It was being said that there was some excitement again at Tudeint, but we didn't have the time to go there and see for ourselves.[8]

We saw an oil refinery in Oil City. The crude oil is first distilled in large iron retorts, and the distillate that remains, generally called tar, is used exclusively as fuel, being fed to the fires under the retorts drop by drop, a very cheap method.

The distilled and already clear petroleum is then further cleaned with sulfuric acid and marketed. Crude oil here gives generally some 75 percent refined petroleum. A barrel holds 42 gallons of petroleum, while generally a barrel holds 30 gallons of other fluids.

One notices at once that the population here is rather coarse. On the trains this was very easy to see. Among such a moving and floating population the female element is being represented only by a certain class of women. In Pithole this must have been most noticeable, but on the trains also these women, apparently all traveling free, were well represented.

Mr. John Huidekoper is superintendent for a Philadelphia company and runs four wells for them, which now give only some eight barrels per day.

THURSDAY 26 JULY 1866

After having said farewell to the several members of the Huidekoper family, we departed from Meadville at 8 am and arrived in Buffalo at 10 pm.

FRIDAY 27 JULY 1866

Back to Niagara, picked up our baggage at the Clifton House and in the afternoon, with pain in the heart, departed from Niagara forever and went by train to Rochester and Charlotte on Lake Ontario. There we meet the steamer to Montreal and after only a few minutes we are steaming over the mirror-like lake. Beautiful evening and a pleasant moon in the night sky.[9]

SATURDAY 28 JULY 1866

In the morning the skies are threatening, and it doesn't take long before a heavy shower comes down, preventing me from really enjoying the Thousand Islands. Forested as they are, they should present a pretty view in the wide river. In Ogdensburg we change boats and quickly steam down the St. Lawrence and through the several rapids. Long Sault, Cedar, and Lachine Rapids are the most important, but I wonder why they fail to make a great impression on me. Have most rocks been removed, or is it my own fault that these highly praised rapids don't live up to my expectations? At least I didn't have any sense of danger at all. But it is true that there are elements of ruggedness and turbulence. It is strange to see the quietly flowing river suddenly change into a wild sea, without any visible cause. Underwater rocks must be the reason, for apart from a few places, there is no great drop in the level of the water. The rocks can also be recognized by the upstream flow of the big waves in the rapids. The impact must be strong, and one should not forget that when coming down the river, the more so on a steamer, the current always seems to be slow moving. To my disappointment the banks of the St. Lawrence are more built over than I had expected.[10]

The arrival in Montreal is fine, and I was most impressed by the immense tubular bridge across the river, 1¼ mile long and resting on twenty-four piers in the river and two abutments, cost $7,000,000. Stayed in St. Lawrence Hall.[11]

SUNDAY 29 JULY 1866

Wrote letters, and made a tour 'around the mountain.' Montreal is very nicely situated, at the foot of Mont Royal, half on the mountainside and along the wide river. Most houses are neat and tidy, although never very high. In almost every street trees have been planted on both sides, which gives the town a pleasant but somewhat somber look. The quay along the river is nice, although the view across the river is not always free because of the many ships and steamers moored there. But as the quay is fairly high one can see more than, for instance, in Rotterdam.

MONDAY 30 JULY 1866

Grey Nunnery and other sights, both very interesting. In the evening by steamer to Quebec.[12]

TUESDAY 31 JULY 1866

Arrival in Quebec at 7 am, and changed at once for the steamer to Saginaw.[13]

WEDNESDAY 1 AUGUST 1866

Occupied with the boat tour to Saginaw, but spoilt by the rain.

THURSDAY 2 AUGUST 1866

Quebec, Montmorency Falls.[14]

FRIDAY 3 AUGUST 1866

Indian Lorette, departed by train in the evening.[15]

SATURDAY 4 AUGUST 1866

Arrival in Gorham and by stage to the Glen House.[16]

SUNDAY 5 AUGUST 1866

Sunday, rain and letters.

MONDAY 6 AUGUST 1866

Glen Ellis Falls, rain.

6

In Boston and New England

August–September 1866

TUESDAY 7 AUGUST 1866

To Boston.

WEDNESDAY 8 AUGUST 1866

Delivered my letters of introduction. Dinner with George Wm. Bond outside at Jamaica Falls.[1]

THURSDAY 9 AUGUST 1866

Dinner with William Sturges Bond in the Union Club.

FRIDAY 10 AUGUST 1866

Jasigi, Braggiotti, Blake.[2]

SATURDAY 11 AUGUST 1866

Dinner with Phillips in our hotel.[3]

SUNDAY 12 AUGUST 1866

Sunday, had tea with Bond in the open.

MONDAY 13 AUGUST 1866

I had heard of a Methodist camp meeting being held in the neighborhood, so we went on our way to attend that meeting, at least for a part. The place was at Yarmouth on Cape Cod, the southeastern tip of Massachusetts. In a crowded train and after many delays we finally arrive there at the campground just after noon.

In a small grove about 160 tents have been pitched, each for a fairly large number of visitors, and the total of all believers present must have run into the thousands. In every tent something is going on, here is singing, there praying. The biggest and best attended is the Centenary Church—this is a centenary festival and therefore very special. A crowd of women and a few men are gathered there, sitting on low benches or in the straw, but mostly kneeling. The congregation is strongly moved by the spirit and prayer; singing and confessions of conversion—from women chiefly—are alternating continuously. In the center four men are sitting, with the most horrible fanaticism on their faces, who are constantly working to elate the spirits even more. Whenever a moment of relaxation seems to come, they set a furious example of fervor. One of them especially by way of a very fervent prayer—fervent mostly by constant repetitions, big words, and violent movements—encourages confessions of several nervous women. And during this all, the four alternate with "Hallelujah," "Glory to God," "That is so," "True, true," and such expressions to raise the fervor ever higher. Those confessions, of course, always mean that the patient only now feels the "true joy" of being accepted as God's child and that his own personal will has made way for God's will. Naturally weeping and great nervousness are a constant feature of such a meeting. The singing of the old, almost merry Wesleyan hymns, went very well, and had a good effect.

Left the meeting at 2:30 pm, and traveled back to Boston with an old Methodist, member of the organizing committee of the camp meeting, and a Unitarian. A lot of discussion. The latter told me that the virtuousness of the women in Boston, especially that of the married ones, left a lot to be desired.

TUESDAY 14 AUGUST 1866

To the city jail with Mr. Bond. This edifice has been constructed in a most remarkable way in the shape of a Grecian cross, with three arms for cells and the fourth for all other services. The rows of cells are placed back to back with doors giving on corridors along the outside of the arms of the cross. Instead of solid doors the cells each have a barred door and ditto window, and in this way the prisoners have plenty of fresh air and reasonable lighting from the large windows. Five rows of cells on top of each other, each with an iron gallery for communication. The system with barred doors has the advantage of perfect ventilation, but for the prisoners there is no privacy at all, as wild animals in a cage, and with the drawback that communication between them cannot be prevented. The last is of limited importance only, as the inmates here are only of the following categories:

1. Detainees, who are unable or not allowed to post bail, either from poverty or because of the nature of their crime, for instance murder here in Massachusetts.

2. Those serving time instead of paying a fine. Longest term here is three months. In case of fines lower than $10 the judge has the right to give a remission and order his release. For fines over $10 this is impossible.

3. Those serving terms of a few months only. The longest conviction here among those detained now was 18 months.

Work is not compulsory. The population is too much floating for anyone to contract out for work, and even in the case of a longer detention only some little housework is being expected of them, and they don't wear hoods or uniforms, all very American. The only thing they seem to do is read the newspapers. A newsboy comes in daily to hand these out, and at the time I was there almost everyone was doing this. A few were sleeping; nobody did any work, although if one would want to, it would certainly not be refused to them. There were several blacks among them.

The building is splendid and well maintained, neat and tidy. The system of the barred doors and the unusual situation of the cells in the middle with the galleries outside seem to be the most remarkable features.[4]

The City Hall is also well built and well equipped, with more than enough desks, etc.

WEDNESDAY 15 AUGUST 1866

Dinner at Mr. Blake's place, chief of Blake Brothers & Co. He lives in Brookline, 4 miles from Boston. His youngest son, Arthur Blake, had agreed to meet us at the Boston & Worcester depot in Boston, and with him we steamed to Brookline in the continuing downpour, where the old gentleman Blake was waiting for us with a carriage. He drove us to his place, very prettily situated and furnished with good taste. He has developed this estate from a piece of primeval forest by cutting away all the shrubbery and low growth and laying out a beautiful lawn under the remaining high oaks and hickories. Only low firs border the paths, but for the rest there is no attempt at all at further development, but the good maintenance and neatness of it all showed abundantly that someone with real good taste has been at work here. The house is built solidly of granite and though simple, very well laid out and furnished. A big wood fire in the open chimney makes us forget the dampness of the atmosphere, and a good dinner brings us in a pleasant mood. Miss Blake, Miss Austin, a niece, are the ladies. After dinner Mr. Bradford, one of the associates of the house, turns up.[5]

THURSDAY 16 AUGUST 1866

At 1 pm departed for Lynn, with Mr. Jasigi, for whom we had an introduction by Joseph Thoron. He is spending the summer there with his wife and ten or twelve children, all still very young. We are well received and the house is very neat, and it is quite clear that Mr. Jasigi is very well off. A Miss Reggio, daughter of the Italian consul, a perfect example of a Southern European woman, is dining with us. Made a tour to Nahant in the afternoon, a small peninsula much frequented by Bostonians in the summer, in the company of Mrs. Jasigi and Miss Reggio. A fine carriage and lively horses.[6]

FRIDAY 17 AUGUST 1866

To Rye Beach, New Hampshire, a much frequented bathing resort on the ocean, with William Sturges Bond. Arrived around 3:30 pm and we are on our way to meet some young ladies whom he is acquainted with. Our first visit to Gilbert's cottage is a complete washout. During a game of croquet we are presented to the Misses Adams, Miss Whitney, and Miss Wigglesworth, but everyone is so engrossed in the game that we depart with a lot of misgivings. We suspect that we have made fools of ourselves.[7]

A later visit to the Fuller family has a better result. We are very well received and stay for a couple of hours in most pleasant conversation. We meet Mrs. Fuller, Mary, Etta (Henrietta), and Carry Fuller, Julia and Susie Robins and their mother, Mrs. Wigglesworth and her daughters Etta and Annie, and Mrs. and Miss Gould. From this moment on this house will serve us as our headquarters, where we feel most at home and where we spend the most pleasant hours. In the evening we smoke a cigar at Spiers, the general bachelor's quarters. There we meet Mr. Nichols, a medical doctor and pianist, and Mr. Dabney, who plays the flute as I have never heard before.[8]

SATURDAY 18 AUGUST 1866

Had a bath in the sea and visited with the Fullers. As usual here everywhere, ladies and gentlemen take the bath together, of course all in a suitable bathing costume, although I thought some quite insufficient. I still prefer our way of sea bathing. In the afternoon a visit with Mrs. Walker, Miss Charlotte Skinner, Miss Richardson, and Miss Cobb.[9]

In the evening an 'attempt at a hop' in a hall, a dancing pavilion built by one of the regular visitors out of his own pocket. But as the music, provided by a couple of young ladies, is somewhat poor, the dancing dies out quickly and everyone leaves the hall. It would have seemed to be more rational to remain in the hall and convert it into a *conversazione*. It seems that most people have a date for a *tête à tête*, which is much more pleasant for those involved, of course. Even for me the night was not lost, for here I really got acquainted with Miss Robins, and although Mr. Fuller (a cousin of the girls) and Carry Fuller were standing around, I had a long conversation with her. I never saw a more splendid array of beautiful women, all with freshness and all very well grown up and at least three-quarters of them really handsome and nice. An ugly and undeveloped girl is hardly ever seen here. Not a single matron was present; all were young people. The ladies danced without gloves and the gentlemen came out in gray coats, as a proof that this all is most informal. I would have preferred a little more of etiquette.

SUNDAY 19 AUGUST 1866

Sunday, an absolutely boring day here, but we go out for a sailing trip to Shoal Islands, about nine miles out, although this is not quite 'correct' to do on a Sunday. We had a good fish dinner on Star Island. Only Bond, Oyens, and I are in the party. Spent the evening with the Fullers.[10]

MONDAY 20 AUGUST 1866

In the morning a game of croquet with the Fullers and a bath in the sea. In the afternoon Bond, Oyens, and I go out for a ride with Etta Fuller, Miss Robins, and Carry Fuller. Visited Portsmouth with the Navy Yard. Saw new ironclads on the stocks and a new wooden gunboat. At 6 pm the bell rings for the end of the working day and a large crowd of workers pours out from the gates. As the road to Portsmouth is a very roundabout one, they all have boats to cross the wide Piscataqua River. With military drill the boats are boarded, and at least twenty-five or even thirty of them, each with about fifteen men, push off. They are rowed in style, and with the evening sun on the river, they present a very picturesque sight. It will be superfluous to say that our tour was a great success, especially the return in the moonlight; and that we get a little excited by the free and easy companionship of young Americans, as allowed everywhere, does not need to be emphasized either.

TUESDAY 21 AUGUST 1866

In the morning and afternoon croquet. In the evening a stroll with Etta Fuller in the moonlight. We sit talking pleasantly for about an hour on a rock jutting out into the sea and don't get home before 10:30 pm. I won't tell what a Dutch mother would have said about this, but that it is generally quite accepted here is clear from the—also tonight—heavily populated 'rooks.' Everybody keeps saying that the situation is hardly ever being improperly used, on the contrary, the "institution" as it is called, is profitable for both parties. The general idea of a 'flirtation' is not negative, and the ladies speak about it quite naturally and without any inhibition. Mr. Amory with Mary Fuller, Mr. Jones with Etta Wigglesworth, and Mr. Ellis with Miss Annie Wigglesworth don't hesitate to make good use of this permission. How far it is seriously meant I am unable to say.

We also get acquainted with Mr. and Mrs. Jones—a very pretty woman—and Miss Blake, who have come to stay in our hotel for a couple of days.

WEDNESDAY 22 AUGUST 1866

Departed in the morning with a lot of anguish. Spent the day at the Asbury Grove Camp Meeting near Hamilton to make good our somewhat incomplete experience at Yarmouth. The atmosphere at this camp meeting, however, was much less excited and therefore less interesting. The sermon on Ecclesiastes 9:10 was fairly good but a little on the dry side.

NB One of the pleasant meetings at Rye Beach was also that with Mrs. Wigglesworth and Mrs. Gould, the first one a daughter of Nath. Goddard and has copied a lot of letters to Daniel Crommelin & Sons, and the latter the wife of a former correspondent.[11]

THURSDAY 23 AUGUST 1866

Executed several orders and visited people. Public Library, where my umbrella is stolen. Dinner in the Union Club.

FRIDAY 24 AUGUST 1866

To Lawrence, after Lowell the biggest manufacturing town in New England. On arrival I lose Oyens, and after having searched for him in vain, I decide to go to the Pacific and the Washington Mills on my own. Fortunately I have the letters of recommendation in my pocket. Before noon I spend some hours in the first one, the Pacific Mills.[12]

It is a woolen- and cotton-spinning and weaving mill, chiefly of cotton warp and woolen weft. Capital $2,500,000, annual production 40,000,000 yards, four thousand workers, average wage $1½ or $2; the weaving is being paid by piece, 3,400 looms. The manufacturing of the cotton is split in carding, drawing, spinning, dressing with starch, and weaving. The printing is completely done with machines; the cloth is running on a big drum and is being printed by means of thin brass rollers, pressing against the drum. A total of sixteen rollers, meaning sixteen colors, can be used at the same time. A folding machine had my special interest.

A lot has been done for the laborers. The company has built boarding houses for some 900 unmarried women, where also a number of married couples are living. They are making no profit on these and so they are much sought after; usual board is $2.75 a week. For the other employees, watchmen, overseers, etc., the company has built houses too, very solidly constructed and neat. Working hours are 6:30 to 12 and 1 to 6:30, on Saturdays 1 to 5. There is also a library available, with separate reading rooms for men and women. About 1,500 of the 4,000 make use of this, as far as I could see, and about 1,000 books are being lent out every week.

The lecture hall was too small for the present and therefore temporarily out of use. Among themselves the workers had organized a Relief Society and a Savings Bank. The first named had already paid out some $25,000, but I was unable to obtain other figures than this.

When the bell rang at 12, I saw everyone rush outside, mostly girls generally over 18 years old. Most had a sickly look and almost all of them freckled, but dressed after the latest fashion and with a great love of finery. The Pacific Mill has paid out dividends up to 25 percent.

In the afternoon to the Washington Mills. All kinds of manufactures are being produced, printed woolen tablecloths, shawls, worsted, cloth for pants, etc. For the first time I saw weaving with different colors in process. Either the raw cloth or the thread or the finished piece is being dyed, depending on the destination of the finished product and its properties. NB I noticed a machine to turn the fringes for shawls.[13]

Wherever I went, nowhere was a glass of ale to be had. It seems that there is an old liquor law in Massachusetts, generally forgotten in the cities, but still enforced in the countryside and in factory towns such as this one in particular.

SATURDAY 25 AUGUST 1866

Dinner with George Wm. Bond in Jamaica Plains. Maria is still on her couch with a sprained ankle. Game of croquet with Sophia and Miss Gertrude and Cora Weld. General Macy and Ned Robins. General Macy has lost a hand in the war. He was provost marshal of the Army of the Potomac, and he was charged with the paroling of Lee and his officers, and also with the keeping of 8 or 10,000 prisoners. He is a cheerful person and behind his teeth he told me that "by God" he would love to go through another campaign but that he didn't dare to tell anybody. Ned Robins is a brother of Miss Robins of Rye Beach and was on the staff of Gen. Macy.[14]

SUNDAY 26 AUGUST 1866

Sunday, to church in Roxbury with Wm. Bond. Unitarian Church, Dr. Hall, dull and boring, but beautiful singing, a quartet with a seraphine. In the afternoon a drive with Maria and Will, music in the evening.[15]

MONDAY 27 AUGUST 1866

Strolled around, Bunker Hill monument, Cambridge, Harvard University. Empty halls with no one around as it is vacation. Old Elm, at the foot of which Washington accepted the command of the American army in 1775. Longfellow's house. Visited with Blake in Brookline.[16]

Tuesday 28 August 1866

With W. S. Bond to the Norfolk Mills in Rosebury, property of the New England Rosebury Carpet Company. Three kinds of carpet: tapestry, velvet, and Brussels. The first two are woven in the same way, with the thread dyed and so making the pattern in the warp. Before the weaving the thread is stretched on big movable drums and then carried forward on narrow disks carrying the paint, and moving under the big drum on small carriages. It will be clear that only one variety of thread can be handled on the drum at the same time. With notches on the rim of the rotating drum, the worker—more often than not a woman—can decide where the disk with the paint will touch the thread, according to the pattern in question. The disk runs parallel with the pivot of the drum. Four or five colored threads are usually sufficient to make the pattern.[17]

The warp is made in about the same way as with the cotton weaving, only much slower. As the threads are very different in respect of elasticity, the colors would soon run unevenly and the pattern would be unrecognizable if the making of the warp would be left to a machine. Two women are employed to make about 10 feet of warp at a time. The spindles have been placed on a moving apparatus, and the cylinder that receives the warp is fixed. At both ends, on the apparatus with the spindles and on the cylinder, meaning at the end where the warp is being made and where it is being received, a kind of lock—an iron bar with a screw—is fitted, that fixes the warp to prevent a thread being moved. The whole operation is as follows: the apparatus with the spindles (A) is moved away from the cylinder (B) after the lock has been closed. The cylinder cannot move in the wrong direction, and from the spindles at A an amount sufficient for making about 10 feet of warp is being unwound. The women together now quickly check and manipulate the threads to make the pattern perfect. Then the lock at A is closed, that at B opened, and the finished warp wound upon the cylinder.

That warp is then woven into the linen underlay. Two warps of linen thread and the dyed woolen warp are woven together at the same time. At every stroke a long steel pin is pushed in between the linen and the woolen warp. The woolen warp is being drawn over that pin and at the next stroke fixed by the weft between the linen. This is the way the well-known rows of loops in tapestry are formed and the woolen warp with the pattern woven into the cloth. Six or eight of those pins are sufficient to prevent the pulling out of the threads, and every time the machine withdraws the first pin and puts it in again as the last one.

Brussels is woven on the jacquard loom, and as is well known, for every thread of the warp there is [a] separate [device] making a warp of every color in the pattern. With every stroke of the loom all these threads that will form the pattern are retained with a system of cards with holes to accommodate the pins, while all others are falling through and stay out of view. Those threads that are kept above are always of the same number, here generally 260, and every card has 260 holes, and the threads are retained above the cloth, just as with tapestry and velvet, by a steel pin, making Brussels a series of loops too. Almost no others than women are being employed here, and they make between $6 and 7 a week.

It is interesting to see the independence of the workers everywhere around you. Nobody is taking notice of the visitors or the one who accompanies you, generally the owner or the superintendent. Everyone just keeps working and will not even think of touching his cap or taking it off, as is usual in European factories. And your guide will not even think of disturbing a worker to explain something or make things clear for you. You are allowed to look and see and ask as many questions as you want, but you will not be favored with even one minute of a worker's or the bosses' time.

In the afternoon we went with Henry Sturges to Swampscott, where he spends the summer. His wife, formerly Miss Mansom, whom he married against the will of his family, didn't please me much. She is vulgar and has few charms, at least not for me. Her friend Miss Emma Bird I liked much more, although she is not one of the best. Mr. Ned Blake played a game of croquet with us. Visited with Jasigi, where we met Miss Reggio again. She appears the moment when she is informed by Jasigi that we are with him. Stayed overnight with Sturges.[18]

WEDNESDAY 29 AUGUST 1866

Back to Boston. Had my portrait made at Sursell. A couple of visits. Spent the evening with the Bonds. Saying farewell was hard, even when it is only for a short time.[19]

THURSDAY 30 AUGUST 1866

Departed for Newport at 8 am, arrived at 11 am. A bath in the sea. After 1 pm the gentlemen bath in the nude. In the evening a steeplechase on the beach, the first one won by Digby, the second one by Russell. Went to see Alfred Reed in the evening.[20]

No entries for 31 August and 1 September 1866

SUNDAY 2 SEPTEMBER 1866

Dinner with Alfred Reed, Mrs. and Miss Hoffman in the Fillmore Hotel. Visited with Mrs. Morton.[21]

MONDAY 3 SEPTEMBER 1866

Same with the Wards and Mr. McKay.

No entry for 4 September 1866

WEDNESDAY 5 SEPTEMBER 1866

Together with Alfred Reed, Jr., to Providence. Oriental Mills, cotton spinning and weaving mill of A. Reed. New and very neatly arranged; self-cleaning cards. Engineering works of Corliss & Co., screw manufactory. Making of screws in three operations: 1, the striking of the head: the iron wire is cut off at a certain length and put in a solid die consisting of two parts, and the head is then struck on. 2, the burrs are turned off the head and the groove cut with a machine; first the burrs are turned off and the machine then turns about and cuts the groove with a small circular saw; then at a second stroke the screw is treated with the chisel and the burrs caused by the sawing cut away. 3, the cutting of the thread: the screw is fixed with the head in a revolving spindle. On the axle of that spindle a loose part A turns with the spindle. This piece has a large screw thread with another part B, which is pressed on from time to time. When the spindle is revolving, piece A will move also and with every revolution one stroke of the screw thread. Piece A now presses forward the chisel that is to cut the thread while the screw itself is revolving with the spindle and piece A itself. The thread on A is now transferred in a smaller shape on the screw that is being treated. Everything, the picking up and turning of the screw, is done mechanically in a most ingenious way. The shares of the factory were originally $100 and are now valued at $15,000. Dividends are around 100 percent per month. Everything is protected by patents.[22]

To New York.

7

In New York City, New Jersey, and Troy, New York

September–October 1866

THURSDAY 6 SEPTEMBER 1866

Visits.

FRIDAY 7 SEPTEMBER 1866

Met Mr. C. H. Russell, president of the Commercial Bank, by accident. He has known my father and grandfather well and he invites me to visit with him in Newport.[1]

No entry for 8 September 1866

SUNDAY 9 SEPTEMBER 1866

Went to church in Trinity Church. A lot is being made of the singing by the boys' choir, but as usual it leaves me stone cold. The church itself is built in a fine Gothic style of gray sandstone, with handsome stained-glass windows.[2]

No entries for 10–12 September 1866

THURSDAY 13 SEPTEMBER 1866

With Alfred Reed, Jr., to Harper's establishment, chiefly a printing business. A big institution in a fireproof building. Everything is being printed with electrotypes; printing from ordinary types has been discarded completely and every book is stereotyped. Every electrotype can produce about 200,000 copies. Saw a cylindrical printing press that prints four sheets at a time. Marbling. A machine for the folding of the sheets, most curious. When their former building burned down some years ago, they lost—over the insured value—goods and inventory valued at about $1,200,000 (gold dollars of course). Met Mr. Joseph Harper the Second.[3]

FRIDAY 14 SEPTEMBER 1866

Visited the Board of Education, Grand Street, and met Mr. Randall, the superintendent of it all, and Mr. Boese, the clerk and the general manager as far as I could find out. Had a long conversation with them. New York has about three hundred public schools, and according to Mr. Randall at least as many would be needed, despite the large number of private schools. The earlier preference for 'pay schools' seems to have faded away, and the great majority of the children are now being sent to the public primary schools. Later the 'accomplishments' that are being taught in the private schools, but not in the public schools, are seen as more important by many parents. Private schools are completely free, the teachers don't have to pass any examination, and there is hardly any inspection by the government. All teachers in the public schools have to pass certain tests and examinations. The same with the pupils: 75 percent of them have to be promoted to the next grade at the end of term. If not, the teacher will lose his certificate unless he can give some reasonable excuse for himself. In the better schools 90 or even 100 percent will pass, but what are the exams worth in that case?

The annual expenditure is about $2,500,000, with a subvention by the state of some $250,000. But as taxation is set according to the valuation of real property and the subvention according to the number of pupils, New York City pays about $450,000 for education in the state, but gets only $250,000 in return. On top of that 1/20 percent of the valuation of real property, plus the same amount as the subvention by the state, plus more taxation of up to 8 percent per pupil, all to be levied by the Board of Education, and not linked to the rest of the city government.

No entries for 15–18 September 1866

WEDNESDAY 19 SEPTEMBER 1866

Had dinner with Edward King at Hoboken. Pretty country mansion owned by his mother.[4]

THURSDAY 20–SATURDAY 22 SEPTEMBER 1866

Stayed with Thomas Ludlow at Yonkers. Mrs. Newbold of Philadelphia invited me strongly. Cottage Lawn is about 100 acres, sale price now between $2,500 and 3,000 per acre. Valued for the state tax at $40,000 at 5 percent. Rents in New York: the Brown Brothers building, their own offices $30,000. Pacific Mail Co. $25,000.[5]

Heard a story about a town meeting where the bounties of the soldiers who had been drafted were paid out. In charge of the meeting were a drunkard and a thief out on bail.

No entry for 23 September

MONDAY 24 SEPTEMBER 1866

To the Verplancks at Fishkill. We were met at the station by Gulian C. Verplanck, and he drove us to Mrs. Nevils, his sister, who wasn't in. Then to Mr. Delancey Verplanck and the old homestead, bought from the Indians in 1680 by one of the early Verplancks. The place is now occupied by Dr. Verplanck, who is in bad health, and Mrs. Sam Verplanck, whom we didn't see. Afterward to William S. Verplanck, son of G. C. Verplanck. Well received in a most friendly way, and I soon feel at home. His children are Eliza (Mrs. Richards), Mary, Bob, Annie, Jenny, Gelyna, and William. In the evening a hot dispute with Mrs. Richards about politics.[6]

TUESDAY 25 SEPTEMBER 1866

With the Verplancks to Mr. Joseph Howland at his beautiful country estate, 2½ miles below Fishkill.[7]

WEDNESDAY 26 SEPTEMBER 1866

In the country with Mr. Osborn at Garrison's Point. Rain all day and we had to seek comfort around the fireplace.

THURSDAY 27 SEPTEMBER 1866

Seen the Sing Sing Prison. Together with Trenton and Auburn the state prison of New York. Between 1,200 and 1,400 inmates, and everything on the old system. The prisoners sleep in cells but work together in all kinds of shops. Barbaric punishments: an iron hood that has to be worn day and night; the dark hole; showers of cold water over the head, continued for a long time, sometimes until passing out. The buildings are lying in the open on the river bank, without a ring wall; all security is maintained by guards. There have been sharp outbreaks from time to time. NB Ketchum was there too, but he had a lot of freedom of movement because of his 'influential friends.'[8]

No entry for 28 September 1866

SATURDAY 29 SEPTEMBER 1866

Blackwell's Island, Lunatic Asylum, Workhouse, and Almshouse.[9]

Sunday 30 September 1866

Visited with the Scharffs at Newith & Bloomfield.[10]

Monday 1 October 1866

Dinner with the Dutilhs.

No entry for 2 October 1866

Wednesday 3 October 1866

Oyens left New York on the *Java.*

Thursday 4–Saturday 6 October 1866

Stayed with Mr. Joseph Howland at Matteawan.[11]

Friday 5 October 1866

Picnic on the top of South Beacon. Mr. and Mrs. Adrian Verplanck; Mr. Daniel Crommelin Verplanck Nevils; Mary Verplanck and Miss MacKinnon; Mr. and Mrs. Slack; Mr. and Mrs. Campbell; Miss Van Buren; etc.[12]

Saturday 6 October 1866

Dinner with Mr. Chrystie in Newburgh; his wife is related to me through the Ludlows. Miss Addie Chrystie, Mrs. Dashwood.

Mr. and Mrs. Howland have both been very active in the war. He served a long time in the Union Army, was promoted to colonel, and left the service as a brigadier. She, together with her sisters—three Misses Woolsey—has merited a good deal of praise in the hospitals and as a supervisor of nurses. The ample means of Mr. Howland have enabled him and his wife to do a lot of good, and they have not been stingy there. Their most cherished trophy is a handsome Bible presented by the privates of Howland's regiment to Mrs. Howland. In earlier days they traveled a lot in Europe and the East; now he is treasurer of the State of New York. Both are violent radicals and 'go in for [universal] manhood suffrage,' but for the rest most pleasant people, generous and hospitable. They try to do something for everybody, receiving the upper classes in style and building schools for the lower orders. They are very orthodox, prayer in the morning, prayer before meals, Sunday schools, etc. Beautiful estate, neat and well furnished.[13]

Sunday 7 October 1866

Sunday.

No entries for 8–9 October 1866

WEDNESDAY 10 OCTOBER 1866

To Paterson with a letter obtained through Cas. Thoron for Mr. Powers, son of the well-known sculptor at Florence. Saw the New Jersey Locomotive and Machine Works, mostly the property of Mr. Grant. Mr. Powers received me well and showed me everything. After everything I had heard of these works, they disappoint me a little bit. About 600 men at work, 72 locomotives annually, each sold for about $15,000 to 20,000. I couldn't see many machines and instruments that I didn't know. The only thing new to me was the fixing of the wheels on the axles, which is done cold by hydraulic pressure.[14]

Falls of the Passaic. In the evening with C. Thoron to the *Black Crook* ballet, largely based on the *Biche au Bois*.[15]

THURSDAY 11 OCTOBER 1866

Dinner with Mrs. Richards-Verplanck. Mr. Rob. Verplanck.

FRIDAY 12 OCTOBER 1866

To Troy to visit with James T. Munn, as promised earlier. With him a visit to three Misses Seymour, rather vulgar women,[16]

SATURDAY 13 OCTOBER 1866

Seen the Arsenal at West Troy, shown around by Captain Prince. Activities here are now largely confined to repairing the old and used equipment, and the most interesting operations have of course been ended. A machine for the pressing of bullets drew my attention. The casting of pointed bullets has been discarded completely, but for round bullets it is still being practiced, at least partially. Chronograph of Schultz.[17]

The two types of guns (fieldpieces) that have been used and will remain in service for a time are the bronze 12-pounder, invented by Napoleon, a smooth bore, and the 3-inch wrought iron rifled bore. This last piece has steel grooves. It is cast with a steel core a bit larger than the bore, and then drilled out. Also Parrot-guns, both for siege and for service in the coastal fortresses. Iron gun carriages with eccentric axles suitable for running on wheels for better maneuverability. They can also rest on rails, whereby the recoil is largely absorbed. For a long time Captain Prince was attached to the arsenal in Washington and charged with the testing and evaluation of all new inventions. In his arm of the service, the Ordnance, all promotions up to the rank of colonel are given only after an examination.[18]

SUNDAY 14 OCTOBER 1866

Sunday. Choral service in the Troy Holy Cross Church.

8

In Boston, Providence, Albany, and back to New York City

October–December 1866

MONDAY 15 OCTOBER 1866

Rode from Troy to Boston on the Western Massachusetts Railroad. Picturesque landscape, but barren, rocky, and a lot of stones. Negro minstrels with Mr. Fuller.

TUESDAY 16 OCTOBER 1866

Invited by Mr. Bond to stay with him, so I packed up my things and went to Jamaica Plains. Visit with the Fullers.

No entry for 17 October 1866

THURSDAY 18 OCTOBER 1866

Various visits, many introductions. Mr. Philbrick; dined with Mr. Reed.

FRIDAY 19 OCTOBER 1866

Introduced into several schools by Mr. Philbrick, superintendent of schools; I start my visits today. Brimmer School first, master M. Bates. Grammar school for boys between 8 and 14 to 15 years old. Excellent discipline, military atmosphere, different positions taken by the pupils on orders from above, even in praying. Reading aloud together in different tones, 'the whispering, the loud, the conversational etc. (vocal gymnastics).' Generally short lessons of 15 to 25 minutes. A lot of attention, the master in good shape and he knows how to keep the boys awake. The system of teaching by the principal doesn't please me much. The school has about eight hundred boys; Mr. Bates has a class of his own and has only three half days to organize his own school, and moreover he has to check all primary schools in his district, of which he is the principal too, at least nominally. But he has an assistant to teach his own class whenever he is away. In those primary schools all the teachers are standing next to each other, and not surprisingly, this causes a lot of bickering and trouble. I also thought the boys too well trained, with a lot of automatons. Each master has his own class, not his own field of science. For boys of 12 or 13 it may be a good system, but some variety would do no harm in my opinion. Later with Miss Penniman, who did a very good job in teaching, many female teachers. Ventilation left a lot to be desired. Corporal punishment usual, but not frequent; good discipline at the end of classes. Hours from 9 to 10:15, 10:45 to 12, 1:45 to 4.[1]

Ride with Miss S. Bond.

In the evening with Dr. Clarke and his daughter Lilian to a soirée of Mrs. Julia Ward Howe, well known in literary circles. She composed a "Battle Hymn of the Republic," which gained a lot of popularity recently, undeserved in my opinion at least. Gov. Andrew and others, who didn't interest me much; a Miss Deltone pleased me better.[2]

SATURDAY 20 OCTOBER 1866

Visited the several courts with Francis E. Parker. Municipal court, one in every township, for minor offences only, civil $300, no jury. Superior court, civil about $4,000, all crimes except capital crimes; District Attorney Sanger. Various sentences with fines up to $500 for violation of the liquor laws, which prohibit all sales of 'intoxicating liquors.' Supreme court, real estate, court of appeals. Everybody is allowed to defend himself in every court. To be licensed as an attorney requires three years of study. All judges are appointed by the governor and his council 'on good behaviour.'[3]

U.S. district court, U.S. circuit court, circuits of the Supreme Court in Washington: all crimes at sea, patent rights, forgery, and counterfeiting of the coin of the realm, etc. No appeal from supreme court [of Massachusetts] to U.S. Supreme Court.

Dinner with Mrs. Clarke, tea with Mrs. Bond.

SUNDAY 21 OCTOBER 1866

Sunday, in the evening visit with Mrs. Jones.

MONDAY 22 OCTOBER 1866

Visited the Idiot School in South Boston. This school, the first in America, was established nineteen years ago by Dr. Howe in imitation of European examples of the same kind. It is well situated on Dorchester Bay, with a lot of fresh air and seawater and in my opinion answered all the needs of such an establishment.

The classrooms are spacious and well ventilated, and the teaching is well adapted to the low level of development of the pupils. Mrs. McDonald is the headmistress, a most accomplished and handsome woman. About sixty-five or seventy pupils, of which the state is responsible for about fifty-five, the others are being paid for. The main emphasis is on corporal development by way of gymnastics and calisthenics, and all other teaching is simple and easy to digest. The singing was reasonable, and the little exercises such as the reciting of tables of multiplication and the definitions pleased me very well. Generally the children looked happy and in good health. However, many showed the marks of their undeveloped youth on their faces; otherwise they would have been pretty enough.[4]

The Blind Asylum on Dorchester Heights, also founded by Dr. Howe and now some thirty years in operation. About seventy pupils, the course is one of seven years for ages between 7 and 14, and it is seen as a real school. The children have their days off and vacations, and the institution is aiming at enabling the blind to help themselves and make their own living. This they often do with music, although some, especially boys, also make brooms, etc.

Dinner in the Union Club with Francis E. Parker, R. H. Dana, the well-known lawyer and author of *Three Years before the Mast,* and a Mr. Morse. Most pleasant dinner, all were very talkative and full of stories. One of Dana's struck me in particular. When he was in California in 1860, a new governor had been elected, a certain Latham. Immediately thereafter a new U.S. senator had to be elected. Parties were split between two candidates A and B, and no one was thinking of Latham. When Mr. Dana left California, he was very much intrigued by the outcome and he thought that he could estimate the chances of both candidates fairly well. Therefore he was much surprised to hear from someone after his departure that Latham was to be the senator. Upon his question of how this had been possible, he got for answer "O, very naturally, the bulkhead has done it." The case was this: in San Francisco a plan had been drawn up to construct a bulkhead or seawall, for many interested parties a sure way of making a lot of money. In his inaugural address the governor had spoken vehemently against this project, so he had to be removed from office somehow, and the easiest way seemed to be to make him U.S. senator. Dana's friend and spokesman had gone to Sacramento and hadn't had much trouble to drum up enough support to get a majority for Latham. The first question from Dana was whether Latham, whose greatest ambition was to go to Washington, had spoken against the bulkhead only to reach that goal. Parker has many European ideas and is no strong Republican.[5]

TUESDAY 23 OCTOBER 1866

Winthrop School, grammar school for girls, Mr. Swan master. Very good reading, together and each girl separately, mental arithmetic, etc., excellent discipline and order. Mr. Swan defended the system that the principal has a class of his own, as the male element must have a positive influence on the female. In my opinion a male assistant could do the same. Swan complained about the amount of work for a principal. He does have a female assistant who can take over his class anytime.

Wednesday 24 October 1866

Wrote letters and spent the day outside.

Thursday 25 October 1866

Various things. The English High School system of every teacher having a class of his own is making headway here.

Friday 26 October 1866

Various things. Attended a political meeting in Cambridge in the evening. Speakers were Boutwell and Dana. The first one was too narrow and simple in his arguments. His last one was this: Bright is appealing to the fact that in the North the workman has suffrage; how much stronger will his argument be if he could appeal to the Negroes? In that case there will be no class difference anymore, and the English aristocracy will cease to have any influence.[6]

Saturday 27 October 1866

State prison in Charlestown, Mr. Haynes warden. Same kind of building as the jail, neatly executed; there are prisoners for life. The prison system is the same as at Sing Sing. Sleeping in cells, working in shops with perfect discipline. The midday meal is taken in the cells here too. All march inside, get their rations, walk to their cells, and lock themselves in by means of a self-closing door. Punishments: dark cell, after that a dark hole that seems to be worse, both are without a bed or other amenities. The corporal punishments have been abolished. About 530 inmates, but room for 30 more. There is no gaslight in the cells, but from outside enough light is being admitted through the barred doors that they can read until 8 pm. Some are able to continue until 9, but from then to 6 am it is pitch dark and there is nothing else to do but sleep.[7]

Sunday 28 October 1866

Sunday, in the church of Dr. Clarke. Heard Dr. Hill, president of Harvard, give a very dry but well-wrought sermon. This church was built from contributions and then placed as a corporate body under trustees to serve as meeting hall for the Church of Disciples, an independent association of believers, somewhat comparable to the Unitarians. Mr. Bond is a member. The deed has been well thought out, also making arrangements for the circumstance when the Church of Disciples will have ceased to exist. Otherwise the Probate Court would have to decide how to dispose of the assets. This way of church organization is so much different from ours that it is hard for us to fathom everything. Usually the income of the preacher is found in the letting of the pews, but here, as all the seats are free, his income is supplied from voluntary contributions, which are said to be ample and generous.[8]

Monday 29 October 1866

Attended a session of the Circuit Court of the United States. A case of unlawfully obtained prize money. Jury trial. All, except the judges, in light-colored pants.

Tuesday 30 October 1866

Various things. First a visit to the Tombs. The Tombs are located under the courthouse, and all offenders are taken from there to the municipal court that is in session every day and can pass sentences itself or commit to a grand jury. Those that are arrested on Saturday night have to stay in the Tombs all Sunday to appear before the police court on Monday morning. It is partly underground and lacks light and fresh air, but is fairly well heated. Every criminal has his own cell with a couch and a chair and nothing else, but each cell also has a privy, and food is brought in at regular times.

Atheneum. Violent southwester storm. Miss Emily Freeman.[9]

Wednesday 31 October 1866

Spent the day at Harvard, mostly with Arthur Huidekoper, also with Edgar Huidekoper and Don Reed, and dined with some other friends. What a difference with our universities at home! I was there from 10 am until 5:30 pm and I wasn't offered a single drink, not even a glass of ale. Only water at dinner was all that I got, and a filthy pipe the only thing presented. Nobody has cigars, and hardly anybody seems to have access to wine or liquor. A stroll to Mount Auburn gave me the occasion to get to know that famous cemetery, worth its fame, I think. It is laid out very well, and the view from the tower in the center of the park is splendid and worth the climb. Many tombs are located within an iron enclosure to contain several graves. They bury only in one layer. Two big and several smaller monuments, one of them looks like father and mother taking their children for a walk. Walking back I met Longfellow. Handsome head and his gait is still strong and sure, but his occupation less poetic, as he was buying cheese at the grocer's.[10]

Thursday 1 November 1866

Inspected the training ship for convicted boys below the age of 21. All boys sentenced to a stay on the ship are kept at that institution until they turn 21, but in reality they hardly ever stay longer in the ship than one year. There simply is not enough room for them all, with the steadily growing number of convicts. A first step to improve that situation has been taken by the equipping of a second school ship, presently moored in New Bedford. A gift of $5,000 from a certain Mr. Barnard seems to have spurred on this development. Although the institution officially aims at turning the boys into good seamen, actually only half of them are given positions in the merchant marine or the navy. For the others jobs on land are sought, generally at the wish of the parents. But all are being kept under the supervision of the trustees of this state institution until their twenty-first birthday, and whenever they misbehave, they can be put back on the ship at once. Judge Russell seems to be the heart and soul of the affair and still takes a great interest in it.[11]

The education is entrusted to Mr. Sydney Brooks, a former teacher; his wife, the only female element on board, is also living in the ship. She takes care of the boys and teaches them some music. The pupils, about 160 in all, are divided in a starboard and port watch, and in turn each watch has a day of teaching and a day on deck. I found that the actual education is given by Mr. Brooks with a lot of common sense and success. He is following the usual methods, short lessons, much variety, gymnastic exercise, common exercise, more or less adapted to the needs of his pupils. His discipline is fairly good but not as perfect as I have seen elsewhere. Of course, I know that most of the boys had been on board only for a short time, but for a school such as this one I thought the discipline not very strict. The other division I liked much less. That watch is on deck all day but is only put to work if there is something to do, such as rowing someone to the quay, scrubbing the decks, cleaning the hammocks, or washing clothes. It will be clear that for 70 boys this isn't much. For the rest it appears that they are allowed to play; at least today, after noontime, they had nothing to do but play. And in the small space of a ship's deck there is not much to play but for some loafing about, climbing the rigging, playing ball, and for the rest gossiping. In summer the boys go sailing around and then they will have more opportunities to learn useful things. After 4 pm they are allowed to read until sunset—now at 5 pm—and then they are sent off to bed—according to Mr. Brooks at least before 7 pm—so at this time of the year probably much earlier. But even when counting from 7 pm they will have eleven hours of sleep. It is then easy to imagine what the consequences will be when one puts 160 boys, most of them from the lowest orders and all convicted of some crime or misdemeanor and disobedience, together between decks in closely packed hammocks and forces them to stay under the blankets for more than eleven hours. I couldn't think of a better way for encouraging all kinds of vice and immoral acts!

FRIDAY 2 NOVEMBER 1866

Watch manufactory at Waltham. Property of the American Watch Company, Mr. Robbins director. This factory, about twelve years old, has seen a very great success over the last few years. Capital invested $750,000, production 75,000 watches annually, price of silver watches from $25, of gold ones between $100 and $375. About 750 workers, men and women; wages around $4 per day for the men, $1.50–2 for the women; board $3–3.50 per week. Superior kind of workers, all intelligent, neat, and clean. For the first time I saw here a man, an Irishman, who saluted the director. Almost everything is being produced with the help of most ingenious little machinery, and undoubtedly a closer study of all this machinery would show some interesting principle. However, the number of machines is too great for me to watch them all at close quarters, but most seemed to be fairly simple and intended for one operation only. The work is so delicate and has to be executed with such a precision that it would be difficult to combine several operations in one machine. They are mostly improved and self-acting machines, but not yet 'full-fledged' ones. The worker still has a great responsibility and cannot leave too much to the machine. The gear wheels are punched here, but the teeth are later cut in the brass disks.[12]

In the evening to the Boston Museum with Sophie and W. Bond and Miss Freeman. A benefit performance for Miss Annie Clark of *The Flowers of the Forest* and *The Conjugal Lesson*. A good and enthusiastic audience, and again I liked the usual melodramatic tone of the plays.[13]

SATURDAY 3 NOVEMBER 1866

Invited by the mayor, Mr. F. W. Lincoln (an instrument maker), I go at 2 pm with him and several of the commissioners of Public Charities, Mr. Kimball, Mr. Drake, Mr. Manning, and three or four others by steamer *Henry Morrison* to Deer Island. For some years the city of Boston has erected and is maintaining on that island a big institution for the poor and for convicts. After a dinner, fairly good for America, Mr. Payson, the superintendent, and the mayor take me around to see the four divisions assembled here in this building: the almshouse for elderly men and women (not convicted), the House of Industry for convicted men and women (for misdemeanors only and especially public drunkenness), the boys' and the girls' reform schools, both for convicted minors only. The buildings are handsome and solidly constructed, with iron staircases and doors, and well heated and ventilated high-ceilinged rooms. Discipline is all right and the food of good quality, but here again the system of long nights is in force. Both the convicts and the boys in the reform school are sent to bed at 7 pm and have to get up only at 6:30 in the morning. The convicts get no other education than in ethical and religious matters.[14]

The right to pardon is in the hands of the board of commissioners. These commissioners didn't give me a very good impression. They hardly spoke, and when they opened their mouths it was for gossip only. No real good conversation possible. After dinner Mr. Kimball, the president of the board, lay down on a couch and slept. About the institution I couldn't hear more than cheap jokes or smutty stories.

SUNDAY 4 NOVEMBER 1866

Sunday. Went to church at Rosebury, Dr. Putnam, Unitarian, preaching. Dinner at Alfred Reed's with Mrs. Coolidge, Hooper and Frothingham, and Mr. Verploegh, late commissioner on Java, who had come here across the plains from San Francisco. Visit with the Jasigis.[15]

MONDAY 5 NOVEMBER 1866

A quiet day, wrote letters, and in the evening a game of ninepins.

TUESDAY 6 NOVEMBER 1866

Election Day in many states. In Massachusetts all is very quiet. I visited a polling station, where there was little excitement. The Republican Party is so preponderant in Massachusetts that there is hardly any contest, and the outcome never in doubt. Only the election of two colored men as representatives in the state legislature made some noise here and gave sufficient matter for conversation, as this is the first election of its kind. Messrs. Mitchell and Walker are the first of the 'despised race' who are called to a post such as this one. And that a combination of circumstances has caused that Mr. Walker is representing Beacon Street and Commonwealth Avenue makes the case even more special.[16]

Afterward visited the primary schools on East Street. Every class of sixty is called a school and is completely separate and independent from the other classes in the same building. The teacher is the only one in charge of her school and is subordinate only to the principal of the grammar school of her district. Six classes, each with a course of six months, together make up the primary school from where the pupils are promoted to the grammar school. Excellent female teachers.

In the evening a lecture by Wendell Phillips, with the title *The Swindling Congress.*[17]

WEDNESDAY 7 NOVEMBER 1866

Wednesday. Girls' high school; House of Correction almost identical to the House of Industry and the jail. Ball at Miss Reggio's.

No entry for 8 November 1866

FRIDAY 9 NOVEMBER 1866

Primary School on Poplar Street. Boston Museum: *All Is Not Gold That Glitters* and *A Phantom Breakfast* and *Box & Cox*.[18]

SATURDAY 10 NOVEMBER 1866

Various things. Tea with the Fullers at Rosebury.

SUNDAY 11 NOVEMBER 1866

Sunday.

MONDAY 12 NOVEMBER 1866

To Providence. Seen Iveses and Goddards.[19]

No entries for 13–14 November 1866

THURSDAY 15 NOVEMBER 1866

Back to Jamaica Plains.

No entries for 16–17 November 1866

SUNDAY 18 NOVEMBER 1866

Sunday. Church of the Disciples, Dr. Clarke. He preached on the occasion of the recently—at the Unitarian Convention at Syracuse—proposed change in the confession of faith of the Unitarian Church to leave out the declaration that one should try as 'Disciples of God' to propagate on earth the Kingdom of God and his Son. The new proposed version would be to declare that the meaning of life was to live 'in love, charity, truth etc.' Dr. Clarke had voted against the change and now tried to justify himself. People who had opposed the earlier expressions had maintained that they included a creed, and the main principle of the Unitarian Church is that there will be no creed, but liberty for everyone to believe what he liked. The opponents thought these words to be against the chief principle of the Church. After all one should not lock out even those who did not believe in Christ but who were still calling themselves Christians. Dr. Clarke declared that he had nothing against a creed as long as it was not: 1. a test of Christian character; 2. a test of fellowship; 3. a barrier to free thought. And as now in his ideas the name of 'Disciples of Jesus Christ' only signified that one is following Him, be it as the Son of God, or as Godly Man, or even only as a moral teacher, there was nothing binding in that name and it could never be interpreted as a creed.[20]

After the sermon a wedding ceremony. The couple entered the church accompanied only by a groomsman and a bridesmaid, in ordinary clothes. The family came to sit around them quietly. Dr. Clarke read a short service and that was all.

MONDAY 19 NOVEMBER 1866

"*Visites d'adieu.*"[21]

TUESDAY 20 NOVEMBER 1866

Same and same. Said good bye to the Bond family in the evening, and spent the night in Parker House.[22]

WEDNESDAY 21 NOVEMBER 1866

Departed from Boston for Albany by the Western Massachusetts RR. Raw and unpleasant weather, making me think of the coming winter and regret the fine autumn weather that we have enjoyed until now. The railroad traverses the state from east to west and provides a good impression of the character of Massachusetts. The country is hilly, very rocky, and infertile. Most of the large and neat villages that are to be seen now and then make their living in industry. Many strawboard factories.

Albany. Found the name E. Evertsen.[23]

Equal Rights Convention, which could better have been named Women's Rights Convention, as the Negro question came to the table only well toward the end of the meeting. Moreover, the most interesting thing about it was that the platform was filled with women and the position of chairman was taken by a woman, Mrs. Lucy Stone Blackwell. It was most amusing to hear her addressed as Mrs. Chairman. I arrived at the meeting only late but heard enough to form an opinion of the business at hand, an opinion that was not very favorable. A lot of old arguments and a few new ones that were neither here nor there and were proposed without much enthusiasm. A young Negro, Mr. Remond, Mrs. Jones (most pathetic), Mrs. Lucy Stone, and Mr. Pillsbury were the speakers I heard. Also Mrs. Elizabeth Cady Stanton. She had been ridiculed by the *Albany Evening Journal* and had then written a letter to the editor to tell him that she had seven children and a pleasant home and invited him to come and visit her there. He had retorted that he didn't doubt that she should be much more pleasant at home as hostess than as a bad speaker on a platform. Now she objected that the objective of the association was to win over adherents and lull opponents into sleep. Therefore she proposed to present the editor with a bottle of Winslow's Soothing Syrup (a much advertised concoction to keep children quiet). This occasioned loud applause, partly well meant, but also partly derisive. Generally the audience was not very sympathetic, and derisive applause was frequent. Mrs. Jones claimed that if the right to vote was a natural right, everyone should have it and that exclusion from the vote was absolutely wrong. She went on and on in this vein in a kind of 'maundering tone,' comparing the right to vote with the right to live. That a theorem such as this would need some more proof seemed to have escaped her completely.[24]

The next speaker, Mr. Pillsbury, talked about the association and came forward with a new crime perpetrated by the white race against the black. In earlier days, he said, the Negroes were black and mulattos almost unknown. Nowadays two-fifths of the black race is faded and who other than the white race is guilty? "They have been robbed of their color."

Mrs. Stone spoke best of all. She was up in arms against the claim that women shouldn't come to places where the going was as rough as in the polling stations. But, she said, if the men there are so rude, while they live at home with their wives, it is because there are no women at the polls, *at qui ergo*. And if they remain rude there, we women will have our own polling stations where we will invite decent men, who are worth it, to come and vote with us. Most of the women on the platform were equipped with spectacles. Will this make the movement more popular?[25]

Thursday 22 November 1866

Albany, Fishkill. The first snow of the season, a bleak and raw day. To the Verplancks'; heard of the engagement of Mary Verplanck with Sam Johnson.[26]

Friday 23 November 1866

Snow. Mrs. Verplanck told me about the wages of the maids: ordinary maid $2 per week; laundress $10–16, kitchen maid $12–18 per month. To New York in the evening.

No entry for 24 November 1866

Sunday 25 November 1866

Heard Henry Ward Beecher in Plymouth Church in Brooklyn. Flowers on his table. 'Good common sense,' eloquent at times, but less than I had expected. Great clarity and correctness of expression, with always perfect comparisons give him something fascinating, explaining his great popularity. His subject was: 'God's influence on man through his personality only,' illustrated by the edifying influence a single eminent person (e.g., Dr. Arnold of Rugby) can exercise solely by his existence or his presence, without any expression of his will.[27]

Dinner with the Dutilhs. In the evening at the Cotonnets'. Miss Emma Lowndes from Charleston.[28]

MONDAY 26 NOVEMBER 1866

School of Miss Wright, 20th Street, Primary School, for girls only, course of about four years, girls between 5 and 9 or 10 years of age. Miss Matthews, grammar school, only girls until age 16 or 17; geometry, composition well done, handsome hall. Dinner with Osborn.

No entries for 27 November–6 December 1866

FRIDAY 7 DECEMBER 1866

Seen Claflin's Store, together with Stuart's the biggest in the world. Between 500 and 600 clerks, 100 in the counting room only. Last year's sales $70,000,000, income $2 to 3,000,000.[29]

9

In the South:
Charleston and Savannah

December 1866

SATURDAY 8 DECEMBER 1866

Departed for Charleston on board the *Saratoga*. Rain and fog at the time of departure, and we were obliged to anchor in the Narrows until the fog lifted. Around 7 pm we are finally at sea and have fairly heavy weather for the first twenty-four hours, but for the rest of the journey beautiful weather and a calm sea. This was very welcome to me as the room on board was very restricted and the furnishings poor. What this would have meant in heavy weather I don't know, but it must surely be unpleasant. New York–Cape Hatteras is 320 miles, Cape Hatteras–Charleston 280 miles. Cape Lookout, Cape Romain. As the entrance to the harbor is obstructed by a sandbar, with only 9 feet of water at low tide, and 15½ feet at high tide, and as our boat draws 13 feet, we can enter only at high tide. This happens to be at 10 in the morning and in the evening and as the lighthouses have not yet been rebuilt after the war, I assumed that we could enter only the next morning—Wednesday—too late as we were for the Tuesday morning high tide, delayed by several defects of the ship's machinery. To our surprise the captain (Crowell) ventured to enter in the evening, two hours after high tide, and so we arrive in Charleston at midnight after a 65 hours' journey. We stay on board, however, and go to our several hotels only the next morning.[1]

The only passengers I got to know were H. C. Howell, a young traveling salesman from New York, a German (Hegemann?) who had lived in Charleston for many years, and an army officer, Allsworth, who shares my stateroom. With the last named, a full-blooded Southerner, I had many discussions about politics that really came to nothing, as usual.

Some of his figures may be noted here: wages of Negroes, field hands $10 to 15 per month, domestic servants $12 to 15, everything including board. Most owners—

not planters, about planters he didn't say anything—are glad to be rid of their slaves and value today's system much higher than the old one. During the war the price of gold skyrocketed to 5000 percent, meaning $1 in gold for $50 currency. But he had also knowledge of a barrel of flour worth $10 in gold being sold for $1,200 currency. It is clear that this was the cause for much speculation, and the bribery to be declared officially unfit for army service must have been unbelievable. Later desertion grew to enormous proportions.

He claimed that the planters didn't want a return to the slave trade as they maintained that this would have depreciated the value of their old slaves, making the growing of cotton before the war already highly unprofitable. This could never have been a reason to go to war, as he said. He told me that field hands were worth only $500 before the war. He disregarded all stories about the punishing of those men who taught the Negroes, but he did say that for helping slaves to flee to the North the death penalty could still be imposed, although never really enforced. At the occasion of testamentary manumission the testator also had to provide funds to make the freed slave leave the state, this being the cause that there are hardly any freedmen in South Carolina. He also claims that the president against the Congress can count on the regular army and 300,000 men from the South. He calls all Northerners "the most vile, lying, cheating, hypocritical set of people on earth."

One of the waiters amused me by ventilating the same opinion regarding the North, because his father, a shoemaker of about 60 years of age, was suspected there because of his age of not being able to make shoes anymore, something one would have gladly entrusted him with in the South. One other of his complaints was that in school the rich boys got preferential treatment over poor boys. But as this seemed to have happened in North or South Carolina as well, this statement against the North was not very convincing in my opinion.

Regarding Reconstruction, the 'burden' of his argument was this: we don't care, let them do what they want to do in the North, we are just as happy outside the Union as in it again.

No entries for 9–11 December 1866

WEDNESDAY 12 DECEMBER 1866

At first sight Charleston made a very dismal impression. One still can see the craters, only just filled in, made by the bombs during the bombardment of eighteen months, day and night. Furthermore a whole section of the town burned down in the first year of the war, although this fire had nothing to do with the bombardment. The ruins have not yet been cleared away; everything is as it was the day after the fire. The multitude of Negroes, the colorful scarves that the women use as headgear, the market surrounded by tame turkey vultures, the many mules,

The destruction caused by the Civil War to the once prosperous and
dynamic city of Charleston, South Carolina, is graphically revealed in
this 1865 photograph. Churches did not escape the negative impact of the
conflict.   Library of Congress

the gentlemen on horseback, everything combines to provide a real Southern spectacle. But the almost complete absence of carriages, the ruinous exterior of the
houses, and other particulars clearly show the sad situation of the inhabitants.
Nowhere are houses being built, and the vacant lots in the 'Burnt District' are
evidence that everything is dead. Charleston's credit is so low that a plan to give
away city bonds to the lot owners in exchange for a mortgage on their lots fell
through.

Visited with Mr. Wunderlich, our consul. A fire in Mr. Mure's office, just opposite his. Fire engines and a lot of noise.[2]

In the evening visited with Governor Aiken, who has suffered a lot during the war, just as all Lowndeses, Hugers, and others. All planters, whose wealth consisted almost uniquely in slaves, are ruined. They have given everything, and because of the emancipation they have lost the last they had. Only their land is left, but with the labor problem and the scarcity of capital, that land cannot be made profitable. Some have borrowed northern capital at outrageous rates of interest, and generally they have not been able to pay off their debt, partly because of the unfavorable season for almost all crops, and also because of the insufficient number of hands available and consequent lack of care. Of course, Governor Aiken claims that the Negroes are lazy and will never be willing to work. He estimates the cotton crop at 1,000,000 bales, while in New York the same crop is estimated at 2,300,000, but mostly from Texas. He asserts that the Mexican War and the annexation of Texas were not provoked by the South. He did concede that the position of the South in the slavery question in Missouri, Kansas, and Nebraska had been an attempt to maintain the majority. In his opinion this was foolish, as slave labor was not suitable for Kansas or Nebraska. If they had kept quietly within the framework of the old slave laws and not sought any extension of the system, the question would never have come to a head. The slaveholders possibly would have emancipated their slaves of their own free will, partly because that kind of labor would become unprofitable in the long run, as had already happened in Virginia and Tennessee. But when he pointed out that under the old regime a crop of 10 million bales would have been possible, his solution of the problem became very doubtful in my opinion. He takes a gloomy view of the future and hopes that the importation of coolies will solve the labor problem. He maintains that 2,000,000 Negroes have run away, and the available labor decreased with that number.[3]

Aiken, just as Mr. Wilkinson—whom I visited later and where Mrs. Wilkinson and Lou and Ella made me a hearty welcome as an old friend—expect that the Negro will fall back into barbarism instead of improve. Everyone is depressed and concedes that all are ruined completely, and that the wealth of the country in horses and mules has decreased. Reconstruction will take a long time, especially as long as northern capital will remain wary because of the political instability.

Naturally all are angry at Congress, and the general expectation is that the Radical party will carry everything before it. They see themselves reduced to the status of territories, which wouldn't even make much of a difference, as the state legislatures cannot do anything without the consent of the military commanders, who don't even hesitate to reverse arrests of the courts. Small wonder that deep despondency and indifference are widespread. Many are really devastated.

The usual Southern gaiety has not greatly suffered, however, which I witnessed at a party at two Misses Mackay's, where Lou and Ella Wilkinson took me. Dress was very simple, most so with the gentlemen who came in their sports coats, but the dancing wasn't less enthusiastic. I liked the girls, but they could not hide their hatred of the Yankees, that goes so far that they refuse to greet an U.S. officer, whom they had known before, on the street.

Thursday 13 December 1866

Dinner at Mr. Wunderlich with Louis Manigault, of an old planters' family, and Mr. Lanen, the French consul. The first named was not so very pessimistic about the Negro labor question as Mr. Wilkinson, who firmly believes that the black race will fall back into a state of barbarism and will never learn to work.[4]

Did a tour in the afternoon, low sandy land, swamps here and there, and lots of pines. Magnolia Cemetery, grave of Mrs. White.[5]

Friday 14 December 1866

In a rowboat with Willis Wilkinson to the points of interest in the harbor. Mr. Willis, now about 26 years old, has witnessed everything. For three years he was chief of ordnance under Longstreet and took part in the flight of Jefferson Davis, although he was not present when the latter was arrested. He told me a lot about the sufferings from hunger and misery of the people throughout the South.[6]

Fort Pinkney, Fort Johnson, one of the most important batteries for the bombardment of Charleston, Fort Sumter and Cummings Point (Yanhice, Fort Putnam). Fort Sumter, formerly three stories high, is now nothing more than a heap of rubble. The two top stories have been destroyed and have deposited such a mass of rubble over the lower one that the fort was then more impregnable than ever, as long as the connection with the mainland could be maintained to introduce fresh troops, ammunition, and provisions. As soon as Sherman approached Charleston, Fort Sumter had to be evacuated too. Here as elsewhere in other batteries everything was still as it was at the end of hostilities. The guns are still pointed as when the last shots were fired. All around this made a picture of destruction and devastation as I have never seen before. Cummings Point on Morris Island was fiercely defended by the Confederates and was such a difficult position that fresh troops had to be brought in daily from Charleston. When finally taken by the Northerners, it became the foremost battery against Charleston. From here their shells flew a distance of five miles and kept the population of Charleston in permanent alarm for a year and a half.[7]

In the evening visited with Mrs. Hayne, where Mr. Buvard Hayne, her son, whom I had met at the Cotonnets, had invited me. Mr. Hayne's brother was the well known 'nullificator' of 1832. Eldest daughter was the lovely Mrs. Barnwell, Miss Hayne, Mr. Theodore Hayne. The most typical Southern family I have met until now. The mother is a most pleasant woman, with all the special characteristics. All were extremely well-bred, with a measure of French polish and lightheartedness, but without any real warmth and depth. For one evening most pleasant and charming, but in the long run by far not what those damned Yankees are.[8]

Here I witnessed the real Yankee hatred to perfection. They are made out—but always half laughing—as the original, perfect villains. Most lamented seems to be the loss of all personal comforts: no servants, no carriages, no money is the continuing refrain, and this seems to weigh heavier than anything else. Real serious, deeply felt anger I haven't seen anywhere. Although half laughingly, I here heard the theory of the 'divine institution' too, and I believe it was more seriously meant than it seemed at first sight. They did acknowledge the existence of a law against the education of Negroes, but keep telling me that it was a dead letter. They did concede that Negroes were maltreated sometimes, and admired their behavior at present. Buvard did agree that Captain Wirtz had fully deserved his fate. For the rest I must say that this evening was among the most pleasant, maybe even the single most pleasant evening I have had in America.[9]

SATURDAY 15 DECEMBER 1866

Bad weather, cold and rainy. A couple of visits; cotton gin and rice mill. In the afternoon a visit with Mrs. Wilkinson and Mrs. Gibbes. Mrs. Gibbes is an archetypical Southern woman, a bit like Mary St. Clair. 'Lolling in her rocking chair,' she talked incessantly in an indifferent and nonchalant tone. Her stories all boil down to the same topic, but are not very consistent in regard of the Negroes. She said that if only the Yankees and the Freedmen's Bureau would be gone, everything would adjust itself, the Negroes would fall back into their old habits and go to work as usual, and everything would be fine again. Everybody keeps telling himself that only if one would leave us to ourselves, we would manage quite well. But will the North do that in view of the still prevailing atmosphere?[10]

I have no doubts that the treatment of the Negroes has generally been good. Mrs. Wilkinson confirmed to me that whoever maltreated his slaves was ostracized from society, and others pointed out the interest masters had in good treatment of their slaves. Slaves cost between $1,200 and 1,500 for a field hand, $1,500–2,000 for a house servant, sometimes as high as $2,500. Undoubtedly of course, there were exceptions, especially in the backwoods and among the smaller slaveholders.

Fiercest against the Yankees are the ladies. Lou Wilkinson said to me this very evening, "I wish I could have a rope around all their necks and hang them all," and when her mother objected—on my behalf—she said "Oh, but I wouldn't like to see all the corpses dangling in the air, but I do wish they were all hanged." Later, when she talked about the possibility of being a Yankee herself, "Oh, I would put a rope round my own neck and hang myself first, and I would take it nobly, not like those mean Yankees." The hatred against the flag is general: "that ugly grid-iron flag," said Mrs. Hayne. The men are indifferent and only think of recovering their material prosperity. In general this is a frivolous people, without any depth and seriousness, and it is mostly this that they cannot bear to see in the Yankees.

More and more people confirm that the reason behind the war has been the idea that the North intended to abolish slavery and by doing so infringe on their rights. After the election of Lincoln, an abolitionist in their opinion, the question came to a head, and the South felt constrained to dust off their favorite doctrine of 'states' rights.' They were convinced that they had the right to leave the Union, and the responsibility to take this step rests squarely with their leaders, and especially with those under oath to maintain the Union. In my opinion they saw the near future as too dark. In itself the breaking up of such a Union, when a part of the people is clearly unhappy with it, does not seem to be such a crime, at least as far as I can see. One cannot bind people for eternity, and whenever one has really valid reasons, most insurrections are justifiable. On the other hand, it is undeniable that the other party had the right to maintain the existing government and Union. Both parties fought for opposite principles, both defensible in their own right.

One of the standing claims is that the people of the South are so much more 'gentlemanlike, generous, magnanimous' and what not than those 'mean, sneaking, hypocritical Yankees.' Mrs. Wilkinson once answered an officer, who had said to her—most impolitely—"We'll soon put down all that aristocracy and make tinkers and tailors of you all," "Then Sir, Southern gentlemen will make a profession of those trades." And when another said, "Well, the Union flag is waving over you again," she retorted, "Yes, the stars are there and those that love them may take the stripes with them (on their back)." Boasting of the good society, of the fine carriages, the many servants, the style they had, is the order of the day, and the chief complaint is that the Yankees have taken all that away.

In regard of the sale of domestic slaves, Mrs. Wilkinson told me that most of them were quite indifferent about this as they ended up with good masters anyhow. Only those who had served a lifetime in the same family and had absorbed the family pride would have found it very hard. A Negro coachman, who drove me yesterday, claimed that the Negroes did appreciate their new freedom, and although he too maintained that most had been well treated, he said that some of them still bore the scars of beatings thick as hail on their backs.

SUNDAY 16 DECEMBER 1866

Dinner with Mr. Mure, a simple Scotsman. He was the bearer of dispatches to the British government and was caught on board the *Africa* by the federal authorities and jailed in Fort Lafayette. He was liberated only after a lot of pressure from the British. He is strongly in favor of the South, but he didn't tell me much new. The only thing he told me about was the scandalous looting by Sherman's army. Others, the Wilkinsons among them, did confirm this. Safes were broken open or simply taken, carriages, paintings, and silver were stolen and later identified as in the possession of Northerners. The pockets of the ladies were searched, the watches snatched from their sashes, and rings taken from their fingers. One lady whose silver was stolen went to the commanding officer in Charleston and managed to have him produce the stolen stuff. Before returning it to her he took the best piece and told her, "I'll take this for my pains."[11]

With Mr. Mure to the Presbyterian Church. Later I saw from the Battery the most magnificent sunset I ever witnessed. Afterwards visited with the Wilkinsons and had a long conversation with Mr. Wilkinson. According to him the cause of the war is the same one that I always have seen as the real one, national aversion, that started when they lost their power and wrongly thought that the North was about to declare against slavery. Rights were undisputable. The Constitution was accepted by the states during the convention or later by the legislatures elected for that purpose. Explicitly or implicitly all states had reserved the right to leave the Union whenever it no longer served their purpose. He gave a most despondent lecture on the government, regarding both its morality and its strength. There was a lot of truth in his views of the caliber of the members of Congress and on the tendency to strip the Executive of all its power and on the then unavoidable anarchy and the weakness of a Congress made up of irresponsible and uninterested delegates. Everyone keeps telling about the hatred toward the Northerners. At the earliest opportunity every man between 15 and 60 would be ready with his rifle in his hand to try once more.

MONDAY 17 DECEMBER 1866

Visited Mrs. Hayne in the evening. Fresh impression of the French nature of the South, the liveliness and spirit of Mrs. Hayne. She says that at the signing of the Secession Act people behaved as an excited French multitude. She also tells about the way the gentlemen followed the last mode, especially in the wearing of pantaloons and such. And not only the willingness but even the obvious pleasure to discuss the war and its incidents speak for itself. Theodore Hayne's dictum that there was despite all 'a good deal of fun in the war' is another example of the Southern views, just so as the idea that the duel was a good thing, the bragging about the gentlemanlike character in all its details. The polished and gracious manners, and especially the casual way in which they treat everything, all do remind one of the French nation. New examples of the looting by Sherman's soldiers and the outrages committed. What a strong contrast with the seriousness of the Northerners, who do not like to discuss the war.

A nephew of the family, a planter himself, told me that the Negroes didn't work too badly now. Where he used to plant nine acres 'to a hand,' he could now only have five acres, which didn't seem too bad to me. He supposed that the rice culture would be dead soon, as it was so unhealthy that the remaining Negroes would prefer to work in the cotton fields, causing a severe shortage of labor in the rice fields.

Mrs. Barnwell struck me again as a most lovely woman. Shaking hands was certainly not common here, just as in France.

NB Governor Aiken's slaves always had mosquito nets. Difference between North and South in the way of having tea. Special accent in the speech of the South.

TUESDAY 18 DECEMBER 1866

Took my leave. At the Wilkinsons' I had a long discussion with Mrs. Wilkinson about the present state of things. She was strong in her expressions about the aristocratic feelings of the South and said that she did not pity the young men fallen during the war, but did pity those that had to witness these changes and had to adjust to the changed circumstances, where all 'tone' and gentlemanlike behavior was bound to disappear. She also said that the feelings of the 'low whites' were most unfavorable toward the Yankees. When one of the Livingston's of New York told her that "the Carolinians will <u>have</u> to respect merchants now, will <u>have</u> to go to trade themselves," she answered, "If they have to take to it, Sir, they will feel the degradation of it." Another proof of the aristocratic mentality of the planters, who heartily despised the wholesale trade thirty years ago.

WEDNESDAY 19 DECEMBER 1866

Left for Savannah per *Kate* at 8 am. Around 2:30 pm we arrived at the mouth of the Savannah River; wide at the mouth, muddy, red water, low country with rice plantations on both banks. Arrived in Savannah at 4:30 pm. Comedy, *The Pearl of Savoy,* in the evening. Met a couple of Germans, Herr Koch and Herr Kirchhauff.[12]

THURSDAY 20 DECEMBER 1866

Delivered a couple of letters of introduction, without much result so far. Looked for Mr. Joe Manigault and Mr. Joseph Huger, the first a nephew, the other a brother, of Mrs. Wilkinson, who both own rice plantations outside Savannah. Mrs. Wilkinson had given me very positive letters of recommendation for both. After some time I found at long last Mr. Huger's son, named Prelo, who invites me straightaway to visit with them. He is a young man of about 20, and as almost everybody else, he served for some three years in the Confederate army, which gave him an independent and vigorous air. He strongly reminds me of Alexander Schimmelpenninck. Mr. Huger's plantation is situated in South Carolina on the north bank of the river, separated from Savannah by two branches of the river, with Hutchinson's Island in between. We cross both rivers in a small boat and trek across the island on a primitive path.[13]

The rice plantations here are all situated along the river. They are vast, low-lying fields that have to be flooded from time to time. For this purpose they are crisscrossed by smaller and bigger canals, just like the meadows at home. The vicinity of the Savannah River with its tides of between 5 and 6 feet is a most valuable source for this system. The rice fields, swamps some time ago, with a fine alluvial soil, mostly heavy clay, are about at the level of the average tide of the river. They are surrounded by light dikes that keep out the high water when necessary, but that let in the fertile muddy water by means of small sluices. At low tide the water can be run off again. The parallel ditches are 3 feet wide and spaced at about 50 feet. The muddy silt replaces all fertilizer, while the water itself, although not absolutely necessary, is of great importance for the growth of the plant. Wherever there is no opportunity for flooding the fields, rice is also grown but then only for domestic consumption, as one is completely dependent on the rain at the right time. Without an abundance of water the rice simply doesn't seem to sprout. The large-scale rice growing is practiced only in the manner described here.

When the rice starts growing in the spring a rice plantation is said to be very much like our meadows, and everybody agrees that a rice field makes a beautiful sight in spring and at harvest time. At that time the leaves are still green, while the grains are a golden yellow, and the ears themselves are most graceful. Now, after the harvest, everything looks desolate, and one sees only the stubble on the field. Rice is planted in rows and needs constant care to keep the weeds that grow tremendously in this climate under control. The flooding of the field after the plants have sprouted, and are some 6 inches high, also serves to kill the grass that cannot grow under water.

The evidence of the war is still everywhere around. Both Confederates and Federals crossed Mr. Huger's plantation, the first when the others approached under Sherman. Of course, the latter left a stronger mark because of their influence on the Negroes. Almost every house has been burned or destroyed. Trees and gardens have been cut down and spoiled, the threshers burned or damaged, the valuable steam engines inside taken away and sold. People commonly say that these steam engines, just as most other movable property, were stolen by the Negroes at the instigation of the Yankees, who then bought these things from them on the cheap. The sluices have been neglected or damaged, without the doors, and all ditches are full of mud and weeds. The land itself has not been used for a couple of years, and the original vegetation is taking possession again.

In 1859 an illustrator for *Harpers Monthly* depicted the planting, cultivating, and harvesting of rice in the Low Country of South Carolina, practices that continued into the 1860s and later.   Ernest Lander Coll., Clemson University Archives

It looks as if the present situation will continue for some time. After the war the government seized the land, and the planters couldn't cultivate it. Small homesteads of 40 acres were given over for use by Negroes, and even when the original owners have now been put back in possession they still have to agree with this arrangement. Only last March did Mr. Huger obtain his pardon and get his land back. Last year everybody was forced to start cultivating too late in the season, around February/March, mostly because the Negroes were persuaded that the government was going to give them the land per January 1st. Hence they were not eager to contract for labor before February, while the cultivating season really starts in January. Another reason was the lack of capital, which the planters could get from the North only with great difficulty and at high rates of interest.

All through the season the Negroes didn't work very well, and despite high wages, they could be persuaded to do only half the work. They make $20 a month without board, that is, with a cabin and fuel, but no food. With food they make $15 a month or $1 per day. They run away and it is hard to get help from the Freedmen's Bureau, and altogether they work badly and are lazy now the whip has gone.

The great scarcity of capital for all planters, however, is the first cause of the lack of good crops this year, even when the season has been good for rice growing. For cotton it was less favorable, although the Negroes in the cotton districts were less demoralized than here, where Sherman's army camped longer. The problem is easy to explain. The wealth of the planters consisted of land and slaves. Not only was everything they possessed invested in these two items, but it was used productively and provided them with a large income. What they could put aside was invested again in the same way, or spent on taxes during the war and invested in Confederate bonds in a burst of patriotism. Everybody still keeps large amounts of these but is convinced that they are worthless by now. Emancipation robbed them of the capital invested in slaves, which often ran as high as $100,000 or $200,000, sometimes even $800,000, and which constituted their 'working power.' Now they have lost the capital and the interest from it, they have to hire labor at wages higher than the interest on their former capital, and moreover get less efficient labor for that money. They still have the land, but not a single dollar of capital available, and have to obtain this in the North at outrageous rates of interest. Last year this seemed possible, but after last year's bad harvest, which was chiefly caused by the lack of care for the crops, most planters have plunged heavily into debt.

And apart from lacking the revolving capital, the fixed capital, the land, is also in a bad shape, which has a negative influence on the crops. Restoring the land to its original condition is so expensive that most cannot even think about it. Mills, sheds, and everything else have been destroyed, the ditches are clogged up, and the dikes and sluices in bad shape. Most implements and plows are lost, and horses and mules stolen or dead. Introduction of costly agricultural implements is impossible for most planters. Mr. Huger would like to use the steam plow and the ditcher of Mr. Danvers of Illinois to clean his ditches, but he is unable to find the money for this. Where two hundred Negroes were working before the war, he now has ten or twenty at the most. Mr. Huger used to harvest 60,000 bushels of rice from 2,000 acres, and last year he made only 6,000 bushels from about 500 acres.[14]

The methods of harvesting seem very primitive. The rice is stacked on the land and threshed there with flails, or sometimes with a steam thresher on a boat in the canal. In that case the rice is winnowed at the same time, loaded into a clean boat, and carried to market unbagged. When threshed by hand on the land, the rice and chaff mixed together are brought to the farm, and to winnow it an interesting installation is being used. A plank floor, generally roofed over, is raised on four poles of some 20 feet high, looking a bit like a house on bamboos in the Dutch East Indies. In the plank floor a crude sieve is mounted. On a windy day the rice is carried up in sacks and dumped through the sieve. The rice falls straight down while the chaff is blown away. The rice is carried to market and hulled in specialized mills in the cities.

Of course, it is hard to judge the condition of a plantation after all this destruction. Most of the ones I saw were simple, with a kind of roomy farmers' house only, not the luxurious and opulent houses one generally thinks of. Most are now damaged and not yet quite repaired, missing most furniture, and only a shadow of their former selves. Also, most cotton plantations will have looked more attractive than the rice fields because of their better situation.

After my visit with Prelo Huger to their plantation, we tried to find Captain Manigault, but he was out. When we understood that Mr. Huger Sr. had also gone to the city, we decided to return there, with empty stomachs as there was nothing in the house to eat. On our way back we bought a loaf of bread from a Negro, and thus fortified, we rowed back across both arms of the river. In Savannah we met a certain Mr. Clemson, a real American gentleman, who had come south to see if he could plant rice. His views of the rice business were most unreal and his plans wild, and after only one day, without even seeing a single rice plantation, he returned again. He had calculated his rice at $3 per bushel, while the current price is only $1.50. He thought that he could start a plantation with $5,000, where at least $17,000 is required. He was over six feet tall, with a long beard, and he insisted on treating us on oysters after he had understood that he had been imprisoned with Mr. Huger's brother in the Northern prison at Fort Johnson, Lake Erie.[15]

Friday 21 December 1866

Encouraged by young Huger, I let myself be persuaded to undertake the arduous journey to their plantation once more to get acquainted with his father. The weather is perfect, so despite the discomforts I accept his invitation. Outdoors we find Mr. Joseph Huger, Mr. Arthur Huger, and Mr. King. Both Hugers are archetypical planters and good examples of the present state of that class. The Hugers belong to the wealthiest families of South Carolina. Mrs. Wilkinson is herself a Huger. Joseph Huger estimated his worth at around $300,000 to 400,000. Both are real gentlemen, well brought up, intelligent, well-mannered, and tall men. But both now are virtually poor, and last year only the little credit they still have has provided them with some borrowed capital. They tried hard to adjust to the new circumstances and make a living for themselves and their families. Mr. Joseph has a wife and ten children, and they really live in poverty and show that in their dress, not only outdoors, but also in the city. It is painful to see that they lack almost everything and have to live with the strictest economy. I sat talking with Joseph Huger around a log fire deep into the night after everybody had gone to bed. He is really bitter and most pessimistic about the future. He rails against the government and the Yankees more than anybody else and presages the complete breakdown of the country. He maintained that the North and the West owed their prosperity to the South and were bound to find out that they had been foolish to stop that source of wealth. The West had a huge market for its horses and mules in the South that no longer existed now. They also had false hopes of the rising prosperity of the South because of the 4,000,000 bales of cotton, which dated back to prewar years, but which had only now come to light. The remainder of this old stock was bound to make up part of the so-called crop of this year.

He thought the war was largely caused by jealousy of the wealth of the South. He also said that the Freedmen's Bureau had done a lot of evil by handing out daily rations to the Negroes, which had reduced them, even in their own opinion, to the class of the poor and indigent. His way of talking to his brother and son I found tyrannical and quarrelsome. Is this a result of earlier times?[16]

What I noticed of the treatment of the Negroes didn't influence my views of the former situation negatively. Although they were always considered inferior beings and people didn't hesitate to talk about them in their presence, yet the present-day relations between masters and former slaves, as far as they still remain with them, seem to be fairly jovial, not at all barbaric or hard. They always greet their old slaves when meeting them in the street, and I once saw ladies in Charleston stop to speak to an old and dirty former slave. The young Huger asserted that there is little virtue to be found in Negro women, and that whites too had easy access in that respect. Mr. J. Huger said that he had always been in favor of the slave trade on the assumption that Negroes had a better life in America than in Africa, but he confessed that he didn't think that the majority agreed with him in this case, and he said that even before the war many ladies had already been infected with the anti-slavery venom. He is a real archetypical 'thoroughbred' slaveholder, conservative in every respect and in favor of a strong one-man government, if necessary even the worst despotism, instead of this despotism of the majority. In this almost everybody here agrees with him, influenced by the war no doubt, but also by the prevailing aristocratic tendencies, even favoring a monarchal form of government. Mr. Huger had had an offer for his plantation, formerly valued at $70,000 in gold, of $40,000 in currency. But it is even doubtful if he will be able to make this latter price again this year.

Saturday 22 December 1866

After a frightfully cold night on a couch, the whole company carried me back to Savannah in a sailing boat. The rest of the day I spent in writing my journal.

NB One other claim of Mr. Jos. Huger was the following. The real cause of the war was this: with the growth of democracy and the idea that what the majority wants must be right, the far-seeing people in the North were becoming afraid that their possessions were endangered. For twenty years the cry of the *Tribune* was 'let us vote ourselves farms.' The only way to avoid this danger for a time was to stir up the passions against the South and use the wealth of the South as bait for these masses fond of plunder and pillage. Lo and behold the secret! He was also strongly against the encouragement of immigration and considered this the downfall of the country.

Arthur Huger is a curious type: tall, heavily built, with black hair, hawk nose, and piercing black eyes, and in his short jacket, high boots, and broad rimmed black hat, he strongly reminded me of an old Huguenot. His seriousness and energy that was visible in his stooping posture did much to strengthen this idea. By the way, all these old families, Huger, Porcher, etc., are old refugees.[17]

10

In Georgia and Virginia

December 1866

SUNDAY 23 DECEMBER 1866

Savannah–Augusta, Central Georgia Railroad, 130 miles, from 8 am until 6:30 pm, with a two hours' delay at Millen. It is Sunday. The whole region is nothing more than a vast pine forest, sandy and swampy in places. Only now and then I see a clearing and a settlement of a few houses. The clearings are mostly cotton plantations, also many cabins of Negroes. Here is being demonstrated how the Negroes "squat about," according to the current expression. They build a hut, clear a few acres, and raise corn that yields at least thirty bushels per acre, where a couple of bushels will suffice to feed a family the year round. They have a gun and fishing tackle and use these to supplement their diet with some animal food. According to Mr. Wilkinson and others this is the future of the Negro race. In Charleston I saw many of them getting out in the morning with an old gun and returning later with a squirrel and a couple of birds. This way of life must surely be very attractive to them, and unless more civilization will make them recognize that there are other things to be done and to be wished for, I think that many of them will succumb to that easy way of life. Prelo Huger says that they are so immoral that a woman often will have intercourse with another man while her husband sleeps in the same bed. Men also swap their wives as the old Spartans did, and there is hardly a girl of twelve still a virgin. The train is full of Negroes in cars of their own, with much laughter and amusement; the women smoke pipes. At the depots they also turn up in large numbers, all in their Sunday best, especially the women in multicolored clothes, red scarves and colored handkerchiefs round their heads. Some are dressed after the latest fashion with toreadors, others in long white gowns, covering their heads as well, which gives them a distinct Oriental look. I was amused by many of the children with their round faces and white teeth.[1]

The white traveling public as seen in the hotels and on the railroads is of a most distinctive character, very different from the Northern type. Mostly dark-haired, with long beards, often plump, and always more corpulent than the Yankees. Some have bloated faces, but all have the same expression of apathy and even stupidity. Do they hate the Yankees so much because they feel that they are inferior to them? In this respect there is a strong distinction between "low whites" and the higher classes, who are always intelligent, refined, and well-bred. My friend and cabin mate on the *Saragossa,* Captain Allsworth, was a Southerner and a good example of the race. Most of them are pleasant and kind-hearted, I believe. I never saw so many people kissing each other on the train, even more than I have experienced in some regions of Germany.[2]

Mementoes of the war in many places, burnt houses and such. Only a few remnants of the depot at Millen are still standing. In the wooden shed, now serving as temporary depot, we got a reasonably good dinner. Ladies and gentlemen have their separate dining rooms. While New York is skating, the weather here today is warm and pleasant. I spent a large part of the journey on the platform of the last car of the train, smoking and daydreaming of bonds, promotional parties of bygone days, and the political situation here now.

I have developed a few thoughts about that political situation, perhaps not quite unfounded. The North represents the centralizing and equalizing trends of these days, the South the conservative and somewhat aristocratic ideas of earlier times, in itself not inferior as far as I can see. The great counterweight to the pure democracy was the 'self government' by communities, townships, and states. The North rejects both, especially the doctrine of 'states' rights,' so strongly defended by the South, and in earlier days also adhered to by Massachusetts and other states. The urge for abolition has caused the Republican Party to sidestep these old-established and recognized rights, and the war has confirmed the supremacy of the Union, maybe more so than more prudent and moderate people had wished. The Republicans now judge the doctrine of 'states' rights' completely demolished and even disregard it so far that they want to reform the Southern states into territories. The next step will undoubtedly be the formation of a single strong governmental structure, with provinces. The strong desire to bring some theories in practice is shown in the abolitionist movement, now victorious at long last. With this apparent humanitarian principle the abolitionists have managed—in good faith—to unite the whole of the North to begin a fight against an institution, which only the states in their sovereign capacity had the right to decide upon. Hereby the road toward a centralized system of government was opened, where only the numerical majority will be the power in the land. Originally the 'states' rights' doctrine was generally approved everywhere and formally the South had the right to secede, as far as I can see. Both parties undoubtedly acted in good faith, but the sectional hatred has caused the two doctrines to grow more and more apart.

In regard of the abolition of the autonomy of the towns, one of the most glaring recent examples is the way the State of New York has managed to take a large section of the government of the City of New York into its hands. The foremost reason that things in this country are generally managed reasonably well, even where everything is still loose and undecided, must be that everybody owns—or hopes to own—some property. This ideal of one day becoming a man of means even overrides the problem of the frequent changes in the constitution—in some states every ten or twenty years—and the possibility that each and every decision can always be 'reconsidered.' Everybody always thinks of change, and there is no real class distinction. But if ever an underclass of paupers will come to exist, this will all change. Nowadays there are no upper classes that can be overthrown to some advantage of the lower orders. The 'love of organization and law' must give thanks for its existence to this general attitude, and the common civilization has also played a role. The tendency toward an extension of the democracy is visible in the repeal of the small, but formerly generally recognized, 'qualification' as has been done recently in the Massachusetts constitution. This makes the weapon available. The danger can already be seen in New York, as proven by the story of Ludlow, mentioned earlier. Apparently the majority there is thinking that it can override established rights if it wants to.

The following examples may show that the respect for individual liberty is not very great. New York policeman arrests known pickpockets without a shadow of proof and has them transported to the house of correction on Blackwell's Island. Whenever a town corporation decides to construct a road, the necessary land will be expropriated, not only without compensation to the owner, but he has even to pay some of the costs, as in the case of Thom. Ludlow. Incorporated railroad companies have the right to choose and expropriate the land for their own right of way without approval by the legislation. Liquor law, both wholly prohibitive or only partly, as in New York.

The notion is strong that whatever the majority is doing, it is *eo ipso,* always right, without any question about rights or principles. With the fierce partisanship that is presently reigning, this will be disastrous for the country. The way the Radical party is behaving is proof of this. North and South sometimes remind me—and I am not alone in this—of two quarrelling children. The South keeps telling us that the issue of slavery is of no importance, as it is less profitable than other systems, but we don't want it to be taken from us by force. The North says that if they don't want the amendment, they can stay outside the Union. The South counters that they are happy to stay outside, as it can never get worse than it is now.

The South also maintains that they are happy to give the vote to the Negroes, and that they will control those votes, but they do hate the Negro lovers of the North, who are acting like madmen, which is also my opinion.[3]

One of Mrs. Haynes's anecdotes comes to mind. An old woman, having heard that she was free now, insisted, against many pleas, to leave her master: "She would see what it was, even if it were not bigger than a pocket handkerchief." A funny proof of the 'off-hand' manners of Americans is this one: I was in a bar one evening and had to pay 45 cents; I gave 50; the barman had no 5 cents and asked if I had a nickel, presumably with the intention of giving me a 10-cent bill back. When I said no, he retorted: "Oh, I guess that won't make any difference," and that was his final word.

Monday 24 December

Arrived at Augusta, Planters Hotel. I tried to find Captain Thompson, care of Adam McNatt. Stanton Blake had given me a letter of recommendation for him. However, Mr. McNatt himself is living at some place 33 miles by railroad from here and then another 12 miles from the depot, so I had to give up as I had only one day left. Mr. Nicholson, the friendly owner of the Planters Hotel, recommended a ride in a buggy to get some impression of a cotton plantation. I am driven to a plantation, belonging to Mrs. Eaves, a couple of miles from the city. One of the inspectors or overseers receives me and drives me around. A vast stretch of land, some 1,500 acres along the Savannah River, beautiful clay soil, from time to time fertilized by the water of the river. All cotton in bygone days, but now mostly wheat. My guide thought that the diversification will mean more intensive cultivation instead of the former extensive over-cropping. People now think it wrong to buy their corn for $0.90 or $1 in Illinois or Ohio instead of growing it oneself. The usual complaints about the lack of control over the labor supply. Wages about $10 a month with house and board. Unhealthy climate, fevers and such, he himself had lost all his hair. Bad harvest this year: one-half bale per acre in earlier days, now 1 bale for 5 acres and even less. They had counted on 400 bales but harvested only 150, chiefly through lack of weeding the grass that chokes the cotton plants, and indeed the cotton everywhere had grown much lower than usual. But anyhow, a cotton plantation looks much nicer than a rice plantation. Trees everywhere, Pride of India, Live Oak starting to lose their leaves because of the frost, common American Oak, etc. According to my black driver the Negroes really enjoy their freedom; wages between $7 and 12, and plenty of work for those who are willing to work.[4]

Departed from Augusta at 6:30 am. Tomorrow is Christmas, and at every depot one sees the Negroes in large numbers sitting around big fires, letting off fireworks, and already very excited and mostly drunk. Columbia, Charlotte, Greensboro, Danville, Richmond. Generally the Southerners are more boisterous in the trains than Northerners. Loud talking and laughing everywhere, something one hardly ever hears in the North. The country is mostly barren, proven by the only vegetation one sees of pine forests, and that with such a climate and so much sunshine. Cotton is slowly disappearing, but corn still everywhere around. But pretty country nevertheless, a bit hilly.[5]

TUESDAY 25 DECEMBER 1866

Christmas day and the Negroes have come out in large congregations, all in their Sunday best. Conversation with the conductor, a young man. When I asked him if the Spotswood Hotel in Richmond was good, he answered: "Yes, about the best in town, that's where I am staying myself." His wages were $90 a month; a brakeman makes $1.50 per day. Negroes pay a fare of $7, whites $8. He mentioned prices of consumer goods during the war: a barrel of flour for $1,500 to 2,000! Every trip he made he earned about $500 by bringing goods from Augusta to Richmond. Flour was doing $120–150 in Augusta, $400 in Danville, and in Richmond $800! A railroad conductor's wage was about $400 a month during the war, low, because they were free from conscription.

Arrival in Richmond at 11:00 pm. Conversation with the owner of the hotel. He had been exchange officer for the North, but he had laid down his commission when he was ordered to exchange whites for blacks: "That went against my principles." When I went to bed he said: "Make yourself at home, and when you want anything just mention it."

WEDNESDAY 26 DECEMBER 1866

Stayed at home most of the day, wrote letters home, and walked around in the afternoon. Richmond is a spacious town, lovely built and situated on several hills, with deep ravines in between. It is fast recovering from the deep war wounds, and Main Street has risen from the ashes probably in a better shape than before.

THURSDAY 27 DECEMBER 1866

Walked to the camp of the 11th infantry regiment to see Mr. Robins, 1st lieutenant, now brevet captain. Long visit, his pay $1,800. Most moderate in his views, but no very profound thoughts. When he was talking about the Negroes with little enthusiasm, another man said, "Well, if those are your views, I wonder that you should have fought for the niggers." "By God, Sir," he told me, "I was near knocking him down." These feelings are very common with the people all around; they started fighting for the Union, not for the abolition of slavery.[6]

Visited with Miss Jane S. Woolsey, a former nurse in the hospitals and now since some weeks teaching at an Industrial School for Freedmen. Schools for freedmen

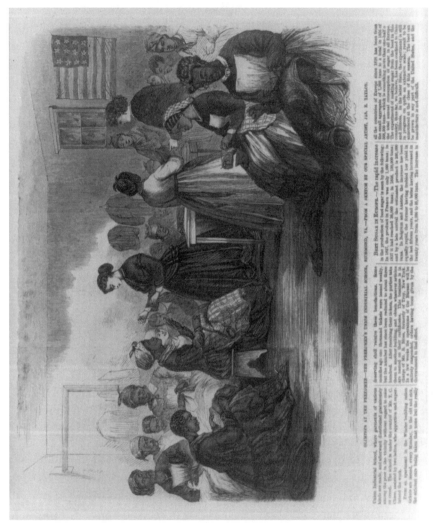

In 1866, the year Crommelin visited Richmond, Virginia, James E. Taylor (1839–1901) made this wood engraving for *Frank Leslie's Illustrated Newspaper* of African American women sewing in Richmond's Freemen's Union Industrial School.　Library of Congress

have been established all over the South by philanthropic societies of the North. The most important are [. . .]. These societies have originated from the remnants of the sanitary commissions and of the old abolitionist associations, and they have divided up the field among themselves, but are all connected with the central organization. For instance, each society has one state where it establishes and maintains the schools. Government provides the schoolrooms, and the Freedmen's Bureau helps where it can. These organizations were so perfect that only a couple of days after the fall of Richmond, thousands of little Negro children were already going to school. Miss Woolsey is, just as many others, of the opinion that those little niggers are brighter than most whites up to a certain age, but then they stop and are passed by the white children. Of course, she is somewhat pronounced in her views, but not as vehement as many radicals. To me she seems to be a most excellent woman, a bit pockmarked.[7]

The affair of Dr. Watson is making a lot of noise here. The story goes as this: A certain Negro driving Major Nichols's carriage almost demolished the carriage in which Dr. Watson's family was riding. Some days later a furious Dr. Watson went for that Negro and wanted to whip him *more majorum*. The man took to his heels, and when Dr. Watson called out after him he kept running, whereupon Dr. Watson shot and killed him. The civil authorities didn't want to indict him and let him go. The *Times* writes that "he was tried by a jury of his peers and acquitted." Then the military authorities took the matter in hand, and Gen. Schofield ordered a military tribunal to judge him. Halfway through the proceedings the president issued an order to stop the trial, making everybody furious.[8]

At night reception at Gen. Schofield's, chief of the military department and of the Freedmen's Bureau. Many people present, dancing in old Jeff Davis's rooms. Miss Woolsey, Capt. and Mrs. Robins, Mrs. Hartwell, Miss Lee, Major White, all Northerners of course. A large number of officers, most of them rather vulgar, the women too. I place Gen. Schofield and his wife in the same category. Gov. and Mrs. Pierpoint, governor of Virginia. It is so cold that all policemen walk around wrapped in plaids, fastened by a large pin with their number.[9]

FRIDAY 28 DECEMBER 1866

Drove around with Capt. Robins. The capitol, with a plaster copy of a statue of Washington, meeting rooms of the former Confederate Congress. Saw the infamous Fort Libby, the Confederate prison for Union prisoners, where thousands were packed together. It is now partly being used as a military prison. Cages with six or seven men, many completely dark. The commander, Major Lawrence, didn't seem to care too much. Apparently he considers his prisoners more like animals than as human beings.[10]

Tried to see Miss Van Lew, the only woman in Richmond who remained faithful to the Union. I had a letter of introduction for her from Miss A. Woolsey, but she wasn't home yet from a visit to Philadelphia. Second visit with Miss Jane S. Woolsey, whom I like very much, a very lovely woman. Colonel Stanton, a real Westerner from Iowa, who as a young man participated in the famous John Brown's raid. Yesterday I saw him at Gen. Schofield's reception in civilian clothes.[11]

In Virginia the free distribution of rations by the Freedmen's Bureau has been terminated, except only in very few cases because of the prevailing cold, and then chiefly for incoming Unionists, mostly whites. According to Major White and Mrs. Van Lew (originally Van Loo, a Dutch name) there is relatively little poverty and malnutrition among the Negroes. There have been only few requests from the several sub-departments for the masses of shoes, clothing, blankets, etc., in store at the Freedmen's Bureau. Miss Woolsey maintains that the prisons in the North were good, especially that in Washington. But she and also Capt. Robins also acknowledge that there have been excesses and malpractices. It is true that Fort Libby and Belle Isle prison island in the James River, where thousands of prisoners were lying without tents or shelter, were in Richmond under the eye of Davis and Lee.[12]

Saturday 29 December 1866

Farewell of Capt. Robins. Many war stories, the first I heard during my stay here, and told with horror in his voice. He is brevet captain; ranks with brevet are being given for gallantry and may be much higher than the real rank in the actual service. They qualify the bearer to use the rank and in some cases also for actual commands, but the pay is not higher. He was not sure what the army was going to do in a possible conflict between president and Congress. He thought that General Grant and every officer would refuse to obey orders from Congress, and it is impossible to fire them except in cases of 'heinous offenses.'

Visit with Major White in the Freedmen's Bureau, and he introduces me to General Brown and Colonel [. . .], inspector of the department. The usual stories of Negroes being swindled by the whites. Local magistrates refuse to issue warrants against whites in case of criminal behavior against Negroes. They pretend that they wouldn't be certain of their lives in such circumstances. Most important business of the Freedmen's Bureau now is supervising the contracts between employers and Negro workers, also the balancing of the supply of labor by transporting Negroes from one place to another. They maintain that Negroes are good workers when well paid, generally $8 per month.[13]

Long farewell visit with Miss Woolsey, but discussion of few interesting topics only. In the evening at 7:30 by train to Baltimore by way of Gordonsville and Washington.[14]

11

To Baltimore and Washington, D.C.

December 1866–January 1867

Arrival in Baltimore at 9:30 am. Straightaway to an Episcopal Methodist black church. All shades of color, from coal black to almost white, some more yellow like Chinese. All kinds of hair, short woolly heads, some with a parting, some with long hair, and one with long silvery white curls. The owner of those curls was sitting in the front row, and he certainly had Negro blood in his veins, but his face, as far as I could see, was less Negroid than most. Most odd are the frizzy heads of elderly people, having become grey, almost white. Most people were well-dressed, especially the women, but sometimes a bit too dashing. The men generally in long black coats. More intelligent faces than in Charleston. Everyone was civil toward me, although I was about the only white in the congregation, but no whispering or stealthy looks. Usually city Negroes are better educated than Negroes from the plantations.

At the singing every line was read first and then sung. The sermon was delivered by a coal-black preacher, at first haltingly, but soon he got into his stride and spoke with fervor. Taken all together it was the most rambling rhapsody I ever heard, without any sense or aim, but he managed to reach the hearts of his audience, and brought some of them to tears and to a real storm of excitement. "Yes, Sir, Amen," etc., with much shouting and moaning that made me feel uncomfortable now and then. Curious expressions in the sermon: "Tom Payne, Bolingbroke, and Voltaire preached against the church, but could not prevail against her." "I believe in the joint godhead and manhood of Christ. I do not know how it was fixed, but I believe in it." "Pray for everybody, not only for the good men, but for the wicked ones too, for the presidents, judges, governors." With his shouts he knew how to generate a frenzy of excitement at the right moment. There was a choir and fairly good singing. The preacher had a large mug of water at hand, and from time to time he took sips of that, preferably in the middle of a sentence. Behind him two fellows were sitting on a couch, who replaced him now and then, for example, in the reading of the hymns, and who were leading the crowd in the signs of enthusiasm. One of his announcements referred to the service that was to start tomorrow, New Year's Eve, at 8 and would continue until midnight to lead the congregation into the New Year, after which everyone would be free until 2 am, or, if he wanted to, to pray until sunrise. Episcopal Church, decorated with greenery for the last Sunday of the year; only a few pretty girls leaving the church.

After dinner a stroll around the town, nicely situated. Washington Monument, beautiful mass with music in the Roman Catholic cathedral, built more or less after Rome's Saint Peter, but with two curious minaret-like towers.

Are American morals generally good or bad? Is my most favorable impression, based on what I have seen and heard, right or wrong? Or are most women lewd and the girls 'fast' and often not much better than older women? I have been thinking about these issues and want to write my opinion down here and now, after slowly having weighed the evidence collected so far. In the beginning I thought to answer these questions in the negative, but now I am forced to reconsider. Trott claims that the custom of deliberately not having children was prevailing everywhere. He had spoken with a lady before he was married. She had two children and told him that these two were enough and that she did not intend to have more, whereupon he remarked that this could not be only her decision. She answered: "Oh, how green are you, when you will be married you will know better." According to Oyens a woman gives her husband permission, explicit or with connivance, to be untrue to her, better than having children herself.

Prelo Huger told me long story about a Northern girl he had met at a ball, and he had been allowed to go a long way with her, even sitting on her lap, alone with her in a deserted room. He claimed to have had much the same experiences with almost every Northern girl he had ever met. My friend from the perfume store told me a story about the many pleasant hours he had had with the pretty schoolmistress in the train returning from the camp meeting at Yarmouth. And most of the married women in Boston were of the same caliber, he said. Casimir Thoron claimed that he had a report from the madam of the largest rendezvous hotel in New York, that many a lady came in that hotel in the mornings whom one would never have expected to see there.

Story told by Mr. Davison, pilot of the *Saragossa,* that one of the surgeons on board had claimed that he had delivered five young schoolmistresses, who had come down from the North to teach at the Freedmen's schools, of nigger babies. The specimen that we had on board was certainly not of the best. Sons' tales of reputedly decent girls, as revealed by the Reeds. Miss Bird, friend of Henry Sturgis's wife. Experiences of Casimir Thoron with the latter's widow. And now recently Capt. Robins, whom I judged not having been 'fast' himself, told me that nine out of ten girls in New York are definitely not decent, and that in Boston much the same was true, at least among the 'shoddy society.' I quite agreed with him as far as I knew the Rye Beach society.

In the *Atlantic Monthly* of January 1867 I found the following statement: "Suppose a preacher should give a plain, cold, scientific exhibition of the penalty which nature exacts for the crime, so common among church-going ladies and others, of murdering their unborn offspring, it would appall the devil." And if someone dares to write this in a widely read monthly such as the *Atlantic Monthly* as if it is a commonly known fact, there must be some truth in it. Just think of all the varied advertisements in newspapers and magazines on this subject! Against the general opinion prevailing about the fastness of the girls, Francis E. Parker maintains that of his university friends four out of five were 'innocent.' But Capt. Robins claims that there is nowhere a faster set to be found than in Boston, somewhat like Harry Sturges and friends.

MONDAY 31 DECEMBER 1866

Delivered my letter for Hollins McKim in the morning. Because of the deep snow I cannot do anything else than write some letters. In the evening to Hollins McKim. In his opinions he is a solid Southerner. In Maryland, and as far as I know in most border states, a law has been passed requiring a sort of 'test oath' for voters that they had never sympathized with the rebels. Because of that law McKim had not voted in the past five years. This is one of the crassest examples of what a majority thinks it can impose on others. The idea itself is not bad, that a majority takes the voting rights away from a minority and then starts infighting over the spoils among themselves.[1]

A second example is the case of Dr. Watson, already mentioned when in Richmond. It all started thus: the Supreme Court had ruled that military jurisdiction in a civilian case could not be allowed in a state. Then all the Radical papers started an outcry that it was a shame that the opinion of one man (the verdict was reached with a 5 to 4 vote) can stop the will of the majority. I cannot say where this will lead to in a country where these positions are being defended by almost everyone.

The affair of the police commissioners was this according to McKim: Governor Swann was a moderate, and he expected the radicals to block his election as senator. The old police commissioners were hot radicals, appointed by a former governor. Swann then thought that by appointing new commissioners he would be able to prevail. But Judge Bond issued a warrant against the new ones and had them locked up in jail, and the old commissioners remained in their post during the elections. When these elections turned out against them, they felt that they were losing support and voluntarily requested their demission. He expects that the moderates now in charge will not let the matter rest here and will probably press charges against Judge Bond.[2]

Tuesday 1 January 1867

At McKim's. The gas service almost the same as at home: $3.30 per 1000 cubic feet, gas meter supplied by the company, many complaints about malfunctioning of the meters, not a legal but a factual monopoly, no verification of the gas meters, nor of anything else. Water is now supplied by the city, its price measured after the width of the facade of the house. A house with one door and two windows $13, for every water closet, carriage, 2 horses, etc., a supplement of $3. Dinner at Wm. McKim with Isaac and Hollins McKim, both with their wives.

Wednesday 2 January 1867

To Washington.

Thursday 3 January 1867

To Annapolis to say farewell to Mary and Etta Fuller. Departed at 7 am, everything thickly covered in snow. One hour wait at Annapolis Junction. The Fuller girls are staying, together with Annie and Etta Wigglesworth, with Captain Walker, connected to the Naval Academy. Large institution, with some 400 cadets.[3]

Friday 4 January 1867

Letters sent to General L. H. Pelouse, adjutant-general of the War Office. He refers me to Colonel Dodge, a very friendly young man, who is also connected with the War Department and is keeper of all rebel colors and flags taken during the war. The flags seem to vary a lot in their colors. The first were red-white-red with a blue field with stars, and then white with a blue field with stars, later it became a blue cross with stars on a red field, but also varied by a cross on a white background only, with or without stars. Colonel Dodge was not very happy with all these trophies and wished that they would be handed over to the states whose troops had taken them. In the end he said: why not have them burned, what good will do these memorials of civil strife? I couldn't have agreed more.[4]

About 10,000 colored volunteers are still in service; their term of three years' service not yet over. They will be disbanded as soon as they can be replaced by regular troops. As listed in the latest army bill, the regular army will be 50,000 strong, 45 regiments of infantry, 12 cavalry, and 8 artillery. Of this total, 4 regiments of infantry and 4 of cavalry will be made up of Negro soldiers. The bill has also determined that each company will be 50 strong, and the president has been given the authority to augment every company to 100 men in times of emergency. This means that an army of some 100,000 will be available almost immediately, complete with all officers and NCOs. Colonel Adam Badeux, Mr. A. E. Newton, Colonel William W. Winthrop.[5]

In the Senate. On the table was the bill for abolishing the 13th clause of the bill passed some time ago about the confiscation of the possessions of the rebels and the power of the president to pardon and grant amnesty. The 13th clause in question concerns only the granting of pardon and amnesty by a general proclamation. Whatever Congress might wish, the power to grant individual pardons cannot be taken from the president because of the provisions in the Constitution. This whole bill is not much more than a puerile manifestation of spite. The House passed this bill suddenly on the first day of this session, and it made a lot of noise because it was seen as a declaration of war. The usual incriminations of pardons having been for sale through women of 'doubtful reputation' were repeated over and over again. Most interesting item of the not very lively debate was a speech by Senator Patterson from . . . in favor of the doctrine of states' rights, trying to prove that neither Jefferson Davis nor 12 million rebels could be charged with treason. When a de facto government is in existence, its adherents and subjects cannot be prosecuted for treason because this also implies that the real government was unable to protect its subjects adequately. The bill was passed with a large majority. Senators with both feet on the chairs.[6]

SATURDAY 5 JANUARY 1867

Visited with Charles Sumner. He appears to be very much preoccupied, and our talk does not amount to much. He does remember Mees, at least he heard from his brother, who died in 1863, of him and has seen some of his letters about currency. He does not hide his feelings. When I asked him if the amendment was going to be passed, he said yes, surely, but meaning only the passing of it by three-quarters of the loyal states only. Of the others he said: "I don't want them to accept it, they are not fit to vote." He was unwilling to concede that this meant also the end of states' rights.[7]

S. G. Golby, registrar of the Treasury. Saw the original accounts kept by George Washington for the benefit of the United States during the years 1775–1783. Everything in his own hand with most remarkable notes added. This document, written by the commander-in-chief in person, shows us in form and contents the patriarchal society of those years. I noted an item "to the barber, $1." Also most remarkable was that the visit George Washington paid to the islands in Boston harbor after the departure of the British did not cost more than $1.15![8]

House of Representatives. Thad. Stevens spoke, but so indistinctly that I could hardly follow him. All jokes that made the House burst out laughing were beyond me. I saw him blow his nose *more Americano.* Skating Park.[9]

When I asked Charles Sumner if there was to be a presidential reception he answered that he didn't know and that he couldn't care less. He wouldn't go there himself, and he could not even understand at all why I would like to go there.

Visited with Riggs, and saw opera *Etoile du Nord,* performed by the company of Max Maretzek. Miss Kellogg.[10]

SUNDAY 6 JANUARY 1867

Visit with Mr. Roest van Limburg, our ambassador. Last year planters from Surinam had tried to get Negroes from the Southern states to work in Surinam. An agent was sent over, and Roest helped in his official capacity. Seward and Gen. Howard, chief of the Freedmen's Bureau, didn't object, although they could not sanction the plan officially. Despite all endeavors our agent couldn't contract a single Negro.[11]

Visit with Charles Sumner and his wife in the evening. A great number of diplomats present and the most radical members of Congress, Ashley, Boutwell. They made it less pleasant for me. After they had made their departure Sumner was still very much distracted, and I was glad to be able to leave.[12]

MONDAY 7 JANUARY 1867

Saw a Freedmen's school, one class only. A lot of discipline, and the children appear to understand the lessons quite well. Here I was struck again as so often before that the pupils are not timid at all when explaining something or asking questions. No mumbling and speaking in half words and unfinished sentences that is so common with us at home. Calisthenics between lessons here too.

House of Representatives. The motion that was discussed yesterday at Sumner's for inquiry if impeachment of the president is justified and legal, was introduced by Mr. Ashley of Ohio. NB This is a real impeachment!

Senate. The bill for the District of Columbia is passed with ⅔ majority. The president is expected to veto it. Speeches of Mr. Cowan (Pennsylvania), Williams (Oregon), Doolittle (Wisconsin), and Reverdy Johnson (Missouri).[13]

NB The session of the House was opened with a long prayer. If this is the custom or only because it is the first day of a week that is almost generally considered to be a special prayer week, I don't know. But the prayer before the session began was a very long and somewhat particular one, with many references to the relatives of representatives who had left their families at home. NB It is customary to open a session with a prayer.

Dinner at Mr. Riggs. Western jokes: "Are you the man that's to ride in the stage? I'm the gentleman that's going to drive you."

TUESDAY 8 JANUARY 1867

Introduced by Mr. Kasson, member of the House, to the floor, and attended most of the session. Passing, also by the House with a ⅔ vote, of the District of Columbia suffrage bill. Resolution introduced and defended by Mr. Kasson against the sale of Negroes as a penalty for serious crimes, something that is still happening in many Southern states. Kasson's motion tended to extend the recently passed amendment of the Constitution—abolishing slavery—also to these cases and make both buyer and seller liable to punishment. His resolution was passed with a great majority, and all rabid radicals came forward to congratulate him. They were especially happy with his way of saying that the invisible wheels of progress, liberty, and new ideas will crush all remnants of the old systems. Those new ideas played a central role in their thinking, and no one hesitated to acknowledge that a great change had taken place and the old had to give way for the new. The poor Constitution has already suffered a lot from those invisible wheels, and the suffering doesn't seem to be over yet.[14]

In general the members seem to treat all matters very lightly. The bills and resolutions proposed are continuously being amended and changed, often without any visible reason. Mr. Kasson included an amendment in his resolution, proposed by another member, who made suddenly a bill out of it, without Kasson wanting this, and hardly knowing what the amendment implied, but simply because some members around him wanted it. Three or four times Kasson sent little notes with changes, making it impossible to know what was really the matter to be voted on. The Senate was supposed to clear this up when the resolution would be introduced there. That this bill will be a serious infraction on the rights of states to organize their own civil laws is without doubt, but after the imposition of the amendment abolishing slavery this is only to be expected.

Dinner at Colonel Badeux, who keeps house with Gen. Porter and wife and Gen. Babcock and wife. Gen. Babcock was absent. Invited were Mr. Foster (president of the Senate) and wife, Miss Delafield, Miss Hamilton, a cousin of Tom Ludlow's, Gen. Jones, formerly ambassador in some South American country, and myself. Very pleasant dinner, Mrs. Babcock was a very pretty young lady.[15]

WEDNESDAY 9 JANUARY 1867

Visited with Colonel Badeux and presented by him to General Grant. He spoke about being in favor the acceptance by the South of the amendment and claimed that, as six years have elapsed since the beginning of the war, the number of those who had been under oath to the United States couldn't be very large. Hence men now of ages between 25 and 31 should be available for the new offices. He said, and I agree with him, that the radicals didn't want the amendment to be passed because they then would be able to carry with them the people, who would otherwise press for the admittance of the former rebels. He also claimed that in case the amendment would be passed, Congress would soon with a ⅔ vote, as prescribed by the amendment, cancel the disqualifications of most returning Southerners and readmit them to all functions. I doubt this very much!

Major W. W. Winthrop, a fervent radical, speaks personally ill of Johnson, especially about his relationship toward his wife, who was said to live in the White House but separate from him. Claims that there is no corruption yet in Congress and not very much in the army, and among the contractors only the Copperheads were cheating.[16]

Arsenal; General Ramsey, seen nothing special.[17]

Visited the Greenback Manufactory again; wages for the girls usually $2 per day. Saw a most ingenious machine for folding envelopes. It was interesting to see the stack of cut but not yet folded envelopes, where one little rod covered with gum lifted only one from the stack and also used the same gum to glue the folded parts together.

Story told by the Riggs girls of a friend from Baltimore, who came here full of Yankee-hatred; when told that if she wanted to go out to parties, she would have to dance with Yankee officers as much as with Southerners, she did, but when an officer asked her permission to visit with her in Baltimore, she had answered in the affirmative but only when he would come without his uniform. Said she: "I will be civil to you because I promised so, but whether my sisters will be, I do not know."

Visit with Miss Kate Riggs. A lot of stories about the arbitrary measures of the Washington government against Southern sympathizers during the war. Tale of a sick woman who had been accused by a Negro of having known something about the murder of Lincoln. She had been forced to walk to the prison together with her husband, notwithstanding her condition. Cases of people taken into custody without their families knowing where they had been taken and if they were still alive or not. A real inquisitorial system seems to have been set up here in this respect. People who had been taken into custody were often released without trial and without being given any explanation or elucidation. She claimed that an attorney, who had been run in but released on the same day and whose papers had been impounded, today still didn't have them back.

Reception at General Grant's. Packed, few pretty women, some beautiful dresses. Spoke some time with Mr. Stansberry, attorney general.[18]

Thursday 10 January 1867

A couple of visits. Went to Mrs. Ira Harris; Miss Harris was in the same box with Lincoln when he was shot. Said goodbye to Mrs. Babcock. Dinner with D. Mackay and had a long conversation about the legality of war. He is from Boston and full of Northern ideals. Heard *Fra Diavolo* with Miss Kellogg and Ronconi.[19]

12

In New York City

January 1867

FRIDAY II JANUARY 1867

To New York, and thought about America for a long time. I feel that in respect of business they are very good at organizing everything. Many things are neatly done and simple, such as the baggage check and express-system, the general character of their railroad carriages, their hotels, etc., but they completely lack the gift of executing these ideas to the smallest detail for comfort and convenience. I think of the design of their water closets in most of the hotels. For American ideas these are practical, well laid out, and praiseworthy. But the way they are usually constructed outside the hotels, without doors or in the open air, or with corridors and landings around, they are most unpleasant.

After arrival visit with Mrs. Dutilh.

SATURDAY 12 JANUARY 1867

Some visits downtown. Diner club. Went to a gambling house or 'hell.' Quite close to Fifth Avenue, fashionably furnished and with a nice supper, drinks and cigars for everyone standing ready, and free of charge. Of course it is then customary to play a little bit, and usually the bank will win enough to make good the cost of the supper. There were few people around so I wasn't very content with having gone there. Faro and roulette tables.

I have forgotten to note down the opinions of General Grant, when I visited him in his office, about General Schofield. He claimed that the radicals do not want the amendment to pass as they think that only in this way they can win the people over to their views and carry them with them. He also thought that once the amendment was passed, Congress would use its right as laid down in one of the paragraphs, to cancel—by a 2/3 vote—the ineligibility of most who were to be locked out under the amendment. In this respect he assumed that the radicals would go further than the conservatives. While the latter would not want to include most of the returning Southerners in this measure, the first named would probably want to push this through. (NB I see that I have made notes of this already before, but the greater precision of this note here be my excuse).

SUNDAY 13 JANUARY 1867

Sunday, went to three churches, Grace Church and two others on Fifth Avenue between 10th and 12th Street. My curiosity was aroused by an article by some author in one of the latest issues of the *Atlantic Monthly*. He raved about the splendor and luxury prevailing there, but the reality disappointed me. Everything is indeed well appointed, and the benches are made of mahogany, but I failed to notice the 'subdued splendor' of the author of the article. In one of the churches the green wreaths and garlands were hanging all around, having been put up before Christmas and staying up as decoration of the building until Easter.[1]

Dinner at Mr. J. Kearny Warren, son-in-law of Dr. Ludlow. The company was formed by his wife, a Mr. Talboys, and two young girls, Nelly Prince and Hattie Travers. They move in the circle of Mr. Jerome, the new millionaire who sets all New York talking because of his liberality with money. Vanderbilt and Belmont also belong to this set. Nowadays this is the most fashionable coterie of New York, and everything they do is markedly 'fast.' Mr. Warren and his family also merit that name: loud laughing and much talking, feeble pleasantries, often improper, such as the teasing of the girls with *amants* etc. Taken all together they are fast indeed, even vulgar. I walked back after dinner with Mr. Talboys, and he told me that his wife was in Europe for a whole year, and when I consoled him with this he said that he didn't really care that much. Even when she was home, they had no real home life, had to accompany her to parties etc. Now he was a free man and preferred to go to those parties as a bachelor. Tonight he seemed to have an appointment too, something that he surely was not going to write about in his next letter to his wife.[2]

Visit with the Kopses. Story by Mrs. John Kops about the poverty of the Southerners. A grandson of Bishop de Hone from South Carolina was driving a [street] car here and a certain Mr. Haywood, of similar old family, conductor. A brother of Friolaeus Huger, Frank, was conductor on a train. She also told me that Mrs. Hayne was a Frapier girl herself, which helps to explain her French character. When the streetcars were introduced in Charleston 1,500 men applied for the posts of driver and conductor.[3]

No entries for 14–15 January 1867

By the 1860s the Episcopal Grace Church, located on Broadway at 10th Street, was, with Trinity Church, one of the most fashionable and richest churches in New York City. When built in 1844, Grace Church was generally thought to be too far out from the existing city, but urban growth soon engulfed the church. Later other churches rivaled the social status attached to Grace Church, including the First Church of Christ, Scientist.   Veenendaal Coll.

WEDNESDAY 16–THURSDAY 17 JANUARY 1867

At home with a swollen cheek.

FRIDAY 18 JANUARY 1867

Said goodbye to Miss Munn. Visited with Mrs. Richards, Osborn, and Mrs. Woolsey. Osborn is paying $20 per year for his water supply.

SATURDAY 19 JANUARY 1867

Had breakfast with Dr. S. G. Howe. Back in 1824 he organized the American support for the Greeks, and now he is doing the same for the rebellious Candiotes and on the point of departing for that part of the world. He thought that this movement was going to end in a general uprising of the Hellenic element and the expulsion of the Turks. When I remarked that it wouldn't be very positive when Russia and others were going to fight over the inheritance, he said, "Oh, that's your business." He didn't care much about the need for more development and education before some republican form of government could be installed. He rattled on about the right of a people to have an elected government of their own, was up in arms against despotism however moderate, and claimed that the consequences of despotism were worse than the worst anarchy. And when I ventured to say that law and justice also have some right to exist, he retorted, "If the majority wants to cut one another's throats, haven't they the most perfect right to do so?" I then said that everything was venal there, and he answered, "Isn't everything venal in Washington?" When I left him he said, "You see, we are terrible rogues," something I couldn't deny.[4]

Various visits. Reception at Mrs. J. Kearny Warren's, she in a most conspicuous dress, a lot of coming and going and a very hospitable table.

General sleigh riding on Fifth Avenue, everybody is doing so. It is interesting to see all those large sleighs with a driver on the box. One can see four ladies who are driven around by their coachman, a dog cart on runners, a sled with a big wooden box, without cover, with five or six men in it. Many handsome sleighs, but I missed the plumes on the horses and the driver in his usual place at the back, as customary in Holland. Strange to see was a sledge with mudguards and shaped as an ordinary carriage at the rear.

Mr. Boese. Coeducational schools, boys and girls, but only in primary schools, where they were sitting all mixed up in class, but this has now been abolished.

SUNDAY 20 JANUARY 1867

To St. Alban's Church, the highest Episcopal Church in America, with Mrs. K. Warren and Miss Travers. Small edifice built after a medieval pattern, big multicolored roof on low walls. Almost Roman Catholic. The clergyman, called Father Morill here, was wearing a green and gold cloth over a white tunic. When the choir boys entered with the clergyman and his assistant, also called Father, a big cross was carried in front. The altar carried all kinds of symbols, a cross in the center with two monstrances at each side, and over that the lamb with a banner, eight high candlesticks, etc. Continuous bowing at the altar; every time the name of Jesus was pronounced during the service, the whole community bowed the head. The assistant, who read the sermon, opened with the sign of the cross, and then read a sermon on the text: "Stand up, those who are asleep." This text was, according to him, taken from an early holy hymn, well known to the 'early Catholics,' because he had found in the English (NB!) words a rhythm, very possibly even a song in honor of the resurrection of Lazarus. Obviously, in his sermon he used a lot of words such as the 'true Catholic faith' and similar expressions. He was wearing a beard like Christ, and both he and the head clergyman were perfect examples of common scoundrels. Especially nr. 1 had a nasal voice and a shifty, sanctimonious, chubby face, worthy of the lowest class of Roman Catholic priests. He announced the services for the coming feast of the Conversion of St. Paul and [. . .]. The Lord's Supper was called the 'Sacrament of Blood of the Lord' and when this was announced—it seems to be celebrated every Sunday, a very close relation to the mass—several small candles were lighted on the altar. At that moment we thought it better to get out.[5]

Dinner at Osborn's, and speaking of St. Alban's, they told me that in the real High Churches in England paintings of the Virgin are still displayed, complete with incense and confession. They also claimed that in St. Alban's at the communion 'the host was raised.' They were not quite certain, however, if the host had really been introduced there, as in England.

According to Osborn the South had never produced more than $200,000,000, not enough for the West to live upon. The Homestead Act gives every man who wants to settle the right to 80 acres (as Osborn thought) of surveyed land free of charge, and after one year he will get the deeds. The problem only is that those lands are in far-away territories, hard to reach. The Preemption Law stipulates that everyone who has already settled will have the right to purchase that land after having been surveyed at the government rate of $1.25 per acre. The U.S. government has kept the odd sections of lands along a railroad; on the Illinois Central those odd sections have been sold long ago.

Children here, even those that are so well brought up as the children of Mrs. Osborn, are very early independent. Fairfield (9 years old) and Freddy (7 years) go to school together every day, from 13th to 40th Street, using the cars of the 6th Avenue line, and Virginia (13 years) goes to one of the skating ponds near 59th Street with Fairfield, who is still in the early stages of the sport.

Wrote some letters, afterward visited with the Cotonnets; Mr. and Mrs. Dutilh, Mrs. Idzard, and Mr. Buvard Hayne, my old acquaintances from Charleston. He told me that planters have more problems in attracting capital from here than last year, something easy to understand. He thought that Northerners are still coming to Charleston in large numbers, and believed that the stories about the return of those who had left are exaggerated.

I remember now that even Osborn, who is a furious radical, acknowledges that without the war the abolition of slavery would have been impossible and unlawful. Heavy snowstorm.

MONDAY 21 JANUARY 1867

Downtown in the morning. Stories of Wessel Scharff about the immorality of the women here. He claimed that nine out of ten women behaved badly, chiefly as a result of the enormous increase of luxury. Rendezvous houses with 'Dentist' on the door. Often a result of the attending of matinees and dinners in hotels afterward. He knew somebody who during a whole week had gone out every day with a different girl or woman, nominally respectable. Introduced at 1, he had reached the pinnacle of his wishes at 5! Dinner with Scharff at the Brevoort House.[6]

Attended a meeting in the Cooper Institute in the evening in honor of the recently passed Columbia District Bill, which gives the vote to all Negroes without restrictions. Garrison, Beecher, etc., had been announced, but didn't turn up. Only Dr. Cheever of the Union Square church was there, and Mr. Gilbert, Reverend Mr. Garnett (black-colored), and other black and white unknown bigwigs were on the platform. The audience was not very large, mostly blacks. Mr. Cheever's speech was a perfect example of how things can be falsely represented. His whole argument was aimed against the constitutional amendment in the understanding that it would give the states the right to exclude a large part of the free population from the 'basis of representation.' Therefore it was a scandalous disregarding of the first principles of the Constitution that intended to have the representation rest solidly on the whole free population and an outrageous injustice toward the Negro population. But he didn't say that the Constitution gave the right to establish who will have the vote and who will decide on the representatives of that part of the free population to the states. According to the Constitution, as it now stands, the 350,000 whites of South Carolina could claim a number of representatives for a total population of 700,000 (white and black) and confine the right to vote to the 350,000 whites. In the amendment they have two options: give the blacks the vote and the representation, or exclude them from both. So instead of the amendment extending the power of the state against the Constitution, as Dr. Cheever tried to foist on his uninformed audience, it will be a restriction of their power. It will be obvious that all kinds of arguments were flying about, such as that they could as well exclude all people with blue eyes or red hair. It is the 'rebellious spirit of the South' that will save us again from a mistake as is the amendment. He did not hesitate to speak of the 'rebel tendencies of the Supreme Court.' His first expression was still stronger, but I didn't quite catch it.[7]

Mr. Gilbert, who seemed to understand the weakness of Dr. Cheever's argument, tried to make it up by claiming that the Constitution originally had intended that all free persons who counted for the basis of representation also would have the vote. In this way he attempted to save Dr. Cheever's untenable statement, by making the basis of representation and the vote one and the same. All Dr. Cheever's arguments were only meant for the right to vote, not for the basis of representation. That Mr. Gilbert's statement is also untenable will at once be clear when one thinks of the fact that for the basis of representation women and children also count, but surely even the most radical persons never thought that the Constitution would allow them to vote as well. Even for free men it doesn't hold, as most early Constitutions included qualifications for the right to vote. Mr. Garnett spoke in a more humoristic vein than the others and told a few good anecdotes. I left when Mr. Howland, editor of the *Anti-Slavery Standard,* came up with a flood of very commonplace invectives against the president.[8]

TUESDAY 22 JANUARY 1867

Visit with Miss Wright, School no. 50, Primary Department. Speaking of my stay in the South, we started talking about the South in general. I had expected her to be a violent radical, but to my great surprise and pleasure I found that she was more Southern, in any case most moderate in her views. Her love for and knowledge of the South originated in 1857 when some gentlemen came over from Charleston to study the New York public school system, with the intention to introduce it in Charleston too. They had tried to persuade her, then in charge of the Normal School, to come with them and organize the same system there, and only strong objections from her relatives and friends had persuaded her not to go. She was full of praise for their manners, their pleasant way of companionship, their assurances and promises that in Charleston she would be able to join in their way of life notwithstanding her position. She wouldn't have to live in a boarding house either, and they were completely indifferent to her views about slavery, as they only wished her to see things with her own eyes and unbiased. "They were giants in mind, blood will tell after all," she said about their qualities, and admitted that she was an aristocrat at heart. The names of those Southerners who were trying to introduce a public school system in Charleston in 1857 were Memminger—later secretary of the treasury of the Confederate States—Bennett, Frost, Coffin, Brewster, and Lasaine. Memminger then had said that many Southerners wished to abolish slavery and that he and those of them with the same ideas only wanted to educate the people in such a way that abolition would be unavoidable. "But they shall not <u>take</u> it from us."[9]

How strong partisanship and the hate in the North against the South were at that particular time will become clear from the following anecdotes. Miss Wright took these gentlemen to a colored school and introduced them to Miss Gwynn, headmistress of the school and an ardent radical, as 'some gentlemen from the South.' The first thing that she did was to have the children sing *Bleeding Kansas,* a violent anti-Southern song, referring to the recent—1856—riots and horrors in Kansas. Governor Arnold of Florida was with her at the moment, and as it happened a certain Mr. Curtis, a singing teacher, entered the classroom. She introduced the gentlemen and the first thing Mr. Curtis said was: "Governor Arnold and a slaveholder." One can easily think with what accent these words were spoken!

From this subject we arrived automatically at the present city government, especially referring to the schools. She complained bitterly. The actual board of education, made up of three school committees for each of the seven school districts, wasn't too bad, and although the members were elected by popular vote and didn't have the high standing of the former members of the Public School Society—appointed by [. . .]—she could not really complain too much about them. Much worse were the boards of trustees, one for every ward and consisting of five members each, which had the immediate supervision of the schools in their ward, and the principals have to do business with them only. They establish all regulations, they appoint the teachers, etc. In Miss Wright's ward and in many others these trustees belong to the lowest orders. They are Irish Roman Catholic politicians, living in tenement houses and knowing so little about schools that they don't even understand what Miss Wright tells them. These folks now have the right, even against the wishes of the principal of a school, to appoint the teachers, and this is more often than not done in favor of daughters, nieces, etc., of those trustees, who need a place but who are completely unsuited for the job. Miss Wright's opposition is totally disregarded, and she then has the difficult task to make these girls at least a little bit fit for the work. Generally she is complaining about the indifference and the total absence of ambition in her subordinates. Some sort of paralysis seems to reign everywhere, and only the system of the big 'halls,' where all classes are sitting next to each other, helps a little bit in fostering the ambition.[10]

Of course, many teachers come from the grammar schools, and are, because of the sort of education they got there, totally unsuited for teaching in the primary schools. They have never heard of phonetics or calisthenics, and Miss Wright is obliged to teach them during the afternoon break to get them to a somewhat higher level. Formerly there existed a daily teacher's college, of which Miss Wright was the principal, but this one was closed as a result of the opposition of the grammar schools. Today there is only a weekly—Saturdays only—teacher's college, for teachers only, but until a short time ago they did there nothing else than continue the studies of the grammar school in useless subjects such as astronomy, etc. Only now, according to Miss Wright, it has more of the character of a real teacher's college. The grammar schools don't take their teachers from one of the higher level schools, as is done in Boston with the high schools, but used to pick the best ones from the primary schools, which does a lot of harm to the primary schools. The earlier custom of paying higher wages for teaching jobs in the second-level schools is no longer in existence. One of the best ways to foster the ambition among the teachers is the system as practiced by Miss Wright of having every class in turn taught in the hall, in her presence—she sits on the platform. She always has two classes rotating at the same time, in a weekly and a daily rotation, and this makes that after ten weeks she has had every class under her eye, each one during a whole week and moreover several times all day long. I don't know if this beneficial system is being followed by all principals, but obviously it needs no recommendation.

She also acknowledged the enormous difference between the Boston and New York teachers, and admired, just as I did, the advantage of having one class for every teacher, without much influence of the principal from above. The result, for the quality of education as well as for the peace between the different teachers, was most satisfying. However, as I did too, in general she preferred the New York system, just as did Philbrick and Dr. Brewer, of whom she spoke as being of the same opinion. Philbrick wanted to introduce the system of halls in Boston. She hoped that the state would take the system of education in its hands, just as was being discussed now. This would certainly lead to a better class of people in charge of this important business. She only was afraid to lose Mr. Boese, whom she valued highly.

Each female teacher needs a license from the city superintendent or one of his assistants, referring to both skills and good behavior, but according to Miss Wright these licenses are given somewhat easily for a pretty face, etc. She tells me that the rule is that no one should be seen as bad or unfit unless his or her guilt is proven. About the question of the state awarding diplomas I couldn't get enough information from her, but she asserted that no one is allowed to teach here without a license from the city. The religion of the teachers is never an object of attention, as it is never for the children: "That's a question we never ask." In the boys' grammar schools the highest classes have male teachers; until about 14 years of age they are taught by women. With a certain amount of regret I took my leave of Miss Susan Wright, and I think that the regret was on both sides. We parted after an exchange of a lot of good wishes for the future.

Had dinner with Ben Richards, together with Sam and Milly Verplanck, children of Delancey. In the evening to the Winter Garden: Hamlet, Edwin Booth.

Several scenes were masterful, and in general his strength lies in the irony, and beautiful was the sequence of the comedy scene "They're but poisoning in jest" and "It's like a camel." His contempt of Polonius after these words is terrible. "To be or not to be" he recited half sitting, half lying down on a chair, and here as everywhere he stressed more the mental and philosophical Hamlet. The dilemmas that he sees terrify him and it is almost with abhorrence that he seeks "Ay, to dream perhaps." Also in "Get thee to a nunnery" he behaves like a madman and it is not quite unjustified that Ophelia is afraid of him. But his last sentences spoken are the more glorious and perfectly right, when he locks her tenderly in his arms and calls out once again, "Get thee to a nunnery." All the sadness of his fate one sees awaiting him, while at the same time one feels the grief that must fill the soul of a Hamlet, when he has nothing better to counsel to a woman whom he loves so much. After the scene with Polonius, "It's like a camel," it struck me that he stood before the window for a moment and let his tired head rest on his arms, how true! In the scene with the praying king his entry was businesslike, but the moment he descried the king, he backed away almost to the other end of the stage.[11]

However, the climax he reached, after the death of Polonius, when he asks with a mixture of abhorrence and joy: "Is it the king?" I did not like the scene with this actor, personified by Devrient with so much dignity and distinction. Hamlet's costume was unusual. At first a purple velvet coat with his legs in dark tights. Then a kind of long black pilgrim's coat with a short cloak with some purple. Then at last in the cemetery scene he wore the costume of a young squire, a short cloak reaching above the knees, with a coat and beret of black velvet, the coat lined with blue, and a sort of blue hood, the beret on the back of his head with blue lapels. The whole transforms Hamlet into a half-troubled nobleman, better than the usual philosopher and 'mawkish' personality. The scenery was handsome too, but the four ladies-in-waiting of the queen were the exception. They were all dressed in white, three of them with a plunging neckline while the fourth wore a high-necked dress.

After the play Booth was presented with a gold medal as a remembrance of his hundredth performance of Hamlet. Afterwards to an 'assembly,' a ball by subscription at Delmonico's.[12]

WEDNESDAY 23 JANUARY 1867

With Miss Abby Woolsey, Miss Smith (engaged to Charles Woolsey), and Miss Sprague (from Albany) to the collection of paintings of Mr. Aspinwall (corner of University Place and 10th Street). Partly old, partly new canvases. Among the first a landscape by Hackaert, a portrait by Rubens, and a ditto by Dorner were good. Of the modern ones a landscape by Church, a dark sea with a lighthouse and clouds colored purple by the setting sun. Also one by Gignoux, fall scenery, but for the rest nothing very spectacular. Dinner with Edward King and reception at Samuel Ward, dull and everlasting.[13]

THURSDAY 24 JANUARY 1867

To William S. Verplanck at Fishkill. Sam Johnson married to Mary Verplanck, he is a cotton weaver. Because of the humid climate the Americans can spin a thread of 1,175 feet per ounce, the English one of 1,000 feet, but the Americans have to keep their factories humid artificially. Reception at Mrs. Knevels's (formerly Miss Verplanck) in honor of the recent wedding of Mary.[14]

FRIDAY 25 JANUARY 186

To a jester's party at Newburgh with Miss Addy Chrystie. In the afternoon to the Howlands, where the Verplanck family stayed over for dinner too. At their departure I said goodbye to them for good.

Joe Howland is paying about 33 percent of his income in taxes. His salary, he is now treasurer of the State of New York, is just enough for his stay in Albany and for the contributions toward the expenses of the Republican Party to which he belongs. These expenses are being apportioned over all who have been appointed in one or other position as Republicans after a certain formula.

SATURDAY 26 JANUARY 1867

Charles Woolsey, Miss Ariane Smith, and Melville Smith have arrived.

SUNDAY 27 JANUARY 1867

Sunday.

MONDAY 28 JANUARY 1867

To Yonkers and stayed with Thomas Ludlow. A young Morris, cousin of Mr. Ludlow, has served in the army but is nevertheless more a Democrat than anything else. Those old New York families seem to lean over to that side. Not surprisingly, T. Ludlow, Gulian C. Verplanck, this Mr. Morris, they all have more conservative ideas than most of the people. Ludlow was as usual fairly somber about the situation the country is in. He estimated the total debt, including state, county, and town debts, at 5,000 million dollars and complains about taxation. He also had some more proofs of the arbitrary ways of the government in respect of citizens during the war. One of his friends had gone to New York and had received several letters to post from a friend in the Astor House. When he came out, he was arrested and taken to a police station, and there all his letters and papers and those of his friend were opened and read. When it turned out that they were harmless, he was set free without explanation.[15]

About 30 years ago Ludlow bought 100 acres at Fordham at $40 an acre, and he recently sold 12 acres for $1,500 an acre. His little pond he has let to someone for cutting and selling the ice, including the use of the icehouses constructed by Tom some time ago. Generally he is making about $1,200 a year from this. He also had a curious story about Southern ideas. When staying with friends in Virginia, they said they were surprised when they saw a rich man walking to the village pump for a pitcher of water; they couldn't understand such a behavior.

A good example of Mr. Leonard Jerome's spirit of enterprise I heard here. He has bought about 100 acres of land near Yonkers for $50,000 with the idea of making a cemetery out of it. In earlier times this setting up of cemeteries was left to the private initiative, and the sale of the actual graves had always been a nice source of income. Nowadays there is a law that restricts this business, but under certain circumstances it still can be a good speculation, although the real big profits are no longer possible. When one transfers 100 acres for free to the community, half of the income generated by the sale of the graves goes to the community for maintenance and betterments of the cemetery, the other half to the donor. A rough calculation has indicated that the total proceeds will be around $400,000, so, although not straightaway but in the course of time, about $200,000 will come to Jerome, amply rewarding him for the interest paid over the original $50,000 and for the duty to take care of the spending of the other $200,000, as the law prescribes.

13

In New York City and Boston and Salem, Massachusetts

January–February 1867

TUESDAY 29 JANUARY 1867

In the morning back to New York. At 3 pm to Fordham, where Mr. Chrystie, brother of the one at Newburgh, has asked me for dinner, chiefly in honor of his wife and her brother, both named Punnett. Their father had a house in St. Albans that had very close relations with Daniel Crommelin & Sons. The Amsterdam house once sent them a tablecloth and napkins, which were still preserved in the family, and today these graced the dinner table. Mr. Punnett was a charming host and friendly, also a man with a clear understanding and large knowledge.

NB The duties when transferring landed property are negligible.[1]

WEDNESDAY 30 JANUARY 1867

With John Scharff to Bloomfield and Newark, long sleigh rides and farewell to the family.[2]

No entry for 31 January 1867

FRIDAY 1–SATURDAY 2 FEBRUARY 1867

Leave taking of all my New York friends.

SUNDAY 3 FEBRUARY 1867

Sunday. Crossed over to Brooklyn despite snow and slush to hear Beecher once more. The underlying idea of his sermon was that conversion was not something that God brought into man from outside, but that it should come from one's self. Just as knowledge, feeling, and such things are not given to someone but are acquired by continuous exercise and effort of those faculties that are necessary for that purpose, so man is not converted as if by magic. A few times this may have been the way of Providence, as in the case of the apostle Paul, but in general even there a slow development is visible. The other six apostles may serve as proof for this. His whole sermon was without doubt 'good sound sense' and now and then flavored with fitting examples and spicy proverbs.[3]

NB When coming up to the pulpit Beecher very composedly took off his galoshes, put away his coat, and then was ready for work. To those people who are always waiting for piety and devoutness he called out: "It should be: work them out, not wait them out." Those who are always wanting to say long prayers, he compared to a sailor taking observations at sea through his binoculars, for five minutes, a quarter of an hour, or maybe half an hour, and being asked what he was doing, answered, "I am taking a long observation." That is not important; it doesn't matter how long your observation is, if it is only well done. If you have looked for half a minute in the right way, the rest of the hour will not improve your observation at all. So close your binoculars and let the clouds cover the sky again; it won't harm you, you know where you are.

In such moments Beecher is sublime and eloquent. In the beginning of his sermon he is usually dull, as if his bulk keeps him down to earth, but as soon as a thought comes to him that he values, he is working himself into an enthusiasm and throws himself wholeheartedly with all the seriousness of his nature into the matter and doesn't leave off until he has explained everything loud and clear to his audience, although sometimes he is near to being ridiculous. The way he elaborated on this comparison of the man taking a long observation was masterful. He was himself taking an observation, swaying to and fro with the movement of the ship, and imitating one who, after a long storm, sees a clearing in the clouds, and 'quick as thought' takes an observation.

Most people, he said, use their dictionary much better than their Bible. When they look into the first they know what they are looking for and find at once a remedy for the problem. And although the Bible gives remedies for all ailments and recipes for all kinds of tastes and moods, people don't know how to use this, but only read their chapter without questioning if this will comply with their state of mind of the moment. Or they read the Bible with 'preconceived ideas,' just as one could study astronomy with a kaleidoscope. In these bursts of eloquence his most noticeable quality is that he knows when to stop. He finishes his sentences sometimes abruptly, but with such an incisive question or a snappy saying that every further word would spoil the effect.

Lunch at Otto Heinze's and said farewell to him and his dear wife. Dinner with Blake. Goodbye to the Cotonnets and Dutilhs.[4]

Monday 4 February 1867

Visited the school of Thomas Hunter, 13th Street at 6th Avenue, boys' grammar school. Class B1, belonging to the 'second grade,' the highest but one, didn't seem to me to be very advanced. Spelling of plain words and very simple arithmetic such as interest accounts, most uncomplicated, didn't seem to be the best way of educating boys of 12 or 13 years old. It should not be forgotten, however, that this class, just as almost all others in high school, has between sixty and seventy boys, which makes everything slow. Bearing this in mind, it even went fairly quickly, but that not much can be done in one hour is evident, when every test is to be executed by sixty boys, and then, faulty or not, everything has to be checked and corrected and the results noted down. To speed things up a number of methods have been introduced, such as sit and stand, raising of hands, the surrender of the slates for correction, etc.[5]

When I attended an examination of one class by Hunter, he gave ten words to write down. Then the slates were handed in, and all boys who had all ten words correct had to stand up on one side of the hall, then those with nine correct to the other side and so on, and in this way he had the results fairly soon. Everything went off in the most perfect order. He tries to examine at least one class every day, and although he is often interrupted in this work, it does stimulate the ambition of the teachers. He also has the system of rotation in the hall, just as Miss Wright.

He sees the same difficulty in getting the right sort of teachers, although he has not the same complaint as Miss Wright about the trustees of the ward forcing unsuitable candidates upon her against her wishes. In his school no one is being appointed but on his recommendation, but he knew about the problems in Miss Wright's ward. In New York City there is no other normal school than the weekly one of 3 or 4 hours, which doesn't amount to much. There is one in Albany for the whole state of New York, from where the city of New York can get a teacher now and then. One is forced to pick them up wherever they are to be found, and this turns out to be difficult enough. New England is a good source, however, and a large number of female teachers of the New York schools come from Connecticut or Massachusetts. Many teachers are drafted from the primary schools, hence the complaints of Miss Wright. Hunter wished for an addition to the New York system in the shape of two or three high schools and two normal schools, one each for male and female teachers. He was in favor of enlarging the number of male teachers in the grammar schools, as he thought that the boys in some classes were getting too old to be under the authority of a woman. The chief problem is financial: for $950 or $1,000 one can get a female teacher of the highest ability, but the males who would want to teach for that wage are worthless. The male head assistants get $2,000 and more.[6]

About the reading of the Bible he gave me the following information. In his school and in most others it is being done, and if a child is not present at the opening, he will lose a 'mark,' which will be of no influence on his progress from class to class, as that progress is governed by his examinations, but it will be of influence for his 'standing,' leading to—if I am correct—a thing like a 'half yearly certificate' or something of the sort. In other schools the Bible is being read, but children of parents who object may be absent, and in other schools again, such as the schools in the Roman Catholic wards, it is not being done at all. Some time ago there was a lawsuit about this. The board of education wanted to withhold the salary of a principal because he didn't read the Bible. In that case the court decided that a principal is totally free to open his classes in the way he wants, and that his salary could not be withheld on these grounds. And as a principal cannot be discharged without the cooperation and approval of the board of trustees of his ward, who in a Catholic ward are, of course, Roman Catholics, to all appearances this case has been taken out of the hands of the board of education.

Packed up, and said goodbye to Osborn.

TUESDAY 5 FEBRUARY 1867

By railroad to Boston; Jamaica Plains, Bond.

WEDNESDAY 6–THURSDAY 7 FEBRUARY 1867

Wrote letters.

FRIDAY 8 FEBRUARY 1867

Attended the session of both houses of the Legislature of Massachusetts. In the house the two Negro representatives, the first ever in any American legislative, were sitting in their appointed places. According to Mr. Bond the standing of most representatives is not very high, and the influence of the masses of the lower orders in the legislative and in the city government is being felt, even if not yet strongly. Especially in Boston the emigration of the 'substantial middle classes' over the past twenty years to the smaller towns in the vicinity has been of influence. In the evening at Macy's. He acknowledged the lack of discipline in Sherman's army and tended to believe all those Southern stories of stealing, etc. In reality, he is rather Southern in his views and feelings, and his sympathies are strongly on that side.

No entry for 9 February 1867

SUNDAY 10 FEBRUARY 1867

Sunday. Dinner with Cas. Thoron at Jasigi's. In the evening with George Bond.

Monday 11 February 1867

Girls' school at Lancaster. About 45 miles away from Boston, the school is situated in a pretty, healthy, and elevated area and most appropriate for the purpose. The several buildings are each surrounded by vast expanses of grass, shaded by old elms, which gives a very pretty and happy look to the whole. This institution, about eleven years old, is organized on the family system and seems to answer all expectations. About 150 girls are housed here nowadays. They are being sent there for three reasons:

1. Petty offenses, and these girls are really convicted, most for petty larceny.
2. 'Stubbornness,' a term that can embrace almost everything, not exactly according to the word, and which gives wide discretionary powers to the judge.
3. Exposure, etc., in cases of vagrancy if the chances of temptation and aberration are great and when these already show their influence. Totally depraved girls, and as far as I could hear, also debauched girls, have been sent there from time to time but taken in by the board of governors only reluctantly, because of the bad influence they will have on the others. These governors have done all they could to convince the probate judges and special commissioners, who have the right to send girls to the institution, that this institution is only meant for semi-depraved children, who are yet only halfway down the ladder to the lowest grade. In recent times they have heeded those requests on many occasions, and the cases of pupils who after their discharge have fallen back into their old vices have become rare.[7]

As I have said before, the pupils are apportioned over the several families. At this moment there are five families, each with some 30 girls, giving a total that can be placed of about 150. Each family is completely separated from the others, and even when at play during the breaks they have no contact with the inmates of the other houses, as each house has a playground of its own, separated from the others by boundary lines, mostly imaginary. The families are made up without any reference to ages or measure of depravity. Newcomers are placed wherever there is room. In general the system seems to function adequately as it answers more than anything to the idea of family and it provides room for good and bad influences because of the difference in age and development, as in every family.

I think that in this school the difference must be felt to a too great extent, the more so with this class of pupils, of which a number have gone from bad to worse, partly from total brutalization and neglect, partly from too early corporal development and too much intelligence. On the other hand it is true that with a number of not more than thirty, one teacher, who is with them all day and who knows them all, should be able to divide them up into two or three groups and keep every group occupied according to the level of their skills. Each family has one matron, who occupies the place of the mother, and who has the general supervision and control, one assistant matron, who teaches in school and in the sewing classes, and one housekeeper, who teaches all domestic skills and chores. Of course, all domestic work is being done in turn by the girls themselves in crews of four or five for cooking, washing, cleaning, and such for a month. This way, after an average stay of two years and three months, they are ready for working as maids in middle-class families. Part of the day is used for the teaching of sewing, knitting, etc., and 3½ hours are spent on general education.

The day starts at 5:30 am (summer) or 6:30 (winter), then breakfast, religious service, in summer conducted by the superintendent in the chapel for all girls, in winter in the several families, one day by the superintendent, four by the matron. After that sewing school for those not charged with the domestic chores, dinner at 12. Then school from 1:30 pm till 5 pm, followed by supper, sewing with reading aloud, and at about 9 pm to bed. After dinner and after supper they have an hour for play, which gives them two hours per day in the open air. But I thought that they looked a bit pale and wan, but, of course, in winter there is not so much opportunity for playing outside as in summer. Three days a week animal food, meat once, soup once, and fish once, and for the rest beans, hulled corn, rice, etc. The matrons of the several houses are completely on their own and independent of the others, only responsible to the superintendent and the board of trustees.

After the girls have spent some time in this institution and when they are found ready for being on their own, they are placed as indentured maids with families that are thought suited to this kind of servant, and where a positive influence on the girls may be expected. However, the institution always keeps an eye on the girls. In this way the influence of the school is spread far and wide, and for the girls the change from complete submissiveness in the institution to a perfect independence in society is more gradual. The pupils remain under the supervision of the trustees till their 21st birthday, in earlier times to their 18th only.

In respect of religion this institution belongs to the evangelical persuasion, unlike most others of this kind, which are un-evangelical and under the great influence of the Unitarians elsewhere. Mr. Marcus Ames, superintendent and chaplain, who showed me around in a most friendly manner, himself belongs to the 'congregational orthodox persuasion' and naturally places his stamp on everything. The general influence of religion is not very strong, it seems, and for Catholics no distinction is being made. At least there is no strong opposition from the side of the Roman Catholic clergy, although they represent some 300,000 of the total population of Massachusetts of 1,000,000. However, at present they try to oppose the current trends by founding reform schools of their own.

In general I saw a lot of order and neatness, and I liked that. A good thing is that they have done away with the large dormitories, and every girl has a room of her own, small it is true, but it gives the girls the necessary privacy and seclusion, invaluable for their feelings and their development.

Visited with Mrs. Lizzie Freeman.

No entries for 12–14 February 1867

FRIDAY 15–MONDAY 18 FEBRUARY 1867

With William Bond to Niagara. Left on Friday 2:30 pm, arrived Saturday 2:30 pm, returned Sunday at 5:20 pm, back in Boston on Monday at 5 pm.

TUESDAY 19–THURSDAY 21 FEBRUARY 1867

Dinner at Charles E. Norton with Longfellow and Lowell.[8]

SATURDAY 23 FEBRUARY 1867

Visited the Normal School at Salem, Mr. Hager principal. One of four in Massachusetts, this one founded in 1857, the first one in 1839. All these schools together produce about one hundred teachers every year. Of the total number of students annually, only half are promoted to the next level. Every class has a written examination of one hour every four weeks, and at the end of each term a difficult exam of one whole week. A complete course takes two years. A primary school in the vicinity provides two classes every day for the practice in the highest level only, and every student of that level has one hour of teaching every two weeks. All the others sit and listen and give their critical comments afterward. For the rest they have a kind of mutual system where every pupil teaches the fellow students of her own class in turn. I never saw a more interesting spectacle than this beautiful school, with these young girls, all 'bright and eager,' all filled with the thought of this future as a teacher, all full of life and energy![9]

Dinner with Mr. Hager, and afterward I saw some relics of the witch trials. In the evening visited with Mrs. Fairbanks and Mrs. Lizzie Freeman.

[Handwritten note: The diary has not been continued further. In all probability the writer returned to the Netherlands shortly after.]

Notes

INTRODUCTION

1. John F. Stover, *Iron Road to the West: American Railroads in the 1850s* (New York: Columbia University Press, 1978).

2. See, e.g., Richard D. Heffner, ed., *Democracy in America* (New York: New American Library, 1956).

3. Charles Dickens, *American Notes for General Circulation* (London: Chapman and Hall, 1842); Anthony Trollope, *North America* (London: Chapman and Hall, 1862).

Good accounts of British visitors to the United States include Roger Haydon, *Upstate Travels: British Views of Nineteenth Century New York* (Syracuse, N.Y.: Syracuse University Press, 1982), and L. Milton Woods, *British Gentlemen in the Wild West: The Era of the Intensely English Cowboy* (London: Collier Macmillan, 1989).

4. Henry Stephen Lucas, *Dutch Emigrant Memoirs and Related Writings* (Assen, Netherlands: Van Gorcum, 1955); Jacob van Hinte and Robert P. Swierenga, eds., *Netherlanders in America: A Study of Emigration and Settlement in the Nineteenth and Twentieth Centuries in the United States of America* (Grand Rapids, Mich.: Baker Book House, 1985); Robert P. Swierenga, ed., *The Dutch in America: Immigration, Settlement, and Cultural Change* (New Brunswick, N.J.: Rutgers University Press, 1985); Robert P. Swierenga, *Faith and Family: Dutch Immigration and Settlement in the United States, 1820–1920* (New York: Holmes and Meier, 2000); Hans Krabbendam, *Vrijheid in het Verschiet: Nederlandse Emigratie naar Amerika 1840–1940* (Hilversum, Netherlands: Verloren, 2006).

For a list of published and unpublished diaries written by Dutch visitors to the United States before 1860, see Pien Steringa, *Nederlanders op reis in Amerika, 1812–1860. Reisverhalen als bron voor negentiende-eeuwse mentaliteit* (Utrecht, Netherlands: Utrechtse Historische Cahiers, 20, 1999, nr.1).

5. J. H. Scheffer, *Genealogie van het geslacht Crommelin* (Rotterdam, Netherlands: Van Hengel and Eeltjes, 1879).

The first "American" Crommelin, Daniel († 1725), lies buried in the cemetery of Trinity Church in New York City, where his damaged headstone remains. The complete Crommelin genealogy is found on the "Stichting Familie Crommelin" website. The webmaster, Govert Deketh, who lives in Geneva, Switzerland, has assisted in sorting out the complicated family relations.

6. Joost Jonker, *Merchants, Bankers, Middlemen: The Amsterdam Money Market during the First Half of the 19th Century* (Amsterdam: NEHA, 1996), 194–200.

7. The Dutch title of Crommelin's doctoral thesis is: *Beschouwingen over de grondbelasting* [*Considerations on Land Tax*] (Amsterdam: Johannes Müller, 1865). A copy is located at The Hague Royal Library nr. 320 A 160.

8. A report of this journey of 1863 is in the possession of Liesbeth Crommelin of Amsterdam, and will be donated to the Stadsarchief of Amsterdam, Daniel Crommelin and Sons Collection. We wish to thank Liesbeth Crommelin for this information.

9. For the Overend, Gurney crash, see M. C. Reed, ed., *Railways in the Victorian Economy: Studies in Finance and Economic Growth* (Newton Abbot, UK: David and Charles, 1969), and Harold Pollins, *Britain's Railways: An Industrial History* (Newton Abbot, UK: David and Charles, 1971).

Sir Morton Peto, through his contracting firm of Peto and Betts, had built the Grand Trunk Railway of Canada, including the magnificent Victoria Bridge across the St. Lawrence River near Montreal.

10. See Muriel E. Hidy, ed., and A. Hermina Potgieter, trans., "A Dutch Investor in Minnesota, 1866: The Diary of Claude August Crommelin," *Minnesota History* 37 (December 1960): 152–60; Steringa, *Nederlanders op reis in Amerika*. See also George Harinck and Augustus J. Veenendaal, Jr., "Transatlantic Transportation and Travelers' Experiences," *Four Centuries of Dutch-American Relations 1609–2009,* ed. Hans Krabbendam, Cornelis A. van Minnen, and Giles Scott-Smith (Amsterdam: Boom, 2009), 318–28.

11. For the problem of the different gauges in use in the United States, see H. Roger Grant, *The Railroad: The Life Story of a Technology* (Westport, Conn.: Greenwood, 2005), and George Rogers Taylor and Irene D. Neu, *The American Railroad Network 1861–1890* (Urbana: University of Illinois Press, 2003).

12. "Circular," Thomas Green Clemson papers, Clemson University Archives, Clemson, S.C.

13. Drew Gilpin Faust, *The Republic of Suffering: Death and the American Civil War* (New York: Knopf, 2008).

14. Charles A. and Mary R. Beard, *A Basic History of the United States* (New York: Doubleday, Doran, 1944).

15. E. Merton Coulter, *The South during Reconstruction* (Baton Rouge: Louisiana State University Press, 1947); Eric Foner, *Reconstruction: America's Unfinished Revolution* (New York: Perennial, 2007).

16. James M. McPherson, *The Struggle for Equality: Abolitionists and the Negro in Civil War and Reconstruction* (Princeton, N.J.: Princeton University Press, 1964).

17. For an examination of sharecropping and the crop-lien system in the American South, see Theodore Saloutous, *Farmer Movements in the South, 1865–1933* (Lincoln: Uni-

versity of Nebraska Press, 1964), and Lawrence Goodwyn, *Democratic Promise: The Populist Moment in America* (New York: Oxford University Press, 1976).

18. See Sidney Andrews, *South since the War: As Shown by Fourteen Weeks of Travel and Observation in Georgia and the Carolinas* (Boston: Ticknor and Fields, 1866).

19. *New York Times,* April 27, 1867; Leo Hershkowitz, *Tweed's New York: Another Look* (New York: Doubleday, 1977), 120–21.

20. Ray Ginger, *The Age of Excess* (New York: Macmillan, 1965).

21. Most of the discussions in the Amsterdam City Council are found in the Amsterdam *Gemeenteblad* for 1874.

22. The Crommelin residence, known as "The Prophet Jonas," burned down on New Year's Eve of 2007–2008. Charles Rochussen (1814–1894), a Dutch painter trained in the Romantic School, worked in Amsterdam from 1849 to 1869 and after that in his place of birth, Rotterdam.

23. Van den Handel, "Crommelin, Claude August," in *Biografisch Woordenboek van Nederland,* to be found on the website of the Instituut voor Nederlandse Geschiedenis (ING, Institute of Netherlands History), The Hague, 14 December 2006. In 1913 the Nobel Prize Committee awarded Kamerlingh Onnes its highly coveted award for his feat.

24. Otto Schutte of The Hague kindly supplied information about Meder.

25. The title translation of the manuscript version held by the Minnesota Historical Society is: "Journey to N. America by Mr. Claude August Crommelin, Amsterdam born 1 March 1840, † 4 November 1874." Crommelin's death, however, is recorded officially as having occurred on 5 November 1874.

26. Rotterdam City Archives, coll. hss. III 4110. The third Claude August Crommelin (1919–1985) had no offspring. The Mrs. De Kanter is Kitty de Kanter-Crommelin (1885–1988), a sister of Dr. C. A. Crommelin (1878–1965). Help for this biographical information came from Liesbeth Crommelin of Amsterdam and Govert Deketh, Geneva, Switzerland.

27. The location of the Crommelin typescript in the Amsterdam City Archives is nr. 654–185. For R. P. J. Tutein Nolthenius, see Augustus J. Veenendaal, Jr., *Slow Train to Paradise: How Dutch Investment Helped Build American Railroads* (Stanford, Calif.: Stanford University Press, 1996). La Tour de Peilz, Canton of Vaud, Switzerland, is situated on the banks of Lac Leman between Montreux and Vevey.

28. The Dutch text of Crommelin's travel diary has recently been published: *Een Amsterdammer in Amerika 1866–1867: Verslag van de reis van Claude August Crommelin door de Verenigde Staten en Canada* [An Amsterdammer in America, 1866–1867: Travelogue of Claude August Crommelin in the United States and Canada], edited and annotated by Guus Veenendaal, with the assistance of H. Roger Grant (Amsterdam: De Bataafsche Leeuw, 2009).

1. From Amsterdam through Belgium and Great Britain to New York

1. Adrien Huet (1836–1899), like Crommelin himself of a Dutch-Huguenot family, civil engineer, professor of mechanical engineering at the Delft Polytechnic, and recognized as

one of the leading lights in the Netherlands in mechanical engineering and steam locomotion. Delft is halfway between The Hague and Rotterdam.

2. Paolo Veronese (1528–1588), Italian painter from Verona, but living in Venice for most of his life; Guido da Siena, painter living in Siena in the second half of the 13th century; Jan Steen (1626–1679), Dutch painter from Leiden; Nicolaes Maes (1634–1693), Dutch painter from Dordrecht, pupil of Rembrandt; Rembrandt Harmensz. van Rijn (1606–1669), recognized as the greatest Dutch painter of the Golden Age; Carel Dujardin (1622–1678), Dutch painter born in Amsterdam but living in Rome and Venice for the greater part of his life; Peter Paul Rubens (1577–1640), greatest painter of the Flemish baroque; Jan van Eyck (†1441), was a Flemish painter, and together with his brother Hubert (†1426) most famous for their altar panels.

3. Emmanuel-Constantin-Premier-Ghislain, baron Van der Linde d'Hooghvorst (1781–1866), one of the founders of Belgian independence in 1830. Charles-Latour Rogier (1800–1885), a Belgian journalist and statesman, who also played an important role in the 1830 revolution. Alphonse Van den Peereboom (1812–1884), Belgian statesman. Pierre-Emmanuel-Félix baron Chazal (1808–1892), a Frenchman living in exile in Belgium, took part in the 1830 insurrection against King William I of the Netherlands and served as a military officer since that year. In 1844 he was naturalized as a Belgian subject and was secretary of war of Belgium 1859–1866.

4. Jules-Marcel-Lamorald Bara (1835–1900), Belgian lawyer and liberal politician.

5. It is not quite clear which one of the brothers Urban Crommelin met in Brussels. Jules Urban was director of the Grand Central Belge, the leading Belgian private railway company, with lines also in the Netherlands. Crommelin must have ridden a train of the GCB from Rotterdam to Antwerp. His brother Maurice Urban was a leading railway engineer, chief mechanical engineer of the GCB, and well known in the Netherlands too. Guus Veenendaal, *Spoorwegen in Nederland van 1834 tot nu* (Amsterdam, Netherlands: Boom, 2004), 173.

The playwright De Girardin must be Delphine Gay (1804–1855), married to Emile de Girardin. She was famous for her literary salons and her writings about the social life in Paris in her time.

6. The two gentlemen Becquet and Gausset have not been identified.

7. George Harry Grey (1827–1883), earl of Stamford since 1845, was an English politician and officer of no great distinction. The Charing Cross Hotel was part of Charing Cross Station of the South Eastern Railway, where the Continental boat trains from Dover arrived. Station and hotel had opened in 1864, only two years before Crommelin's arrival. De Keyser's Royal Hotel was situated on what was later to be known as the Victoria Embankment, Blackfriars, and "conducted in the continental fashion." K. Baedeker, *London and Its Environments: Handbook for Travellers* (Leipzig, Germany: Karl Baedeker, 1892), 8.

8. Morris, Prevost & Co., a London banking firm with close ties to Barings and interested in several French railways since the 1840s. D. C. M. Platt, *Foreign Finance in Continental Europe and the United States, 1815–1870: Quantities, Origins, Functions and Distribution* (London: George Allen and Unwin, 1984), 20–21.

Apparently Crommelin carried letters of exchange for bankers in England and America, to be able to get cash whenever he needed it. At the time this was the usual way for well-heeled tourists to get ready money when traveling in foreign countries.

Simpson's Dining Rooms were located on the Strand and very fashionable. *Baedeker's London,* 12.

Ludwig van Beethoven's opera *Fidelio* was finished in 1805; Italo Gardoni (1821–1882) was a famous tenor, and often the stage partner of Jenny Lind, the "Swedish Nightingale." With Titien Crommelin must mean Thérèse Carolina Johanna Alexandra Titiens (or Tietjens) (1831–1877), a German opera singer (soprano) who after 1859 performed mostly in London. Her Majesty's Theatre or Opera House on the corner of Haymarket and Pall Mall dated back to 1705 and was rebuilt and enlarged many times before burning down in 1867. Restored again after the fire, it finally closed its doors in 1890. *Baedeker's London,* 40. A sortie was a kind of evening cape for ladies.

9. Waterloo Station, of the London & South Western Railway, was opened in 1848 and subsequently enlarged piecemeal. Alan A. Jackson, *London's Termini* (Newton Abbot, UK: David and Charles, 1969), 213–16.

The tree that Crommelin mentions must have been a gleditsia, commonly known as honey locust. Bushy Park, a royal domain of 11,000 acres between Hampton Court and Teddington, was famous for its horse chestnuts, planted in the time of Stadholder-King William III (Dutch William) before 1702.

Balthasar Denner (1685–1749), painter from Hamburg, who worked in London from 1721 to 1728, was famous for his portraits. Bartolomé Esteban Murillo (1618–1682), Spanish baroque painter from Sevilla; Giovanni Antonio de Sacchis (1484–1539), now commonly known as Pordenone after his place of birth; and Jacopo Negreti (1480–1528), known as Palma il Vecchio, to distinguish him from a younger relative Jacopo di Antonio Negreti (1544–1628), known as Palma il Giovane. All were Italian painters of the Renaissance.

The King's Arms was an old inn near the village of Hampton Court, at the entry of Bushy Park. *Baedeker's London,* 322.

10. Bridgewater House, home of the earls of Ellesmere, housed one of the most famous private collections of paintings, mostly from the Dutch school of the 17th century. Willem van de Velde (the younger, 1633–1707), was a Dutch marine painter, and his canvases and drawings were much sought after.

Harriet Catharine Greville (1800–17 April 1866) was the widow of Francis Leveson Gower (1800–1857), since 1846 earl of Ellesmere.

11. All artists listed here by Crommelin are famous or at least well known. Sir Joshua Reynolds (1723–1792) was famous for his portraits. Benjamin West (1738–1820) was an American by birth but settled in London in 1763 and was appointed royal history painter. Sir Thomas Lawrence (1769–1830) again was most famous for his portraits, Sir David Wilkie (1785–1841) for his portraits and genre paintings. Sir Edwin Henry Landseer (1802–1873) was still active as a portrait painter at the time of Crommelin's visit. George Romney (1734–1802) was a portrait painter, Frederick Richard Lee (1798–1879) a fashionable landscape painter.

12. Raphael, officially named Raffaelo Santi (1483–1520), was one of the most famous painters of the Italian Renaissance. His contemporary, the painter and sculptor Michelangelo Buonarotti (1475–1564), was even better known.

13. Julia Margaret Cameron, *née* Pattle (1815–1879), was a famous photographer and well known in London's artistic circles in the 1860s.

The brothers Paul and Dominic Colnaghi operated a bookshop and publishing firm in London.

14. Dalmeyer was a London firm where photographs and photographic supplies could be bought.

15. Thomas Baring (1799–1873), was partner in the House of Baring, the well-known London banking house, since 1828. Ralph W. Hidy, *The House of Baring in American Trade and Finance: English Merchant Bankers at Work* (Cambridge, Mass.: Harvard University Press, 1949), 44.

Jan Both (†1652), was a Dutch painter of landscapes and heroic-moralistic works. Gabriël Metsu (1629–1667), was a Dutch portrait and genre painter, Jean-Baptiste Greuze (1725–1805), a French genre painter, moralist, and portraitist.

16. Henry Peach Robinson (1830–1901), in his time a famous photographer, specializing in portraits and groups.

Leamington, now officially called Royal Leamington Spa, is situated in the county of Warwickshire, southeast of Birmingham.

17. Dulwich lies south of London and was then still a separate community. God's Gift College in Dulwich was founded in the 16th century. The collection of paintings assembled by the art dealer Noël Desenfans for King Stanislaus of Poland in the late 18th century, but never delivered, was bequeathed to Dulwich College early in the 19th century. It was famous for its collection of Dutch masters. *Baedeker's London,* 319.

Guido Reni (1575–1642), was an Italian painter from Bologna, Salomon van Ruysdael (†1670), a Dutch landscape painter of the Golden Age.

18. Joseph Paxton's famous Crystal Palace, originally constructed for the Industrial Exposition of 1851 in London's Hyde Park, had been moved to Sydenham, just south of Dulwich, in 1854. It was used as an exhibition hall but contained little of interest. Part of it burned down later in 1866, shortly after Crommelin's visit. *Baedeker's London,* 312.

19. Apparently Crommelin had already seen a lot of actors in his life. Charles Fechter (1824–1879), a popular English actor, was especially known for his interpretation of Shakespeare's Hamlet. The Lyceum Theatre was situated on the Strand, corner of Wellington Street. Adelaide Ristori (1822–1906) was an Italian tragic actress, who debuted in the United States later in 1866 as Medea in the French Theater in New York; Karl August Devrient (1797–1872) was a Prussian actor, who had been married for some years to Wilhelmine Schröder (1804–1860), a great soprano and opera singer; Rachel was the stage name of Elisa Félix (1821–1858), a French-Jewish tragédienne who was considered the best of her time and had created a sensation in the Metropolitan Theatre on Broadway. Davison has not been identified.

20. Paddington Station, the London terminus of the Great Western Railway, was opened

in 1854 for the traffic to Bristol, the West Country, and South Wales. Jackson, *London's Termini*, 308.

21. Dr. Edward Bouverie Pusey (1800–1882), English theologian and orientalist, professor of Hebrew at Christchurch College in Oxford and one of the leaders of the High Church movement in the Anglican Church.

22. Warwick is a small medieval town southeast of Birmingham. Crommelin must have used the Great Western Railway to get to Warwick from Oxford.

23. The medieval Warwick Castle is close to the town of Warwick; Kenilworth Castle is north of Warwick.

Sir Thomas Lucy, justice of the peace at Charlecote, northeast of Stratford, played a role in Shakespeare's life. His descendants still owned the manor of Charlecote at the time of Crommelin's visit. K. Baedeker, *Grossbrittannien. England (ausser London), Wales, Schottland und Irland. Handbuch für Reisende* (Leipzig, Germany: Karl Baedeker, 1889), 201.

24. Guy's Cliff is just north of Warwick. Saint Mary's Church in Warwick is a gothic building, much rebuilt after a disastrous fire in 1694.

Matlock Bath, famous for its thermal waters and a much sought after spot in the Derbyshire Peak District, is situated north of Derby.

From Warwick Crommelin must first have taken a train of the Great Western Railway to Birmingham and from there with the Midland Railway by way of Derby to Matlock.

25. Chatsworth, north of Matlock, was the famous home of the dukes of Devonshire. To get to Chatsworth, Crommelin likely used the Midland Railway from Matlock to Rowsley, the station for Chatsworth House.

Joseph Paxton (1801–1865), was head gardener of the duke of Devonshire and builder of a big iron and glass greenhouse at Chatsworth. Later he used the same technology for the Crystal Palace, the main building of the Great Exposition in London of 1851, for which he was knighted.

William Cavendish (1808–1891), duke of Devonshire, was a liberal politician and chancellor of the University of Cambridge.

26. It is unclear which Huet Crommelin met in Manchester. There is no one with the initials Th. to be found in the Huet genealogy. Of course, it may also be a mistake of the person who typed out the original manuscript of Crommelin. With no other information available it is also hard to tell which member of the Bake family Crommelin met in Manchester. He might be a brother of Charles François Guillaume de Menthon Bake (1841–1906), a fellow law student of Crommelin at Utrecht University, who had three brothers. Barge has not been identified.

A *divan* was probably a café for smoking and drinking, comparable to a modern nightclub.

27. Rochdale, north of Manchester, was famous for its textile industry. The cooperative movement started here and the Society of Equitable Pioneers, founded in 1844, had already thousands of members and a large accumulation of capital. Mr. Gord has not been identified; most probably he was the manager of the company.

28. The Royal Theatre was located on Peter Street, not far from Manchester Central Station.

Notes to pages 26–28

29. Brown, Shipley & Co., originally W. & J. Brown, was a Liverpool banking house, closely connected with Brown Brothers of Baltimore and New York City. Irene Adler, *British Investment in American Railways 1834–1898* (Charlottesville: University Press of Virginia, 1970), 144. Brown, Van Santen & Co., where Crommelin had relations, must have been a connected firm.

30. The steamship *Java* of the Cunard Steamship Company, launched in 1865, was a large vessel of 2,697 tons and 360 feet in length, with accommodation for 160 passengers, and equipped for the then new screw propulsion. Curiously enough, on November 7, 1866, some months after Crommelin had used the ship, the *Java* collided with a schooner when entering Boston Harbor. The ensuing lawsuits only ended with the verdict of the United States Supreme Court (81 U.S. 189, December 1871) exonerating the captain of the *Java* of all blame.

Birkenhead Park, Wirral, just across the river Mersey from Liverpool, was laid out by Sir Joseph Paxton. Frederick L. Olmsted, the great American landscape architect, was impressed by it and used many of its features in his design for Central Park, New York City.

The great St. George's Hall in Liverpool, opposite Lime Street Station, was opened in 1854 and was used for concerts and meetings. The Chatham's Engineers Band must have been a band from the Chatham Dockyards; Parssa, probably a musician or singer, has not been identified.

31. Queenstown, now named Cóbh, near Cork in the south of Ireland, was usually the last stop in Europe for transatlantic liners.

The Fenians were Irish revolutionaries and nationalists opposing English rule, strongly supported financially by Irish immigrants in America. Violence against everything English was common in Ireland in these years, hence the presence of the English warships.

The *Warrior* mentioned here was the first all-iron warship of the Royal Navy. The ship, launched in 1860, had screw propulsion but was still fully rigged. Michael Lewis, *The Navy of Britain: A Historical Portrait* (London: George Allen and Unwin, 1948), 131–39. The *Black Prince* was an earlier composite wood and iron frigate.

The Latin expression that Crommelin uses could be translated as: Would that it be so.

32. In sailing vessels the first-class accommodation was traditionally located in the stern of the ship, and when steam propulsion by means of paddle wheels was introduced this was maintained, as it was the quietest part of the vessel, with the machinery set up in the middle of the ship close to the paddle wheels. With the new screw propulsion introduced in the 1860s, the boilers and machinery had to remain amidships for reasons of weight distribution, so the screw had to be driven by a long propeller shaft, which often caused serious vibrations and made the stern one of the noisiest and most unpleasant sections of the ship. Because of this Crommelin's complaints appear well founded. The *Oceanic* of the White Star Line of 1871 was the first steamer where the first-class cabins and dining rooms were located amidships, in front of the engine room. The Cunard Line followed soon after with this system. Since then the stern was the place for third-class passengers.

33. The Navesink Hills, on the northeast coast of New Jersey.

34. The last serious cholera epidemic in Western Europe, also in Great Britain and the Netherlands, was to be in the spring and summer of 1866.

The Fifth Avenue Hotel was located on Madison Square, corner of 23rd Street, in New York City.

2. In New York City and Westward to Chicago

1. Hendrik Jan de Marez Oyens (1843–1911), was a young Dutchman with a financial background, like Crommelin. Oyens traveled through the United States with Crommelin for part of the time, and in later years returned many times as a representative of the large Dutch financial interests in several American railroads. Veenendaal, *Slow Train to Paradise,* 75.

By "Schushardt" Crommelin probably means the New York bankers and brokers F. Schuchardt & Sons, with extensive relations in Europe. Mira Wilkins, *The History of Foreign Investment in the United States to 1914* (Cambridge, Mass.: Harvard University Press, 1989), 120. Anthony G. Dulman, of Dutch extraction, was partner in the mercantile and financial house of Dulman & Scharff of New York City. Dulman served on the boards of at least seven American railroad companies as representative of the Dutch interests. Veenendaal, *Slow Train to Paradise,* 100.

Castle Garden, Manhattan, was the place where all immigrants were landed and examined before the opening of Ellis Island for that purpose, but as Crommelin was not an immigrant, he arrived at the regular landing place of the Cunard liners.

2. William Henry Osborn, president of the Illinois Central Railroad from 1855 to 1865 and on the board of the IC until 1882. Because of the large British and Dutch interest in the IC, he always favored good relations with the money markets of London and Amsterdam. Augustus J. Veenendaal, Jr., *American Railroads in the Nineteenth Century* (Westport, Conn.: Greenwood, 2003), 106. Crommelin's expression in French means: Let the ship float wherever it will go.

3. The Cousinery and Thoron families have not been identified, but judging from their names they were descendants of Huguenot families, like Crommelin himself, and probably business relations of the firm of Daniel Crommelin & Sons. One of the Thorons, Casimir, was befriended by Crommelin and is mentioned in this diary several times. By "Blake" Crommelin most probably means Stanton Blake, banker and merchant of New York City, later with his brother W. B. Blake and the Dutchman A. A. H. Boissevain partner in Blake, Boissevain & Co. of Boston and New York City, and with extensive Dutch connections. Wilkins, *The History of Foreign Investment,* 477, 855.

4. Crommelin likely met Jean Joseph Eugène Dutilh (1814–1895), from a Dutch-Huguenot family, founder of the firm of Dutilh & Company in New York City. His wife was Susanna Moon Lydig (†1893). There were also two brothers Dutilh established in Philadelphia, partners in the firm of Dutilh & Wachsmuth, but it is unlikely that Crommelin met them in New York City.

It is hard to say which Schermerhorn Crommelin means here: John Jones Schermerhorn (*1825), New York City merchant, or Simon Jacob Schermerhorn (1827–1901), farmer, banker, and U.S. congressman. Other candidates are Peter Schermerhorn, New York City banker and founder of the Knickerbocker Society, or his son William Colford Schermerhorn (born 1821), lawyer and sponsor of many cultural institutions of New York City. Eric

Homberger, *Mrs. Astor's New York: Money and Social Power in a Gilded Age* (New Haven, Conn.: Yale University Press, 2002), 238–39.

The Wilkinsons of South Carolina included the family of William Wilkinson (1788–1847) and his wife, Amarinthia Wilkinson *née* Jenkins (1790–1879). In 1816 the couple established a cotton and rice plantation, known as the "Summit," on land received from her father, Daniel Jenkins, that adjoined the Toogoodoo River in Charleston County. In 1850 the widow and five of her children lived on the property along with seventy-five slaves, but the Civil War devastated the family fortune, forcing them to sell land parcels and to seek aid from relatives and individuals in the North. After the end of the Civil War the widow and several of her children apparently lived for some time in New York City.

5. From his diary it is not quite clear who Crommelin met at the Morgan house. Dabney, Morgan & Co. was the name of the firm since 1864, with Charles H. Dabney and John Pierpont Morgan (1837–1913) as partners. J. P. Morgan was known as foppish, so Crommelin may well have spoken with him. Dabney was thirty years older than Morgan, and cannot be meant here, but a more junior partner was James J. Goodwin, a cousin of Morgan's, and he must have been the other one Crommelin met. Ron Chernow, *The House of Morgan: An American Banking Dynasty and the Rise of Modern Finance* (New York: Simon and Schuster, 1990), 21.

6. The Atlantic & Great Western Railroad was well known at the Amsterdam Stock Exchange, as several bond issues of this company had been sold there in 1864 and 1865. The A&GW went bankrupt later in 1866, then was reorganized in 1871 and leased to the New York, Lake Erie & Western Railroad, or the so-called Erie Lines. Veenendaal, *Slow Train to Paradise,* 20–23. The line ran from a connection with the NYLE&W at Salamanca, New York, southwest to Dayton, Ohio.

7. Over the years the firm of Dulman & Scharff of New York City did considerable business with Daniel Crommelin & Sons. Wessel Scharff in Newark/Bloomfield was one of the partners of the firm. The amount represented by [. . .] cannot be read in Crommelin's manuscript.

Nicolaas Gerard Pierson (1839–1909) was a Dutch banker and politician. Through his mother he was related to the Oyens family. Young Abrahams, engaged to marry Annie Scharff, has not been identified.

Complaints about the high level of inflation are scattered through Crommelin's diary. And indeed, between 1860 and 1866 the U.S. consumer price index had risen from 100 in 1860 to 191 in 1866, with a maximum of 196 in 1865. So the complaints of Scharff—and others—seem to be well founded. John J. McCusker, *How Much Is That in Real Money? A Historical Price Index for Use as a Deflator of Money Values in the Economy of the United States* (Worcester, Mass.: American Antiquarian Society, 1992), 328.

8. Crommelin was used to the railways in England and elsewhere in Europe, where all lines were completely fenced in to separate them from other modes of traffic and to avoid accidents. In America a railroad was more or less seen as a public highway, open to everybody.

9. Daniel Ludlow (1750–1814), whose mother was a Crommelin and who was the ancestor of the Ludlows Crommelin met, had been agent in New York City of the firm of Daniel Crommelin & Sons around 1800, and president of the Manhattan (Water) Company. P.

J. van Winter, *Het aandeel van den Amsterdamschen handel aan de opbouw van het Ameri-kaansche Gemeenebest,* 2 vols. (The Hague: Martinus Nijhoff, 1927–1933), 1:12. Gerard T. Koeppel, *Water for Gotham: A History* (Princeton, N.J.: Princeton University Press, 2000), 77, 82.

Thomas W. Ludlow (1795–1878), who lived in Yonkers and whom Crommelin met in 1866, was a younger relative of Daniel and founder of a great real estate firm in New York. He too had been in his time representative of the Dutch firm of Daniel Crommelin & Sons. He was married to Frances W. Morris (†1868).

At the time of Crommelin's visit, Yonkers was still a pretty country village with neat villas, country houses, and old farms overlooking the Hudson River.

A federal income tax had been introduced during the war; after many complaints and protests of rich and influential New York bankers and merchants, it was finally abolished in 1873. Sven Beckert, *The Monied Metropolis: New York City and the Consolidation of the American Bourgeoisie, 1850–1896* (Cambridge: Cambridge University Press, 2001), 229.

10. The *New York Herald* was owned and published by James Gordon Bennett, from 1866 ably assisted by his son of the same name, who became a leader of the New York jet set with his exclusive New York Yacht Club. Lloyd Morris, *Incredible New York: High Life and Low Life from 1850 to 1950* (Syracuse, N.Y.: Syracuse University Press, 1996).

Sir Samuel Morton Peto (1809–1889) was an English railway contractor and financier, and strongly involved in the Canadian Grand Trunk Railway, but also in the Atlantic & Great Western, mentioned before, as well as in other railroad schemes worldwide. Jack Simmons and Gordon Biddle, eds., *The Oxford Companion to British Railway History from 1603 to the 1990s* (Oxford: Oxford University Press, 1997), 376. Sir Morton Peto's book that Crommelin refers to is *The Resources and Prospects of America,* published in London in 1866. Irene Adler, *British Investment in American Railways 1834–1898* (Charlottesville: University Press of Virginia, 1970), 103. Apparently Crommelin was unaware of the financial problems of the firm of Peto & Betts. In June 1866 the overextended firm would fail, as a result of the collapse of the London bank of Overend, Gurney and other banks, some weeks earlier.

11. Thomas Boese (1827–1904) was a son of French immigrants and active in New York City education and in the Democratic Party. From 1853 to 1874 he was clerk of the Board of Education of New York City. Miss Susan Wright (1827–1908) was the long-time principal of School no. 50 in New York City, and a great advocate of basic education, consisting of reading, writing, and arithmetic.

12. William Howard Day (1825–1900), well known as a black abolitionist and public speaker, educated at Oberlin College and from 1867 superintendent of the schools of the Freedmen's Bureau in Maryland and Delaware. S. S. Randall served as superintendent of New York Public Schools.

Crommelin's words in German at the end of this paragraph mean: I can play the violin.

13. The Dutch De Bruyn Kops family was related to the Crommelins. Gerrit Willem de Bruyn Kops (1794–1860) emigrated to the United States in 1849 and became a farmer. He had five sons and three daughters, who accompanied him; only one of them returned later to the Netherlands, while all the others stayed in America. The eldest daughter, Maria

Cornelia (*1825), never married and kept a boarding house in New York City during the 1860s, so she must be one of the "Kopsjes" Crommelin met here in her own boarding house. The eldest son, Jan (John) (1827–1888), ran a cotton exporting business in New York City together with the Liverpool firm of Clason & Cy. He was married to Jane Washington Davidson (1839–1887), and apparently they were staying in the boarding house of his sister. Lena, also mentioned by Crommelin, was the younger sister Helena Petronella de Bruyn Kops (*1833). She never married and was living in New York City, teaching music. Three of the brothers, Hendrik Pieter (1830–1908), Jacob Christiaan (1831–1900), and Karel Jacob Adriaan, the youngest of the family (*1835), settled in Minnesota, Hendrik as a farmer near Faribault, Jacob as a Presbyterian minister in Faribault, and Karel first as a farmer with his brother Hendrik, and later in Grand Forks, North Dakota, where he opened a hotel. Hendrik married Anna Sucre in 1859, and Karel married her sister Mary one year later. The Sucre girls came from Bohemia and were originally named Cukr. Crommelin will meet them all later in this story. (Information supplied by C. J. de Bruijn Kops of Abcoude, the Netherlands).

The National Academy of Design, founded in 1828, was set up to be the American equivalent of the French Ecole des Beaux-Arts or the British Royal Academy. It occupied a building on Fourth Avenue and 23rd Street. Delmonico's, since 1862 established on the corner of Fifth Avenue and 14th Street, was already the most fashionable of the New York City restaurants. In 1876 it moved uptown to a location on Fifth Avenue and 26th Street. Homberger, *Mrs. Astor's New York,* 196.

Crommelin's dinner companion Ralli must have been one of the partners of the firm of Ralli Bros., an Anglo-Greek company active in the grain trade in America. Wilkins, *The History of Foreign Investment,* 319.

14. Richard Warren (†1908), was commissioner of the Board of Education, New York City.

15. The Academy of Music, seating 4,000 and located on the corner of 14th Street and Irving Place, was founded in 1853, and burned down on May 22, 1866; it was rebuilt in the same place. The Academy was well known for the Italian operas performed there. Homberger, *Mrs. Astor's New York,* 227–31.

J. Kearney Warren (1821–1895), was a leading banker in New York City.

16. Gulian Crommelin Verplanck (1786–1870), was a well-known American lawyer, politician, and author and related to the Crommelin family. An early member of the Crommelin family, Charles (1675–1740), born in Paris, emigrated to New York by way of Amsterdam and married there. A daughter, Marie Crommelin, married in 1737 a Guillaume Verplanck. His son Daniel Crommelin (1707–1788) married in Amsterdam in 1736 and had a daughter, Judith Crommelin, who married Samuel Verplanck in 1761. J. H. Scheffer, *Genealogie van het geslacht Crommelin* (Rotterdam, Netherlands: Van Hengel and Eeltjes, 1879), 53, 80. The Christian name of Gulian also is known in the Crommelin family.

Hendrik Dirk Kruseman van Elten (1829–1904), was a Dutch landscape painter and etcher and a great traveler. In 1865–1866 he worked for a time in New York City and from 1879 chiefly in Paris.

"Kopsjes" is the affectionate form of the formal plural "Kopses."

17. Cold Spring is located on the eastern bank of the Hudson, just north of Garrison, and opposite West Point. The party must have used the Hudson River Railroad, soon to be incorporated in the New York Central System, and already under the influence of the Vanderbilt interests.

In 1853 Osborn had married Virginia Reed Sturges, daughter of Jonathan Sturges, a New York merchant and one of the original incorporators of the Illinois Central. Through his father-in-law Osborn became involved in the IC.

18. From Albany Crommelin's party must have used the New York Central Railroad all the way to Niagara Falls.

19. The famous suspension bridge across the Niagara Falls, which was also used by trains, was considered one of the wonders of the world. The Canadian Great Western Railway was controlled by the New York Central, and the Michigan Central also had friendly working agreements with the New York Central system.

20. Crommelin writes St. Clair River but actually he must have been ferried into Detroit across the Detroit River. The St. Clair River is to the northeast, connecting Lake St. Clair with Lake Huron.

3. From Chicago through Illinois and Northward to Minnesota

1. Crommelin must refer to Anthony Trollope's *North America,* where he describes his stay in Chicago in vol. 1, 235–44, although Trollope himself doesn't mention the stockyards in his book. Mrs. McLane *née* Scharff must have been a daughter of Wessel Scharff, whom Crommelin visited in Newark, New Jersey.

2. John M. Douglas was president of the Illinois Central as successor to Osborn from 1865 to 1871 and again from 1875 to 1877. Marvin Hughitt was general superintendent of the IC but made his name later as president of the Chicago & North Western. Joseph F. Tucker was general freight agent of the IC. John F. Stover, *History of the Illinois Central Railroad* (New York: Macmillan, 1975), 106, 135; H. Roger Grant, *North Western: A History of the Chicago & North Western Railway System* (DeKalb: Northern Illinois University Press, 1996), 43–44. The Remmer mentioned is probably John Remmer, who in 1862 was a rising member of the superintendent's office of the Illinois Central.

Crommelin seems to give only half of the information needed here. To visit the model farm of Osborn near Chatsworth, roughly between Kankakee and Bloomington, Illinois, the route from Centralia would have been the IC main line northeast to Chicago as far as Gilman, and from there west to Chatsworth over the then new Toledo, Peoria & Warsaw Railroad. Another possibility would have been to follow the IC north from Centralia as far as El Paso and from there go east over the TP&W to Chatsworth. The Peoria & Oquawka Railroad was chartered in 1849 to build a line from Peoria westward to the Illinois River at Shokoken opposite Burlington, Iowa, by way of Galesburg. In 1862 the Chicago, Burlington & Quincy Railroad bought the P&O. Richard C. Overton, *Burlington Route: A History of the Burlington Lines* (Lincoln: University of Nebraska Press, 1976), 16, 49. Onarga is situated on the IC main line from Chicago to Centralia just south of Gilman. Frank Osborn was a son of William H. Osborn.

3. Crommelin refers to the region in the Netherlands known as the Betuwe, between the Lek and Waal Rivers, both branches of the Rhine River. Mattoon, Illinois, is situated south of Urbana/Champaign.

4. Probably Charles Danforth, who had established the Locomotive and Machine Company in Paterson, N.J., later known as Danforth, Cooke & Co., still later as Cooke & Co.; from 1901 it was part of the American Locomotive Company (ALCO). Harold Davies, *North American Steam Locomotive Builders and Their Insignia* (Forest, Va.: TLC Publishing, 2005), 46.

5. Samuel J. Hayes was master of machinery of the Illinois Central Railroad.

6. Crommelin may well mean Walter Loomis Newberry (1804–1868), an important Chicago entrepreneur in shipping and railroads. He was deeply involved in the Chicago & North Western Railway and was a philanthropist who is best known for his bequest that created the Newberry Library in Chicago. Robert J. Casey and W. A. S. Douglas, *Pioneer Railroad: The Story of the Chicago and North Western System* (New York: McGraw-Hill, 1948), 22, 63.

7. The 97-mile-long Illinois and Michigan Canal, with seventeen locks between Chicago and La Salle, was opened for traffic in 1848. David M. Young, *Chicago Maritime: An Illustrated History* (DeKalb: Northern Illinois University Press, 2001), 42.

8. The future Sanitary and Ship Canal would run 28 miles between Damen Avenue in Chicago and Lockport, linking the South Branch of the Chicago River to the Des Plaines River. A series of locks allowed the canal to reverse permanently the flow of the Chicago River. This public-works project, completed only in 1900, was designed to be both a transportation route and a means to improve the water quality by sending the city's sewage south into the Illinois-Mississippi river system instead of Lake Michigan. Louis P. Cain, *Sanitation Strategy for a Lakefront Metropolis: The Case of Chicago* (DeKalb: Northern Illinois University Press, 1978).

9. Kinsley's Restaurant at 133 Adams Street was still operating forty years later. K. Baedeker, *Nordamerika: Die Vereinigten Staaten nebst einem Ausflug nach Mexico. Handbuch für Reisende* (Leipzig, Germany: Karl Baedeker, 1904), 308. Opened in 1866, Crosby's Opera House quickly became a symbol of the cultural awakening of Chicago. Unfortunately the great fire of October 1871 consumed this large, attractive brick structure. Eugene H. Cropsey, *Crosby's Opera House* (Madison, N.J.: Fairleigh Dickinson University Press, 1999).

10. The correct name of this railway was La Crosse & Milwaukee Railroad, since 1863 part of the Chicago, Milwaukee & St. Paul Railroad. August Derleth, *The Milwaukee Road: Its First Hundred Years* (New York: Creative Age Press, 1948), 85.

11. The Steamboat *Key City*, operated by the Northwestern Union Packet Company, served Mississippi River communities between St. Louis and St. Paul. During the Civil War the vessel hauled a large number of refugees from the South and Union troops headed to battle. William J. Petersen, *Steamboating on the Upper Mississippi* (Iowa City: State Historical Society of Iowa, 1937).

12. Parts of the Minnesota pages of Crommelin's diary have been published by Muriel E. Hidy, "A Dutch Investor in Minnesota, 1866," in *Minnesota History* (December 1960): 152–60.

Crommelin has incorrectly dated the age of St. Paul. The settlement began in the late 1830s, known locally as Pig's Eye, and emerged soon after as St. Paul. By 1857 the comment was made that "St. Paul is comparatively an infant city, with a population of probably 10,000 souls, but here 'every man counts.'" Harriet E. Bishop, *Floral Home; or, First Years in Minnesota* (New York: Sheldon, Blakeman, 1857), 125.

13. Johan H. Kloos was a Dutch engineer sent out by the Amsterdam financial house of Kerkhoven & Co. to supervise the construction of the St. Paul & Pacific Railroad, which was financed almost completely from Holland. Augustus J. Veenendaal, Jr., *The Saint Paul & Pacific Railroad: An Empire in the Making, 1862–1879* (DeKalb: Northern Illinois University Press, 1999).

14. George Loomis Becker was president of the St. Paul & Pacific RR from 1864; Hermann Trott, a native of Austria, headed the Land Department of that company. Big Lake, northwest of St. Paul on the line to St. Cloud and beyond, on what was then known as the First Division of the St. Paul & Pacific Railroad.

15. Edmund Rice (†1889) was the original incorporator and first president of the St. Paul & Pacific and its predecessor, the Minnesota & Pacific Railroad. The St. Paul & Pacific never built a line from St. Paul to Winona and beyond, but other railroad companies did, so providing a connection with the rest of the country.

Crommelin must mean La Crescent, Minnesota, on the Mississippi, just across the river from La Crosse, but his geography is a bit muddled as La Crescent is south of Winona. Apparently he had no good map at hand.

16. Edwin C. Litchfield, one of the brothers Litchfield, important railroad contractors, who were involved in the St. Paul & Pacific Railroad and also in the Northern Pacific Railroad.

17. Beginning in the early 1800s, the Metís people, descendants of white fur traders and native Indians, used large two-wheeled wooden carts for transport of upward of 700 to 800 pounds of goods. The key component of those "Red River Carts" was the wooden axle, which supported the entire weight of the cart and load and was likely the part to fail. Fort Abercrombie, North Dakota, is situated on the Red River of the North, just north of Breckenridge, Minnesota.

18. Monticello is on the west bank of the Mississippi, Buffalo south of Monticello, Rockford still further south. It appears that Crommelin's party rode the train to Big Lake on the branch line, and then found the engineers working on the main line west of Minneapolis. Why they didn't take a train on the main line is not clear, but possibly to see as much of both lines of the StP&P being extended from St. Paul in one and the same visit. Captain Overton may be George A. J. Overton, a pioneer resident of Buffalo.

19. The year 1848 witnessed a series of democratic revolutions in Europe, especially in France, Germany, and Austria, where Hermann Trott had been active.

20. John Other Day, a Sioux Indian with a white wife, helped many whites to escape during the great Sioux uprising of 1862 in Minnesota. William Watts Folwell, *History of Minnesota*, 4 vols. (1921; reprint, St. Paul: Minnesota Historical Society, 1956–1969), 2:117.

21. Crommelin surely means Lake Minnetonka.

See for information about the members of the De Bruyn Kops family whom Crommelin met in Minnesota, ch. 2, note 13.

22. The Lake Superior & Mississippi Railroad, constructing a line from St. Paul to Duluth, never attracted much Dutch capital.

23. Crommelin likely misunderstood the name of Lake Waconia.

The typescript gives Benton, but Crommelin must have meant Benson, Carver County, southwest of Minneapolis.

24. Crommelin does not supply the name of the gentleman in question.

25. The *Phil Sheridan,* a big steamboat of 728.6 tons, was owned and operated by the Northwestern Union Packet Company, and carried passengers and freight between St. Louis and St. Paul since 1866. Petersen, *Steamboating on the Upper Mississippi.*

4. In Chicago and by way of Cincinnati and Washington, D.C., to Philadelphia

1. By 1869 Mr. Moring was no longer listed as officer of the Columbus, Chicago & Indiana Central Railway, the successor of the Chicago & Great Eastern Railway.

2. David L. Phillips was land agent of the Illinois Central and a good friend of President Lincoln. Carlton J. Corliss, *Mainline of Mid-America: The Story of the Illinois Central* (New York: Creative Age Press, 1960), 121. Mr. Johnson has not been identified.

3. The Chicago & Great Eastern started life in 1861 as the Chicago & Cincinnati Railroad, and in 1863 was renamed Chicago & Great Eastern. As such it existed until 1868 when it was incorporated into the new Columbus, Chicago & Indiana Central Railroad. After many other takeovers, in 1921 it became part of the Pennsylvania Railroad System. The line ran from Chicago to Indianapolis by way of Logansport and Frankfort. Apparently Crommelin had orders to look into the possibility of Dutch participation in the C&GE, but it never attracted any Dutch capital. William D. Edson, *Railroad Names: A Directory of Common Carrier Railroads Operating in the United States* (privately published, 1999); Veenendaal, *Slow Train to Paradise.*

The young Morton mentioned by Crommelin here may well have been a son of Levi Parsons Morton, head of the banking firm of L. P. Morton & Co., which had many European connections.

4. The Asylum for the Blind in Indianapolis was housed between 1848 and 1930 in a large building that filled the block between Meridian Street and North Pennsylvania Avenue, and North and Walnut Streets.

5. Über den Rhein was the common nickname of that part of Cincinnati north of the Miami and Erie Canal, where most Germans were living. The Miami and Erie Canal was known to the locals as the Rhine. Gore Vidal, *1876: A Novel* (New York: Ballantine Books, 1976), 313. Daniel François Auber (1782–1871) was a French composer of many operas, of which *Fra Diavolo* of 1830 was one of the best known.

6. Gilmore, Blake & Ward, bankers of Boston, were a correspondent of Barings. Gilmore later set up shop for himself, and Blake Brothers remained in Boston. Vevey, Switzerland, is situated between Lausanne and Montreux on the north shore of Lac Leman, and Sillig's school was a well-known boarding school there.

7. Mr. Bohlander and Mr. Sargent have not been identified. Clifton Heights, the name

of the hills north of Cincinnati's city center. Avondale is just north of the old center of Cincinnati, east of Clifton Heights.

8. Crommelin must have used the Baltimore & Ohio Railroad from Cincinnati to Washington.

9. George Washington Parke Custis (1781–1857), who was the adopted son of George and Martha Washington and Martha's grandson by blood.

10. George Riggs was an American merchant and banker whose firm had an early partnership with George Peabody. Kathleen Burk, *Morgan Grenfell 1838–1988: The Biography of a Merchant Bank* (Oxford: Oxford University Press, 1989), 2, 3.

Crommelin does not give the name of the Prussian envoy, but he must have meant Friedrich Josef Marie, Freiherr (since 1858) von Gerolt (1840–1887), since 1861 envoy extraordinary of the Kingdom of Prussia to the United States. The German Empire dates only from 1871, so before that year most of the more important German states had diplomatic representatives of their own.

W. W. Corcoran was originally partner of Corcoran, Riggs & Co., with extensive relations in England and on the Continent; later he was a treasury official in Washington. Ralph W. Hidy, *The House of Baring in American Trade and Finance: English Merchant Bankers at Work, 1763–1861* (Cambridge, Mass.: Harvard University Press, 1949), 386.

11. The Mr. Clarke whom Crommelin mentions could possibly be Mr. Clark, member of the firm of E. & W. Clark & Co. bankers of Philadelphia. Irene Adler, *British Investment in American Railways 1834–1898* (Charlottesville: University Press of Virginia, 1970), 134–35. Since 1874 the federal department that prints U.S. currency has been known officially as the Bureau of Engraving and Printing. At the time of Crommelin's visit the recently established facility was called the "First Division, National Currency Bureau."

In 1829 the firm of Daniel Crommelin & Sons had sold bonds to the tune of $1,500,000 of the cities of Washington, Georgetown, and Alexandria on the Dutch market. These bonds were intended to fund the share of the three cities in the construction of the Chesapeake and Ohio Canal. The canal company went bankrupt in 1834, and to guarantee the payment of interest, sale of sections of the three cities to the Dutch bondholders, legally possible according to the original contracts, was seriously considered. To avoid the shame of parts of Washington, D.C., falling into the hands of Dutch banks, Congress stepped in and paid off the creditors. Veenendaal, *Slow Train to Paradise*, 11.

12. In 1814 Elisha Riggs, merchant of Baltimore, and father of Crommelin's friend George Riggs, took fellow American merchant George Peabody (1795–1869) into partnership, trading under the name of Riggs, Peabody & Co. and specializing in dry goods imported from England. Elisha Riggs retired from the firm in 1829, and Peabody became senior partner. In 1838 Peabody settled in London, became more of a banker than a merchant, and was deeply involved in American railroad finance. Mr. Chilton has not been identified.

13. The Philadelphia, Wilmington & Baltimore Railroad, strongly under the influence of the Pennsylvania Railroad, operated the ferry *Maryland* since 1854 to cross the Susquehanna River. A permanent bridge is said to have been opened toward the end of 1866, but apparently it was not yet in service at the time of Crommelin's crossing. George H. Burgess

and Miles C. Kennedy, *Centennial History of the Pennsylvania Railroad Company* (Philadelphia: Pennsylvania RR Co., 1949), 388–93.

14. The Continental Hotel in Philadelphia was still operating in 1902 at 9th and Chestnut Streets. The Girard Trust Building was just opposite on Chestnut Street.

The Dutch national colors are also red, white, and blue. Apparently Crommelin had heard about the Prussian-Austrian war of 1866, when Prussia overran Austria and its allies Hanover, Hesse, and Saxony. Hanover, bordering on the Netherlands, was annexed by Prussia, hence Crommelin's concern about the new powerful neighbor.

15. Throughout the 19th century, the Fourth of July was the grand American holiday. It would not be until the 20th century that Thanksgiving and Christmas surpassed Independence Day in overall importance.

Andrew Gregg Curtin (1815–1894), was governor of Pennsylvania 1861–1867. Winfield Scott Hancock (1824–1886), general of the U.S. Army. George Meade (1815–1872), general of the U.S. Army, who earned laurels at Gettysburg. John White Geary (1819–1873), general of the U.S. Army, former governor of Kansas Territory, and strongly anti-slavery. Mr. Griffiths of Philadelphia has not been identified.

16. Fairmount Park, the pride of Philadelphia, was laid out on both banks of the Schuylkill River, and no visitor omitted it from his travel schedule.

17. Holmesburgh (today's Holmesburg) is an old neighborhood in northeast Philadelphia.

18. The Eastern Penitentiary in Philadelphia, the first prison of the so-called Pennsylvania System of isolation of the prisoners, each in his own cell. It was situated between Fairmount Avenue and Brown Street.

19. Girard College was founded in 1831 by Stephen Girard as a boarding school for white orphan boys. The House of Refuge was situated nearby on Poplar Street.

20. Theodore Minis Etting (1846–1927), son of Jewish parents from Philadelphia, officer in the U.S. Navy and later a marine lawyer. U.S. Navy Commodore Thomas Turner was on special duty at the Philadelphia Navy Yard 1865–1867. The U.S. Navy Yard in Philadelphia itself, established there in 1801, had moved to League Island only in 1865.

21. Crommelin must have seen the *New Ironsides,* a steam-powered wooden frigate with an armored citadel and sixteen Dahlgren 11-inch guns. It was commissioned in 1862 and spent most of its active life in bombarding the forts around Charleston harbor. It was accidentally destroyed by fire when lying in the Philadelphia Navy Yard in December 1866. Frank M. Bennett, *The Monitor and the Navy under Steam* (1900; reprint, Cranbury, N.J.: Scholar's Bookshelf, 2005), 76–77.

22. The former Confederate warship seen by Crommelin was probably the *Atlanta,* taken after a short battle by the USN monitor *Weehawken* in June 1863. It saw little service as a USN ship. Bennett, *The Monitor and the Navy under Steam,* 180–82.

23. Crommelin's sketch mentioned here is unclear and could not be reproduced. The *Dictator,* a large monitor designed by John Ericsson, constructed by the Delamater Iron Works of New York City and finished only toward the end of the Civil War, was never used, and no more of the same type were built. William H. Roberts, *Civil War Ironclads: The U.S. Navy and Industrial Mobilization* (Baltimore, Md.: Johns Hopkins University Press, 2002), 188, 206.

5. New York City, Albany, Niagara Falls, Pennsylvania Oil, and Canada

1. The two gentlemen Mackay could well have been the brothers Donald and Nathaniel McKay, owners of a locomotive factory and shipyard in East Boston, Massachusetts. Harold Davies, *North American Steam Locomotive Builders and Their Insignia* (Forest, Va.: TLC Publishing, 2005), 166. Mr. Chapman has not been identified.

2. Albany, New York, was originally a Dutch West India Company settlement named Beverwijck, close to Fort Oranje. The Dutch tradition was slow to die out, and Dutch street names still remain.

3. Trenton Falls, New York, is situated just north of Utica, but was not on the main line of the New York Central, which Crommelin must have taken on his way from Saratoga Springs to Niagara Falls. Could he mean Little Falls, east of Utica, which is on the NYC main line?

4. Clifton is on the Canadian side of the Niagara Falls.

5. A roundabout way, as Crommelin must have headed west from Buffalo on the NYC as far as Erie, and from there southeast to Corry, Pennsylvania, and then southwest to Meadville in the northwestern part of Pennsylvania.

Titusville, east of Meadville, was the place where Edwin L. Drake struck oil in large quantities in 1859. An oil boom soon developed along Oil Creek south of Titusville all the way to Oil City, where Oil Creek runs into the Allegheny River. Cities such as Pithole and Petroleum Centre sprang up but died a few years later when the oil had run out, as Crommelin describes. He found no opportunities for Dutch investments. For the history of this oil boom see Brian Black, *Petrolia: The Landscape of America's First Oil Boom* (Baltimore, Md.: Johns Hopkins University Press, 2000).

6. The Huidekoper family originated in the Netherlands. Harm Jan Huidekoper (1776–1854), the founder of the American branch of the family, left for America in 1795 and became a clerk for the Holland Land Company in 1799 and its agent in Meadville, Pennsylvania, in 1804. He had seven children, among whom Alfred Huidekoper (1810–1892), married in 1834 Catherine Cullum; Edgar Huidekoper (1812–1862), married in 1838 Frances Shippen; Frederick Huidekoper (1817–1892), married in 1853 Harriet Nancy Thorp. All three had children, several of whom Crommelin met while in Meadville. Apart from his job, Harm Jan Huidekoper was also active in the Unitarian church in Meadville and was one of the founders of Meadville Theological School. The John Huidekoper mentioned the next day by Crommelin was a cousin of Harm Jan's sons.

7. From Meadville Crommelin must have taken the branch of the Atlantic & Great Western to Franklin, seat of Venango County, and extended from there to Oil City in 1865–1866. J. T. Henry, *The Early and Later History of Petroleum, with Authentic Facts in Regard to Its Development in Western Pennsylvania* (1873; reprint, New York: Augustus M. Kelly, 1970), 288. The A&GW was one of the American railroads that were well known on the Amsterdam Stock Exchange. William Reynolds, *European Capital, British Iron, and an American Dream: The Story of the Atlantic & Great Western Railroad* (Akron, Ohio: University of Akron Press, 2002).

Reno, Venango County, on the Allegheny River, is just west of Oil City, and connected to Pithole by a railroad line. Today Pithole has completely reverted to nature, with only the names of the streets marked in the woods, while Oil City still exists and has a population (in 2000) of 11,504.

8. Probably meant is Tidioute in Warren County, higher up the Allegheny River, formerly the property of the Holland Land Company, where new oil wells were being developed at the time of Crommelin's visit.

9. Apparently Crommelin expected not to return to Niagara Falls, but eventually he went there once more toward the end of his American journey. Charlotte, New York, is situated on Lake Ontario north of Rochester.

10. Ogdensburg, New York, on the St. Lawrence River.

11. The twenty-four-span Victoria Bridge of the Grand Trunk Railway at Montreal, designed by Alexander McKenzie Ross and Robert Stephenson, was constructed across the St. Lawrence River between 1854 and 1859. It was considered one of the wonders of the modern world. William D. Middleton, *Landmarks on the Iron Road: Two Centuries of North American Railroad Engineering* (Bloomington: Indiana University Press, 1999), 22–25.

12. The Grey Nuns, officially the Order of Sisters of Charity of the Hospital General of Montreal, date from the 1730s, when Canada was still French, as a Roman Catholic order committed to the care of orphans, the ill, and the elderly. Soon after the order's founding these sisters became known as the Grey Nuns because of the color of their attire. In February 1918 the organization gained international attention when fire engulfed a wing of the convent complex and at least fifty-three young children died in the flames.

13. Crommelin must mean the Saguenay River that falls into the St. Lawrence about 100 miles downstream from Quebec.

14. The Montmorency Falls in the St. Lawrence River are just east of Quebec.

15. The church and convent of Notre Dame de Lorette is situated northwest of Quebec, now part of a suburb of Quebec.

16. Gorham, New Hampshire, is situated on the northern edge of the White Mountains and on the line of the Grand Trunk Railway from Quebec to Portsmouth, New Hampshire. The Glen House was a famous hotel in the White Mountains near the Glen Ellis Falls; it burned in 1894 and was never rebuilt.

6. In Boston and New England

1. Jamaica Pond and Falls, southwest of Boston, now a suburb of Boston, but then a fashionable place to live. George William Bond may have been associated with Geo. W. Bond & Co. (along with Thomas Hilsen), wool brokers, of Jamaica Pond, and possibly a former correspondent of the firm of Daniel Crommelin & Sons. Apparently his children William, Maria, and Sophie befriended Crommelin.

2. Jasigi was likely a partner in Jasigi, Goddard, & Co., and Francois Braggiotti was a merchant, whose business was located at 34 Central Wharf in Boston.

3. Mr. Phillips has not been identified, and was probably a banker or merchant.

4. The Boston City Jail, also known as the Charles Street Jail, was constructed between 1848 and 1851 to plans of Gridley James Fox Bryant in conjunction with the Rev. Louis

Dwight, a widely respected prison reformer. The humanitarian scheme of the Auburn Plan of the 1790s, pioneered in England, inspired the Boston facility. The jail was constructed in the shape of a cross with four wings of granite that extended from a central octagonal rotunda with a 90-foot atrium. These wings permitted officials to segregate prisoners by sex and category of offense. George Cushing, *Great Buildings of Boston: A Photographic Guide* (New York: Dover, 1982).

5. Brookline, now a suburb of Boston, was then a separate community southwest of Boston. By "the old gentleman Blake" Crommelin probably meant John R. Blake, who headed the long-established firm of Blake Brothers & Co. of Boston, Massachusetts, with many contacts in Amsterdam and elsewhere in Europe. The firm actively sold the federal government's debt at home and abroad. Gamaliel Bradford was an associate of Blake Brothers & Co., located at 38 State in Boston.

6. Lynn, Massachusetts, on the coast northeast of Boston, was then a fashionable watering place.

Nicholas (Niccolo) Reggio (1807–1867) became one of the most successful merchants of Boston, Massachusetts. Born in Smyrna, Ottoman Empire, this immigrant also served as consul for five nations: Sardinia, Sicily, Spain, the Ottoman Empire, and the Papal States. His business focused on imports like dates, figs, and wines from the Mediterranean region. Joseph Varacalli, ed., *The Italian American Experience: An Encyclopedia* (New York: Garland, 2000), 536. Nahant Peninsula is just east of Lynn.

7. Rye Beach is situated south of Portsmouth, New Hampshire.

8. The ladies met by Crommelin cannot be precisely identified. It is known that the family of Edward Wigglesworth (1804–1876) of Boston spent the summers at Rye Beach, New Hampshire, and were joined by a Fuller family and a Lucretia Dana Goddard Gould (1798–1874). Wigglesworth Family Photographs II, Massachusetts Historical Society.

Doctor Nichols has not been identified. Dabney is probably Charles W. Dabney, ship owner and businessman, who became a partner in Dabney, Morgan, & Co. Jean Strouse, *Morgan: American Financier* (New York: HarperCollins, 2000), 41–44, 112, 117–18.

9. In the watering places on the Dutch coast, such as Scheveningen near The Hague, at that time ladies and gentlemen bathed separately, but in Ostend, Belgium, mixed bathing was the rule. K. Baedeker, *Belgique et Hollande: Manuel du voyageur* (Coblenz, Germany: Karl Baedeker, 1869). The ladies met here by Crommelin have not been identified.

10. The Shoal Islands in the Atlantic Ocean east of Cape Cod.

11. The Asbury Grove Methodist campground at South Hamilton, Massachusetts, opened in 1859 and continues today. Hamilton is just south of Newburyport.

12. Lawrence is situated north of Boston and not far from the border with New Hampshire, and Lowell is northwest of Boston; both were factory towns, with most of the machinery driven by waterpower. The Pacific Mills were incorporated in 1853 in Lawrence to manufacture dress goods of wool and cotton. Starting with 1,000 looms, it had already grown to 3,500 looms by 1865 and was considered one of the most successful manufacturing corporations in the United States. Toward the end of the 19th century it employed about 5,500 men and women. Victor S. Clark, *History of Manufactures in the United States,* 3 vols. (1929; reprint, New York: Peter Smith, 1949), 1:453, 463.

13. The Washington Mills, also in Lawrence, were even bigger than the Pacific Mills in the same town, employing some 6,500 men and women around 1900.

14. George Nelson Macy (1837–1875), was a Harvard College–educated native of Nantucket, Massachusetts. During the Civil War he served in the 20th Massachusetts Volunteer Infantry and rose from first lieutenant to major general. Macy experienced extensive combat engagements, including the bloody Battle of Gettysburg, where, at Cemetery Ridge, a minié ball shattered his arm, resulting in an amputation and later use of an artificial limb. After the war he became an officer of the Suffolk Savings Bank in Boston, and he died in February 1875 of an accidental gunshot wound.

Crommelin may be referring to Ned Robbins (1828–1898), who later served with the Bureau of Indian Affairs of the U.S. Department of the Interior. The two Weld girls have not been identified.

15. By the mid-19th century West Roxbury, Massachusetts, had become a bastion of the liberal Unitarian Church. Dr. Nathaniel Hall, pastor of First Parish Church (Unitarian) in Dorchester, Massachusetts, served that congregation from 1835 to 1875. A seraphine was a simple reed organ, invented in 1833.

16. Washington's Elm stands at the northwest corner of Cambridge Common. Henry Wadsworth Longfellow (1807–1882), the famous American poet, lived in Craigie House, Cambridge, from 1837 until his death.

17. Crommelin probably means the Norfolk Mills in Roxbury, south of Boston, and the Roxbury Carpet Company.

18. Swampscott is situated on the coast northeast of Lynn. Henry Sturges was a brother of Mrs. Osborn.

19. The name is unclear in the typescript; probably he was a photographer.

20. Alfred Reed had opened the large and prosperous Oriental Mills, located on Admiral Street in Providence, Rhode Island, in 1860.

21. In Crommelin's time Newport, Rhode Island, already enjoyed the status of a popular "watering place" for the rich and powerful. Hotels sprang up from 1840 to serve visitors. The three most famous hotels were the Ocean House, the Bellevue House, and the Fillmore Hotel. The Fillmore, a large wooden multi-storied structure, opened in 1858 and was located near the corner of Bellevue Avenue and Catharine Street. At the time of Crommelin's stay it was operated by Francis B. Peckam; it closed in the late 1860s.

Mrs. Morton has not been identified; probably she was the wife or widow of a former business relation of Daniel Crommelin & Sons.

22. Providence, Rhode Island, was a center of textile manufacturing, with many different plants, mostly driven by waterpower. The Oriental Mills were among them. The Corliss Engine Works in Providence was famous for its stationary steam engines. Providence was also well known for its plants making files and screws. Clark, *History of Manufactures,* 1:506, 523.

7. In New York City, New Jersey, and Troy, New York

1. Charles Handy Russell (1796–1884), was since March 1866 president of the Bank of Commerce, New York City.

2. Trinity Episcopal Church, on Broadway opposite Wall Street in lower Manhattan, was one of the richest and most fashionable churches of New York City.

3. Harper Brothers, Printers and Publishers, in New York City, had operated under that name since 1833. After a devastating fire in 1853 they rebuilt between Cliff and Pearl Streets. The Joseph Harper the Second met by Crommelin must have been Joseph Wesley Harper (1830–1896), son of Joseph Wesley Harper (1801–1870), one of the four brothers who owned the firm.

4. Edward King was a prominent stockbroker and member of the New York Stock Exchange and had a country house in Hoboken, New Jersey. At the time of Crommelin's visit Hoboken was still largely unspoiled by urbanization.

5. Mrs. Newbold of Philadelphia has not been identified. She may have been the wife or widow of a former correspondent of Daniel Crommelin & Sons.

Brown Brothers, bankers, had their office at 59 Wall Street, New York City.

6. The members of the Verplanck family met by Crommelin are probably the following: James de Lancey Verplanck (born 1805), younger brother of Gulian Crommelin Verplanck, whom Crommelin has already mentioned earlier. Then William Samuel Verplanck (1812–1885), son of Gulian C. Verplanck. Samuel Verplanck (born 1840) was a son of James de Lancey Verplanck. Eliza Fenno Verplanck (born 1838, married 1862 to Benjamin Richards), Mary Newlin Verplanck (born 1840), Robert Newlin Verplanck (Bob, born 1842), Anna Verplanck (Annie, 1846–1891), Jeanette Verplanck (Jenny, born 1849), Gelyna Verplanck (born 1852), and William Edward Verplanck (born 1856), were all children of William Samuel Verplanck. The Mrs. Nevils (Knevals), mentioned by Crommelin, is probably Elizabeth Verplanck (1800–1888), younger sister of Gulian C. Verplanck, who married a certain John W. Knevals. Apparently Crommelin did not quite catch her name.

7. Joseph Howland (1834–1886), born into a powerful merchant family grown rich in the China trade, led a distinguished life, being a military officer, a New York State politician, and a philanthropist. His father, Samuel Shaw Howland, was a longtime partner in the shipping firm Howland & Aspinwall. During the Civil War Joseph Howland was a general in the Union Army, and treasurer of New York State 1866–1867. S. R. Harlow and H. H. Boone, *Life Sketches of States Officers* (Albany, N.Y., 1867).

8. The New York State prison of Sing Sing was situated near Ossining on the Hudson River. Despite a great number of guards, escapes did happen now and then, and in 1877 a surrounding wall was finally constructed, with armed guards at intervals. Denis Brian, *Sing Sing: The Inside Story of a Notorious Prison* (Amherst, N.Y.: Prometheus Books, 2005), 44. Edward B. Ketchum, former inmate of Sing Sing, was a young man associated with the New York City banking firm of Ketchum & Sons. In 1865 he was arrested on charges of security forgeries.

9. Blackwell's Island, in the East River, bought by the City of New York in 1828, housed the New York City Asylum for the Insane, opened in 1848, the charity hospital, the penitentiary, the almshouse, the workhouse, and other public institutions.

10. Bloomfield, New Jersey, is situated northwest of Newark. Newith must be close by but has not been identified. Apparently the Scharff family lived outside Newark, although Crommelin mentions earlier, on May 19, that he visited with the Scharffs at Newark.

11. Crommelin probably means Matawan, New Jersey, south of Aberdeen.

12. Adrian Verplanck was a son of Gulian Crommelin Verplanck. The other guests have not been identified, except that Daniel Crommelin Verplanck Knevals was the son of Elizabeth Verplanck and John Knevals.

13. There were several sisters Woolsey: the best known is Abby Howland Woolsey (1828–1893), social worker, educator of nurses, abolitionist, and founder of the Woman's Central Association of Relief, which did welfare work during the Civil War; she never married. Her sister Jane Stuart Woolsey (1830–1891) was also active in the WCAR, was an army nurse and later resident director of the Presbyterian Hospital in New York City; Jane also never married. Two other sisters, Georgeanne and Eliza, were also army nurses during the Civil War.

14. Mr. Powers, Jr., manager of the New Jersey Locomotive Works, has not been specifically identified. He was, though, the son of Hiram Powers (1805–1873), an American sculptor who had made a name with his statue of a "Greek Slave." The senior Powers lived in Florence, Tuscany, from 1837. The New Jersey Locomotive and Machine Company was incorporated from an earlier factory in 1851, and located in Paterson, New Jersey. In 1863 or 1864 the New York financier Oliver D. Grant acquired a controlling financial interest, and in 1867 the name was changed to Grant Locomotive Works. Harold Davies, *North American Steam Locomotive Builders and their Insignia* (Forest, Va.: TLC Publishing, 2005), 83–87.

15. The Passaic River runs through Paterson, New Jersey, and powered numerous early industrial factories.

16. James T. Munn, Troy, was probably a businessman or factory owner in Troy, New York.

17. The Troy Arsenal was officially known as the Watervliet Arsenal, was founded in 1813 during the War of 1812, and is located about 8 miles north of Albany, New York, near Troy. It remains an active U.S. Army facility. Captain William Prince had ties to the federal arsenal in Washington, D.C.

The chronograph of Schultz was probably an instrument for testing military ordnance, whereby the time taken by a piece of shot to pass over a known distance can be precisely measured.

18. Parrott guns were a system of rifled ordnance, invented in the mid-19th century by Captain Robert Parker Parrott (1804–1877). Both the U.S. Army and the U.S. Navy used his 8-inch and 10-inch guns and found them of considerable value. Warren Ripley, *Artillery and Ammunition of the Civil War* (New York: Promontory Press, 1970).

8. In Boston, Providence, Albany, and back to New York City

1. John Dudley Philbrick (1818–1886), a well-known educator, was superintendent of public schools in Boston.

2. Julia Ward Howe (1819–1910), poet, author and woman suffrage leader; she married Dr. Samuel G. Howe in 1840. In 1862 she wrote the "Battle Hymn of the Republic." Her father was Samuel Ward, a well-known and affluent stockbroker in New York City.

John Albion Andrew (1818–1867), was Republican governor of Massachusetts 1861–1866.

3. Francis Edward Parker, lawyer, was partner with Richard H. Dana in a Boston law firm.

4. Dr. Samuel Gridley Howe (1801–1876), a well-known medical doctor who had been active in helping the Greeks who were revolting against Turkish rule between 1825 and 1831. Back in America he became interested in the education of blind and deaf-mute students in the Perkins School for the Blind and was founder in 1850 of the Massachusetts School for Idiotic and Feeble-Minded in Boston. In 1867 he returned to Greece to help the people of Crete, then also known as Candia, who had risen against the Turks ruling over the island.

Dorchester Bay is located south of Boston.

5. Richard Henry Dana, Jr. (1815–1882), lawyer and author. His *Two Years before the Mast* appeared in 1840 and was an instant bestseller. The Morse mentioned here could well be Samuel Finley Breese Morse (1791–1872), born in Charlestown and a fairly well-known sculptor and painter. He was professor of literature, the arts, and design at New York University, co-founder of Vassar College, and inventor of the code used with the electromagnetic telegraph.

Milton Slocum Latham (1827–1882) was elected governor of California in 1860, but served only a couple of months as such before being elected to the U.S. Senate.

6. John Bright (1811–1889) was a radical English politician and great friend of Charles Sumner and President Abraham Lincoln. He was much in favor of universal suffrage and vehemently anti-slavery and anti-Confederacy, despite the poverty caused in his district of Rochdale, Lancashire, by the stoppage of cotton imports.

7. The Massachusetts State Prison was located in Charlestown, just across the Charles River from Boston.

8. James Freeman Clarke (1810–1888), well-known Unitarian minister, founder of the Church of the Disciples in Boston in 1841. He was married to Anna Huidekoper, of the Dutch-American Huidekopers, daughter of Harm Jan Huidekoper, who was also an active supporter of the Unitarian Church. Dr. Thomas Hill (1818–1891), was a Unitarian clergyman and scientist, and president of Harvard College between 1862 and 1868.

9. The Boston Athenæum, founded in 1807, and located in the center of Boston, had a famous library, only open by appointment. Miss Emily Freeman has not been identified.

10. Mount Auburn cemetery, in Cambridge, west of Harvard College, where already at the time of Crommelin's visit a number of famous Americans were buried.

11. Judge Thomas Russell had a long and distinguished public-service career. In 1852 he was appointed to the Boston Police Court, and later served as collector of the Port of Boston, minister to Venezuela, and a Massachusetts railroad commissioner. George M. Barnard, a director of the Alliance Insurance Co., had a school ship named in his honor.

12. The watch manufactory at Waltham, Massachusetts, was known for the degree of mechanization in making the standardized brass parts for watches and clocks. Robbins, the director, has not been identified. Waltham is west of Boston.

13. Annie Clark (†circa 1905), was a popular actress with the Boston Museum Theatre, and known as the "idol of Boston."

14. F. W. Lincoln, a popular mayor of Boston, won repeated elections in the 1850s and 1860s on the Citizen's ticket. Moses Kimball was long associated with the Public Chari-

ties of Massachusetts and in the 1870s served as chairman. F. B. Sanborn, *Supplement to the 12th Annual Report, the Public Charities of Massachusetts* (Boston, 1876). Deer Island lies in Massachusetts Bay, east of the city of Boston, and housed "hundreds" of residents.

15. Dr. Alfred Porter Putnam (1827–1906), was ordained in 1855 as Unitarian minister at Roxbury, and became a famous preacher and writer of hymns. Crommelin always refers to Rosebury instead of Roxbury.

A. Fitz Verploegh was "assistant-resident," or deputy supervisor, of the residency of Krawang, south of Batavia on the island of Java in the Netherlands East Indies, until February 1865. The transcontinental railroad was only to be finished in 1869, so Mr. Verploegh must have traveled the greatest distance in a wagon train or stage. The other guests at the dinner party have not been identified.

16. Edward G. Walker and Charles L. Mitchell, elected in 1866 to the Massachusetts House of Representatives from Boston, were the first men of color to sit in any state legislature. *Negro Year Book: An Annual Encyclopedia of the Negro, 1914–1915* (Tuskegee Institute, Alabama, 1915), 152. The districts named by Crommelin were the areas where only Boston's upper ten were living, hence his ironic remark.

17. Wendell Phillips (1811–1884), famous abolitionist, advocate of women's rights, and much sought after as an orator.

18. Apparently all three were popular plays of the time.

19. Crommelin met members of the most powerful families of Providence, Rhode Island, the Iveses and Goddards. Described as "old money," these families had profited in the colonial triangular trade and later in land speculation and other business activities. In former times they may also have done business with Daniel Crommelin & Sons, hence Crommelin's visit.

20. During the mid-19th century the "Second Unitarian Controversy" divided this liberal faith. On one side were rational "traditionalists," centered at the Harvard Divinity School, who clashed with their opponents, headed by Ralph Waldo Emerson, who embraced the emerging Transcendentalist movement that argued there existed a spiritual state that transcends the physical and empirical. Sydney E. Ahlstrom, *A Religious History of the American People* (New Haven, Conn.: Yale University Press, 1972).

21. *Visites d'adieu* means "a round of good-byes."

22. The Parker House hotel was located on School Street in the center of Boston.

23. The Evertsen family from Zeeland was well known in the Netherlands for the number of naval captains and admirals in the 17th century.

24. The American Equal Rights Association was founded by Elizabeth Cady Stanton in 1866, and apparently Crommelin attended its first convention. Lucy Stone Blackwell (1818–1893) was active as a women's suffrage leader in the 1860s and 1870s. Parker Pillsbury (1809–1898) was a newspaper editor, reformer, and women's rights activist. Susan Charlotte Jones (1832–1911), women's rights activist, was tied to the Unitarian Church, working closely with Harm Jan Huidekoper, founder of the Meadville Theological School in Pennsylvania, and his son Frederick Huidekoper. Elizabeth Cady Stanton (1815–1902), was a well-known woman suffragist, author, and public speaker.

25. Literally translated as "and who therefore."

26. Mary Newlin Verplanck married Samuel William Johnson on December 18, 1866.

27. Plymouth Church, where Dr. Henry Ward Beecher preached for more than forty years, was located on Brooklyn Heights, just across the East River. Since 1847 Beecher (1813–1887) had been minister of Plymouth Church, and he had become famous as an abolitionist and a popular public speaker. His sister was the well-known Harriet Beecher Stowe, author of *Uncle Tom's Cabin.* Dr. Thomas Arnold (1795–1842) was an English educator and best known as director of the Rugby Public School and professor of modern history at Oxford University.

28. Emma Huger Lowndes (ca. 1831–?), was the daughter of a wealthy Charleston planter, Charles Tidyman Lowndes (1808–ca. 1884). After the Civil War she married James Scott, also from a prominent area family.

29. Horace Brigham Claflin (1811–1885) opened his first dry goods store in New York City in 1843, and after several moves built a large department store in 1861 on Broadway and Worth Street in downtown Manhattan. Alexander T. Stewart (†1876), opened his big department store in 1846 on Broadway and Chambers Street. At his death he was believed to be one of the richest men in New York.

9. IN THE SOUTH: CHARLESTON AND SAVANNAH

1. Cape Lookout is located on the North Carolina coast, east of Morehead City. Cape Romain is on the South Carolina coast, just to the northeast of Charleston.

2. C. Ed. Wunderlich was Dutch consul for the Carolinas and Georgia since mid-1866.

Robert Mure (†1871), was born in Great Britain but later became an American citizen; as a businessman in Charleston, he was asked by the Confederate government to carry diplomatic mail during his frequent business trips to England. He was arrested in New York by the federal authorities; his diplomatic mail was not molested, but letters from private individuals from South Carolina were seized. It was proven that the British consul in Charleston had been in contact with the Confederate authorities, contrary to his duties as consul accredited only to the U.S. government. James Barnes, *The American Civil War through British Eyes* (Kent, Ohio: Kent State University Press, 2003), 217.

3. William Aiken (1806–1887), was governor of South Carolina 1844–1846.

The leading families in the Low Country of South Carolina included the Hugers and the Lowndes. The Hugers, displaced French Huguenots, settled in colonial South Carolina, and the Lowndes, who came from English stock via the British West Indies, also arrived before the American Revolution. Not surprisingly, intermarriage occurred often between these elite planter and business families.

4. Louis Manigault (born ca. 1829), was the son of a distinguished Huguenot family, in America since 1691. After his studies at Yale, Louis Manigault managed the family-owned rice plantations in Berkeley District, South Carolina, and Argyle Island, Georgia. During the Civil War he served as personal secretary to Dr. Joseph Jones, a Confederate army surgeon, based in Augusta, Georgia.

Arthur Lanen arrived in Charleston in 1863 and immediately became acting consul for the French government, although without permission from the Confederate government. When he left Charleston is unknown, but he was apparently still in business at the time of Crommelin's visit. Milledge L. Bonham, Jr., "The French Consuls in the Confederate States," *Studies in Southern History and Politics* (1914).

5. Magnolia Cemetery, located in Charleston County, South Carolina, was established in 1849 and became a popular burial place for the elite of the Low Country, including the "Mrs. White" who has not been identified.

6. James Longstreet (1821–1904), brigadier of the Confederate forces, 1862 lieutenant-general. Jefferson Davis (1808–1889), president of the Confederate States of America 1861–1865, had fled from Richmond when that city was about to fall into the hands of Union forces under General U.S. Grant, and was arrested on May 10, 1865, near Irwinsville, Georgia.

7. Among the forts around Charleston were Castle Pinckney, on an island in Charleston Harbor, Fort Moultrie on Sullivan's Island, Fort Sumter, also on an island in Charleston Harbor, and the federal arsenal in Charleston. Stephen Wise, *Gate of Hell: Campaign for Charleston Harbor, 1863* (Columbia: University of South Carolina Press, 1994).

8. The Hayne family was well connected with South Carolina families such as the Middleton, Pinckney, and Rutledge clans, powerful landholding and professional families in the South Carolina Low Country. Best known member of the family was Robert Young Hayne (1791–1839), member of the U.S. Senate, known as a great advocate of states' rights. Hayne was also a leading force behind the construction of the South Carolina Canal & Rail Road Co. and an advocate of a railroad to connect Charleston with the Ohio River, the ill-fated Louisville, Cincinnati & Charleston Rail Road.

9. Heinrich Hartmann Wirtz (1822–1865), a Swiss immigrant better known as Henry Wirz, was commander of Camp Sumter, a Confederate prison stockade near the Andersonville, Georgia, railroad depot. Of the 45,000 Union prisoners, some 13,000 died from malnutrition, severe overcrowding, poor sanitation, lack of medical supplies, and absence of clean water. Captain Wirz was the only Confederate officer tried and executed for war crimes. Ovid Futch, *History of Andersonville Prison* (Gainesville: University of Florida Press, 1968).

10. The Mrs. Gibbs whom Crommelin met is likely the wife of H. P. Gibbs, a Charleston businessman who invested heavily in the Charleston & Savannah Rail Road Co. Mary St. Clair has not been identified.

11. Fort Lafayette, located in New York Harbor and opened at the beginning of the War of 1812. During the Civil War this fortification served as a prison camp for Confederate soldiers.

12. These Germans in Savannah, Koch and Kirchhauff, were likely merchants.

13. Joe Manigault, probably the son of Louis Manigault, mentioned earlier. For at least three generations one wing of the French Huguenot Huger family owned a large rice plantation on the north side of the Savannah River in Beaufort County, South Carolina. In 1866 the plantation was owned by Dr. Joseph Alston Huger, a Harvard-educated physician, and operated by his son Joseph Alston Huger (1843–?), who was much interested in rice growing.

Alexander, baron Schimmelpenninck van der Oye (1839–1918), was a Dutch nobleman and apparently well known to Crommelin.

The two branches of the Savannah River, the Front and the Back Rivers with Hutchinson's Island in between, separate Georgia from South Carolina.

14. It is not quite clear what Crommelin meant about the steam plow and ditcher of Danvers (Danforth?). Although the first steam-powered ditcher did not appear until the late 19th century, when James B. Hill founded the Buckeye Steam Ditcher Company in Ohio, steam-powered farm equipment began to appear by mid-century. In 1858 Joseph Fawkers used a 30-horsepower engine and plow at a demonstration at the Illinois State Fair and shortly thereafter received a prize from the U.S. Agricultural Society in Chicago. Crommelin may have seen similar equipment during his visit to Illinois.

15. Most probably this Clemson was Thomas Green Clemson (1807–1888), son-in-law of planter and politician John C. Calhoun. Clemson took a keen interest in all matters of agriculture, including rice production. He is best remembered for his will that led to the establishment of Clemson Agricultural College of South Carolina, today's Clemson University.

The Federal prison on Johnson's Island, located on Sandusky Bay in Lake Erie, housed thousands of Confederate prisoners of war. During its three years of operation only about 200 inmates died, low for prison camps during the Civil War.

16. In March 1865 the U.S. government set up the Bureau of Refugees, Freedmen, and Abandoned Lands, commonly called the Freedmen's Bureau. This bureau, which disbanded in July 1869, did much to help freedmen adjust to post-slavery conditions.

17. In the mid-19th century Henry Francis Porcher and John Courturier Porcher, both members of the French Huguenot Porcher family, were prominent plantation owners in St. John's Parish in the Low Country of South Carolina.

10. In Georgia and Virginia

1. The distance between Savannah and Augusta on the Central of Georgia Railway is 133 miles. Millen, 54 miles from Augusta, was the junction with a Central of Georgia line to Macon.

2. When boarding the ship in New York Crommelin called it the *Saratoga,* but later he uses the name *Saragossa.*

3. The Fourteenth Amendment to the Constitution, approved by Congress in June 1866, prohibited the states from abridging equality before the law. A second clause provided for a reduction in a state's representation proportional to the number of male citizens denied suffrage. Eric Foner, *Short History of Reconstruction 1863–1877* (New York: Harper and Row, 1990), 114–15.

4. Captain Thompson has not been identified. Adam McNatt owned a plantation, formerly with slaves, near Jefferson (later Vidette), in Burke County, Georgia. The Planters Inn in Augusta, Georgia, was one of the first resorts in the South, and popular with Northerners who wanted to escape the winter. Mrs. Eaves, plantation owner near Augusta, Georgia, has not been identified.

5. Apparently Crommelin traveled over the Charlotte, Columbia & Augusta Railroad to Charlotte, and from there on the Richmond & Danville Railroad to the Virginia capital.

He makes no mention of a change of trains in Charlotte, although it is most doubtful if there were through trains.

6. Brevet Captain Robins of the U.S. Army has not been identified.

7. Miss Jane Stuart Woolsey. In his manuscript Crommelin has not noted the names of these societies.

Crommelin uses *Negers* (Negroes) when talking about people of color in general and *nikkers* or *nikkertjes* (niggers) when he mentions black children.

8. Crommelin probably means the Richmond *Times*. See about this affair of Dr. J. L. Watson: Robert Selph Henry, *The Story of Reconstruction* (Indianapolis: Bobbs-Merrill Co., 1938), 204.

More majorum translates as "in the custom of the greater number."

9. Jefferson Davis (1808–1889), president of the Confederate States of America 1861–1865. General John McAllister Schofield (1831–1906), general of the U.S. Army, was chief of the Military Department of Virginia but not the head of the Freedmen's Bureau there; in 1868–1869 he was secretary of war. Crommelin writes Pierpoint, but must mean Francis Harrison Pierpont (1814–1899), governor of Virginia since 1865; he was removed from office in 1868. Henry, *Story of Reconstruction*, 326.

"Plaids" refers to the belted plaid costume, or "great kilt."

10. Fort Libby, located close to the center of Richmond, at what was later the intersection of Main and 20th Streets, was during the Civil War a prison for Union prisoners of war. As such it acquired a bad name.

11. Elizabeth Van Lew (†1900), nicknamed Crazy Bet, of Dutch descent (Van Loo), a fervent abolitionist, was a spy for the Union in Richmond, using her eccentricity to hide her spying activities. The Colonel Stanton mentioned must have been Thaddeus Harlin Stanton, but contrary to Crommelin's note, he was not one of the conspirators in the famed John Brown's raid at Harper's Ferry, Virginia, in 1859. In 1862 Stanton did raise a company of Iowa volunteers and later served as paymaster-general for the U.S. Army. Upon the fall of Richmond to Federal forces, Stanton served as the army paymaster in the Virginia capital and subsequently acted as auditor of public accounts for the state. *New York Times,* March 26, 1895.

12. The Freedmen's Bureau was set up to help the newly liberated slaves with getting education, food, and work. Its first commissioner was General Oliver O. Howard. Foner, *Short History of Reconstruction,* 64–69. Its food program, mentioned later by Crommelin, was seen by some as the best means to make the former slaves lazy, and in the fall of 1866 it was discontinued by Howard. Bell Isle was a Confederate prison on an island in the James River in Richmond. Robert Edward Lee (1807–1870) was general of the Confederate forces. From June 1862 he commanded the Army of Northern Virginia, the most important unit of the Confederate armies.

13. Colonel Orlando Brown was commissioner for the District of Virginia of the Freedmen's Bureau. Henry, *Story of Reconstruction,* 60. The name of the other colonel cannot be read.

14. Gordonsville, Virginia, is located northeast of Charlottesville, and Crommelin must have traveled in a rather roundabout way between Richmond and Baltimore.

11. To Baltimore and Washington, D.C.

1. Hollins McKim served as a partner with S. Sterett McKim in the Baltimore investment and brokerage firm of McKim & Co., and was probably a business relation of Daniel Crommelin & Sons. The act mentioned by Crommelin was known as the "Ironclad Oath."

2. Thomas Swann (1809–1885), Unionist governor of Maryland 1865–1868. Judge Bond is likely Judge Hugh Lennox Bond (1828–1893), who served on the Criminal Court of Maryland from 1860 to 1867.

3. John Grimes Walker (1835–1907), assistant superintendent of the Annapolis Naval Academy 1866–1869 under Rear Admiral David Dixon Porter (1813–1891), one of the most noted naval heroes of the Civil War.

4. General Lorenzo Thomas served as adjutant general of the U.S. Army throughout the Civil War. General L. H. Pelouse must have been assistant adjutant general, beginning in 1861 in Cincinnati, Ohio. It is possible that Crommelin is referring to Colonel Theodore A. Dodge (1842–1909), who served in the 101st New York Volunteer Infantry.

5. Adam Badeux (1831–1895), colonel of the U.S. Army, 1864 military secretary and chief aide-de-camp of General Ulysses S. Grant. After the war he had a diplomatic career. For Major Winthrop see note 16. The other gentleman has not been identified.

6. Crommelin does not give the state where Patterson came from. He must mean John J. Patterson (nicknamed Honest John), senator from Pennsylvania and son-in-law of President Andrew Johnson. Robert Selph Henry, *The Story of Reconstruction* (Indianapolis: Bobbs-Merrill Co., 1938), 495.

7. Charles Sumner, U.S. Senator from Massachusetts, abolitionist and Radical Republican. With Mees Crommelin probably means Willem Cornelis Mees (1813–1884), Dutch political economist and president of the Netherlands National Bank from 1863 and an internationally renowned authority on currency matters.

8. S. B. (not G.) Golby, from Vermont, was registrar of the U.S. Treasury between August 1864 and September 1867.

9. Thaddeus Stevens, abolitionist and one of the most radical members of the House of Representatives, opponent of President Andrew Johnson. By *more Americano*, "in the American habit or manner," Crommelin refers to blowing one's nose without the use of a handkerchief.

10. The opera *Etoile du Nord* was composed by Giacomo Meyerbeer and first performed in 1854. Max Maretzek (1821–1897) was an opera impresario of Czech origin who came to the United States in 1849, making a great name there for himself by the lavish productions he organized of operas by famous European composers such as Verdi, Meyerbeer, and others. Miss Clara Louise Kellogg (1842–1916) was a famous American opera singer (soprano) of the time; in 1867 she performed in London for the first time with great success.

11. Theodorus M. Roest van Limburg (1806–1887), Dutch lawyer and politician, Dutch envoy in Washington 1856–1868, minister of foreign affairs 1868–1870. Slavery had been abolished in Dutch Surinam in 1863, and labor there was scarce after that date. William Henry Seward (1801–1872) was secretary of state of the United States 1861–1869.

12. James M. Ashley (1824–1896), member of the House of Representatives from Ohio;

George Sewell Boutwell (1818–1905), U.S. senator from Massachusetts, and 1869–1873 secretary of the treasury under President Ulysses S. Grant. Both were leaders of the Radical Republicans in Congress, and strongly opposed to the politics of Reconstruction as advocated by President Andrew Johnson (1808–1875), president of the United States 1865–1869.

13. Edgar Cowan (1815–1885) served as a Republican U.S. senator from Pennsylvania between 1861 and 1867; Thomas Williams, member of the House of Representatives from Oregon; James R. Doolittle, U.S. senator from Wisconsin; Reverdy Johnson, U.S. senator from Maryland (and not Missouri as Crommelin states). The District of Columbia bill that Crommelin mentions was a measure to enfranchise blacks in that district. President Johnson vetoed it, as expected, but in January 1867 it was passed over the president's veto. Foner, *Short History of Reconstruction,* 120.

14. John A. Kasson (1822–1910) member of the House of Representatives from Iowa 1863–1867, chair of the committee on coinage, weights, and measures, and as such he crafted the Metric Act of 1866. He was again member of the House 1873–1877 and 1881–1884, and ambassador to Germany in 1884.

15. Andrew Porter (1820–1872), brigadier general of the U.S. Army, important staff officer under George B. McClellan during the Peninsula Campaign in 1862; Orville E. Babcock (1835–1884), West Point graduate of 1861, brevet brigadier general and aide-de-camp of General U.S. Grant, later private secretary of Grant as president of the United States; by General Jones, former ambassador somewhere in South America, Crommelin may have meant Major, later Brevet General, William Price Jones, but his connection to the State Department is not known; Charles Foster (1818–1904) was U.S. Senator from Ohio.

16. Major William W. Winthrop, a native New Yorker. After his service in the U.S. Army he became an advisor to the U.S. Bureau of Military Justice.

Copperheads were a group of strident northern Democrats who opposed the Civil War, demanding an immediate peace agreement with the Confederate government. Their opponents gave these "Peace Democrats" their name because of their alleged venomous and dangerous actions.

17. George Douglas Ramsey (1802–1882), U.S. Army officer; commander of the federal arsenal in Washington, D.C., 1861–1863, 1863 chief of ordnance, 1866–1870 again commander of the Washington arsenal.

18. Henry Stanberry (1803–1881), attorney general of the United States 1866–1868.

19. On April 14, 1865, Clara Harris (1845–1883), daughter of U.S. Senator Ira Harris of New York, and her fiancé, Major Henry Rathbone, accompanied President and Mrs. Lincoln to Ford's Theater in Washington, D.C., and both were present at the assassination of the president.

Mr. D. Mackay might well be Donald McKay, a famous clipper ship designer from Boston, who had, with other partners, established a general locomotive and marine business in East Boston in 1863. The plant closed in 1869 after building about one hundred locomotives, but continued to flourish as a shipyard. John H. White, *A Short History of American Locomotive Builders in the Steam Era* (privately published, 1982), 59–61.

Giorgio Ronconi (1810–1890) was an Italian opera singer (baritone), who performed mostly in London but also in America.

12. IN NEW YORK CITY

1. The new Episcopal Grace Church, on Broadway and East 10th Street, was consecrated in 1846, and was easily the most fashionable of all New York churches, where only the "aristocracy" came. Eric Homberger, *Mrs. Astor's New York: Money and Social Power in a Gilded Age* (New Haven, Conn.: Yale University Press, 2002), 112–16.

2. Leonard W. Jerome (1834–1891) was a new millionaire who had made his fortune during the 1857 financial crisis, and was the leader of the New York social elite of the 1860s and 1870s. In 1866 he had opened his fashionable Jerome Park horse racing track and club in Fordham, New York. The Vanderbilt mentioned here is probably William Henry Vanderbilt (1821–1885), son of the famous "Commodore" Cornelius Vanderbilt and active in the New York Central & Hudson River Railroad and other Vanderbilt lines. August Belmont (1813–1890), born in Germany, was the representative of the Rothschilds in New York. He became an American citizen in 1844 and was U.S. minister to The Hague, Netherlands, 1853–1857, where he negotiated a commercial treaty that opened up the trade of the Dutch East Indies to American merchants. He had established his own firm, A. Belmont & Co., in New York City and retained his close contacts with the Rothschilds. In New York he was active in politics as a Democrat, and was, with the others mentioned here by Crommelin, a social leader in competition with Mrs. Caroline Schermerhorn Astor. Miss Hattie Travers was probably a daughter of William R. Travers, a New York City businessman operating in the circle of the Vanderbilts, who had set up a race track near Saratoga Springs together with Commodore Vanderbilt and other tycoons. Miss Nelly Prince and Mr. Talboys have not been identified.

Amants means in this case "boyfriends."

3. Crommelin means drivers and conductors of one of the many horse tramways in the city. Bishop de Hone, an Episcopal clergyman, was well connected to the high society of the Low Country, South Carolina. One of his three daughters married into the prominent Middleton plantation family, and a son also married into local wealth, so the remarks about his poverty must have been exaggerated.

4. Candia is an older name for the island in the Mediterranean now known as Crete, where the population was rising against Ottoman Turkish rule in those years.

5. St. Alban's Church (Episcopal), was located on East 47th Street west of Lexington Avenue, and generally known as Church of the Epiphany. Father Charles William Morrill served as the long-time rector of St. Alban's Church. At [. . .] some words cannot be read in the text.

6. Brevoort House, one of the more fashionable hotels in New York City, was located on the corner of Fifth Avenue and Clinton Place.

7. The Rev. George Burrell Cheever (1807–?) served from 1846 to 1870 as pastor of the Church of the Puritans, located on Union Square in New York City. The Rev. Henry Highland Garnet (1815–1882), born into slavery, was pastor of Shiloah Presbyterian Church in New York City.

8. The *National Anti-Slavery Standard* served as the official publication of the American Anti-Slavery Society. This weekly journal began in 1840 and lasted until ratification of the Fifteenth Amendment to the U.S. Constitution in 1870.

9. Christopher Gustavus Memminger (1803–1888), secretary of the treasury of the Confederate States of America 1861–1864. The other Southern gentlemen have not been identified.

10. At [. . .] the name of the former authority cannot be read.

11. Matilda (Milly) Verplanck (born 1842), was a younger sister of Samuel. The actor Edwin Booth was the best known performer of Shakespeare's *Hamlet*. After his younger brother John Wilkes Booth had shot President Lincoln, he retired, but returned to the stage in January 1866. Lloyd Morris, *Incredible New York: High Life and Low Life from 1850 to 1950* (Syracuse, N.Y.: Syracuse University Press, 1996), 63.

12. Delmonico's Restaurant opened in 1846 at 25 Broadway and was soon the most fashionable restaurant in New York City. Charles Lockwood, *Manhattan Moves Uptown: An Illustrated History* (New York: Barnes and Noble, 1995), 82.

13. William Henry Aspinwall (1807–1875) was a rich New York merchant with worldwide operations, founder of the Pacific Mail Steamship Company in 1848, and known as a protector of the arts. He was related to the Howland family. Jakob Philipp Hackert (1737–1807), German landscape painter of some renown. It is not clear which one of the Dorners Crommelin means. Johann Jakob Dorner the elder (1741–1813) and his son Johann Jakob Dorner the younger (1775–1852) were both German painters popular in their times. Frederick Edwin Church (1826–1900) was an American landscape painter and at that time easily the most popular American artist. Régis François Gignoux (1816–1892) also painted American landscapes, including the Hudson River and Niagara Falls.

14. Elizabeth Verplanck (1800–1888) daughter of Gulian Crommelin Verplanck, and married to John W. Knevals.

15. The Ludlow family was long identified with the history and growth of Yonkers, New York. Crommelin likely refers here to Thomas W. Ludlow, Jr.

13. In New York City, Boston, and Salem

1. Fordham, Westchester County, North of Harlem, retained its rural character well into the 19th century. Mr. Punnet apparently was an old business relation of Daniel Crommelin & Sons.

2. Bloomfield, New Jersey, northwest of Newark.

3. Roebling's Brooklyn Bridge was opened only in 1884, so Crommelin had to take one of the many ferries to get to Brooklyn from Manhattan.

4. Otto Heinze (1831–1891) headed the firm of Heinze, Lowy & Co. and was a founder of the German-American Insurance Company. His son, F. Augustus Heinze (1869–1914), became famous as one of the "Copper Kings" of Butte, Montana. Otto Heinze's company must have been a relation of Daniel Crommelin & Sons.

5. Dr. Thomas Hunter (1813–1915) spent a long and distinguished career in public education in New York City, serving for 37 years as the first president of the Normal College, today's Hunter College of the City University of New York.

6. A New York College for the Training of Teachers was founded only in 1889, but a Normal College for Women had been established earlier.

7. The Lancaster Industrial School for Girls, founded in 1854, southeast of Lancaster, Massachusetts, was the oldest female training school in the United States and early on gained the reputation as one of the most progressive correctional institutions for women.

8. Charles Eliot Norton (1827–1908), born in Cambridge, Massachusetts, graduated from Harvard College in 1846 and went into business. In 1851 he ended his commercial activities and devoted himself to literature, translating, for example, Dante's *Vita Nuova* and the *Divina Commedia*. Between 1864 and 1868 he gained considerable fame as editor of the high-brow *North American Review*, the first literary magazine in the United States. The magazine promoted improvements in public education and administration, rehabilitation of prisoners, and government service for the well-educated. Linda Dowling, *Charles Eliot Norton: The Art of Reform in Nineteenth-Century America* (Hanover, N.H.: University Press of New England, 2007). James Russell Lowell (1819–1891), American writer, abolitionist, professor at Harvard, and editor of the *Atlantic Monthly*, another widely read and influential magazine.

9. Daniel Barnard Hagar (1820–1896), served as long-time principal of Salem Normal School in Salem, Massachusetts, a tenure that lasted from 1865 until his death. His school, present-day Salem State College, was a progressive institution that opened in 1854 to train "young ladies who wish to prepare themselves for teaching."

Index

Corliss & Company, machine factory in Providence, Rhode Island, 70, 160n22

Corruption. *See under* United States

Corry, Pennsylvania, 57

Cotton, cotton production, 10, 66, 67, 91, 106, 130, 159n12. *See also under* United States, Agriculture in

Cotonnet, family, of New York City, 86, 92, 125, 133

Cottage Lawn, Yonkers, New York, 31–32, 72

Cousinery, Mr., merchant [?] of New York City, 29, 147n3

Cowan, Edgar (1815–1885), U. S. senator from Pennsylvania, 116, 170n13

Credit Mobilier of America, 11

Crete (Candia), 123, 163n4, 171n4

Crimean War, 54

Crommelin family, 2, 3

Crommelin, Charles (1675–1740), merchant of New York City, 150n16

Crommelin, Claude August (1840–1874), writer of the diary, 1–15

Crommelin, Claude August (1878–1965), scientist at Leiden University, 13–15, 141n26

Crommelin, Claude August (1919–1985), of Atlanta, Georgia, 14–15, 141n26

Crommelin, Claude Daniel (1795–1859), merchant of Amsterdam, 3, 32

Crommelin, Daniel (†1725), 140n5

Crommelin, Daniel (1707–1788), merchant of Amsterdam, 3, 150n16

Crommelin, Daniel, en Soonen, trading company of Amsterdam, 3, 5, 14–15, 51, 66, 132, 148nn7, 9, 155n11, 158n1

Crommelin, Judith, wife of Samuel Verplanck, 150n16

Crommelin Marie, wife of Guillaume Verplanck, 150n16

Crommelin, Robert Daniel (1841–1907), 13

Crooks, William, engineer of the St. Paul & Pacific Railroad, *44*

Crosby's Opera House, Chicago, 41, 152n9

Crowell, Mr., captain of the *Saratoga,* 88

Crow Wing, Minnesota, 44

Crystal Palace, Sydenham, London, 22, 144n18

Cumming's Point, fort near Charleston, South Carolina, 92

Cunard Line, 6, 146n30

Curtin, Andrew Gregg (1815–1894), governor of Pennsylvania, 53, 156n15

Curtis, Mr., music teacher in New York City, 127

Custis, George Washington Parke, adopted son of George Washington, 51, 155n9

Dabney, Charles W., partner of Dabney, Morgan & Company, bankers of New York City, 64, 148n5, 159n8

Dalmeyer, photographic supply store in London, 21, 144n14

Dana, Richard Henry (1815–1882), author and lawyer of Boston, 7, 78–79, 163n5

Danforth, Charles, director of a machine factory in Paterson, New Jersey, 39, 100, 152n4

Danville, Virginia, 106, 107

Dashwood, Mrs., in Newburgh, New York, 74

Davidson, Jane Washington, wife of John de Bruyn Kops, 34–35, 121

Davis, Jefferson (1808–1889), president of the Confederate States of America, 92, 109–110, 115, 166n6, 168n9

Davison, Miss, fiancée of Arthur Sturges, 35

Davison, Mr., English actor, 23

Davison, Mr., steamboat pilot, 112

Day, William Howard (1825–1900), abolitionist and education expert, 33, 149n12

Deer Island, in Massachusetts Bay, 82–83

De Hone, Dr., Episcopal clergyman of South Carolina, 121, 171n3

De Keyser's Royal Hotel, Blackfriars, London, 19, 142n7

Delafield, Miss, in Washington, D. C., 117

Delamater Iron Works, New York City, 156n23

Delaware River, 54

Delft, Netherlands, 18, 142n1

Delmonico's, restaurant in New York City, 34, 129, 150n13, 171n12

Deltone, Miss, in Boston, 77

Democracy in America, book by Alexis de Tocqueville, 1

Denner, Balthasar (1685–1749), German painter, 20, 143n9

Derbyshire, England, 23, 24, 25

Desenfans, Noël, art dealer, 144n17

Fillmore Hotel, Newport, Rhode Island, 69, 160n21

First Church of Christ, Scientist, New York City, *122*

Fishkill, New York, 73, 86, 130

Fisk, Jim, American railroad tycoon, 11

The Flowers of the Forest, stage play, 82

Fordham, New York, 131–132, 172n1

Fort Abercrombie, North Dakota, 46, 153n17

Fort Johnson, Charleston, South Carolina, 92

Fort Lafayette, U.S. prison in New York Harbor, 94, 166n11

Fort Libby, Confederate prison in Richmond, Virginia, 109–110, 168n11

Fort Moultrie, Charleston, South Carolina, 92

Fort Pinkney, Charleston, South Carolina, 92

Fort Putnam, Charleston, South Carolina, 92

Fort Sumter, Charleston, South Carolina, 8, 30, 92

Foster, Charles (1828–1904), U.S. senator from Ohio, 117, 170n15

Fourteenth Amendment, 9–10, 167n3. *See also under* United States, Constitution of

Fra Diavolo, opera by Daniel F. Auber, 50, 119, 154n5

France, 2

Franklin, Benjamin (1706–1790), American statesman, 52

Freedmen's Bureau. *See under* United States

Freeman, Miss Emily, 80, 82

Freeman, Miss Lizzie, 138

Fremont House, hotel in Chicago, 36

Frost, Mr., from Charleston, South Carolina, 126

Frothingham, Mr., at Boston, 83

Fuller family, 76, 84

Fuller, Carry, 64–65

Fuller, Henrietta, 64–65, 114

Fuller, Mary, 64–65, 114

Fuller, Mrs., 64

Gardoni, Italo (1821–1882), Italian opera singer, 19, 143n8

Garnet, Henry Highland (1815–1882), pastor of Shiloah Presbyterian Church, New York City, 125–126, 171n7

Garrison, William Lloyd, abolitionist and public speaker, 125

Garrison's Station, New York, on the Hudson River, 35, 73

Gausset, Mr., Belgian businessman [?], 19

Gay, Delphine (1804–1855), French playwright, wife of Emile de Girardin, 19, 142n5

Geary, John White (1819–1873), general of the U.S. Army, 53, 156n15

Georgetown, D. C., 51, 155n11

Georgia, 10

Gerolt, Friedrich Josef Marie, Freiherr von, Prussian envoy in Washington, D. C., 51, 155n10

Gibbs, Mrs., wife of H. P. Gibbs, businessman of Charleston, South Carolina, 93, 166n10

Gignoux, Régis François (1816–1892), French-American painter, 130, 172n13

Gilbert, Mr., abolitionist and public speaker, 125–126

Gilmore, Blake & Ward, bankers of Boston, 154n6

Gilmore, Dunlop & Company, bankers of Cincinnati, Ohio, 50

Girard College, Philadelphia, Pennsylvania, 53–54

Girard Trust Building, Philadelphia, Pennsylvania, 53, 156n14

Girardin. *See* Gay, Delphine

Glen Ellis Falls, New Hampshire, 60

Glen House, hotel near Gorham, New Hampshire, 60, 158n16

Goddard, Nathaniel, business relation of Daniel Crommelin & Sons, 66

Goddard, family, of Providence, Rhode Island, 84, 164n19

Golby, S. B., registrar of the U. S. Treasury, 115, 169n8

Goodwin, James J., banker of New York City, 148n5

Gord, Mr., manager of the Cooperative Spinning Mill, Rochdale, England, 25–26

Gordonsville, Virginia, 110, 168n14

Gorham, New Hampshire, 60, 158n16

Gosschalk, J., Dutch architect, 12

Gould, Jay, American railroad tycoon, 8, 11

Index

Turnbull, Miss Agnes, school teacher of New York City, 34

Turner, Thomas, commodore of the U.S. Navy, 54

Tutein Nolthenius, Julie Elisabeth, daughter of the following, 3, 13

Tutein Nolthenius, Julius Hendrik, husband of Elisabeth Weymar, 3

Tutein Nolthenius, Rudolph P. J., Dutch engineer, 14–15

Tutein Nolthenius & De Haan, Amsterdam banking firm, 3, 13–14

Tweed, Boss, New York politician, 11

Über den Rhein, German quarter of Cincinnati, Ohio, 50, 154n5

Union Pacific Railroad Company, 11

Unitarian Church, in America, 6, 62, 67, 79–80, 83–85, 137, 160n15, 164n20, 24

United States of America: Abolitionists in, 106; Agriculture in, 10, 36–38, 46–47, 91, 97, 106; Army of, 67, 110, 114–115, 118; Congress of, 8–9, 51–52, 89–91, 95, 110, 115–116, 118, 120; Constitution of, 9, 10, 95, 115, 117, 125; Corruption in, 11, 78, 118, 123; Declaration of Independence of, 52; Democracy in, 1, 5, 79, 102, 105; Dutch investment in, 5, 37, 39, 43–48, 51–52, 155n11; Elections in, 83, 86; Freedmen's Bureau of, 9, 99, 101, 109–110, 116, 167n16, 168n12; "Greenback Manufactory" of, 5, 118, 155n11; Hospitals in, 73; Hotels in, 28, 32, 36, 60, 69, 120; House of Representatives of, 9, 115–117; Immigration in, 2, 35, 38–39, 45, 48; Inflation in, 30–32, 86, 107, 148n7; Judicial system in, 77; Liquor laws in, 67, 77, 105; Manufacturing industry in, 8–9, 66–71, 75, 82, 85, 159n12; Morals in, 59, 62, 64, 112–113, 120–121, 125; Navy of, 54–55, 65; Oil industry in, 57–59; Patent Office of, 52; Political situation in, 9–11, 31–32, 83, 86–89, 94, 104–105, 115–116, 118, 120, 125–126, 130, 170n16; Prison system in, 5, 54, 62–63, 73, 79, 158n4; Railroads in, 1, 5, 7, 11, 30–31, 35–38, 41–45, 47–48, 76, 85, 148nn6, 8, 151nn17, 19, 2, 154n3, 155n13, 167n1; *see also under* individual rail-

road company names; Relations of, with Great Britain, 94; Religion in, 5, 6, 61–62, 66–67, 79–80, 84–86, 111–112, 121, 124, 134–35; Senate of, 115–117; Supreme Court of, 77, 113, 126; Taxation in, 8, 10, 30–31, 72, 130, 149n9; Treasury of, 115; War Department of, 9, 114. *See also* Johnson, Andrew

Urban, Jules, Belgian railway director, 19, 142n5

Urban, Maurice, Belgian railway engineer, 19, 142n5

Utica, New York, 35

Utrecht, Netherlands, University of, 3

Van Buren, Miss, in New Jersey, 74

Vanderbilt, family, 7, 121

Vanderbilt, William Henry (1821–1885), railroad director, 121, 151n17, 171n2

Van Lew, Elizabeth (†1900), abolitionist and Union spy in Richmond, Virginia, 110, 168n11

Velde, Willem van de (1633–1707), Dutch marine painter, 20, 22, 143n10

Veronese, Paolo (1528–1588), Italian painter, 18, 141n2

Verplanck, family, 7, 73, 86

Verplanck, Adrian, 74, 162n12

Verplanck, Anna (1846–1891), daughter of William Samuel Verplanck, 73, 161n6

Verplanck, Daniel Crommelin, 74

Verplanck, Eliza Fenno (*1838), daughter of William Samuel Verplanck, 73, 161n6

Verplanck, Elizabeth (1800–1888), sister of Gulian Crommelin Verplanck, married to John W. Knevals, 73, 130, 161n6, 172n14

Verplanck, Gelyna (*1852), daughter of William Samuel Verplanck, 73, 161n6

Verplanck, Guillaume, 150n16

Verplanck, Gulian Crommelin (1786–1870), American politician and lawyer, relative of Crommelin, 35, 73, 130, 150n16

Verplanck, James de Lancey (*1805), brother of Gulian Crommelin Verplanck, 73, 128, 161n6

Verplanck, Jeanette (*1849), daughter of William Samuel Verplanck, 73, 161n6

Verplanck, Mary Newlin (*1840), daughter

Augustus J. Veenendaal, Jr., retired as Senior Research Historian at the Institute of Netherlands History in The Hague, is the editor and author of numerous books that have been published in both the Netherlands and the United States. His works include a multi-volume edition of the correspondence of Anthonie Heinsius, Grand Pensionary of Holland, 1702–1720; *Slow Train to Paradise: How Dutch Investment Helped Build American Railroads;* and *Spoorwegen in Nederland. Van 1834 tot nu.*

H. Roger Grant, Kathryn and Calhoun Lemon Professor of History at Clemson University, is author or editor of twenty-seven books, most of them on railroad history. He has written company histories of the Chicago & North Western, the Chicago Great Western, the Erie Lackawanna, the Georgia & Florida, and the Wabash railroads. His latest book, *Twilight Rails: The Final Era of Railroad Building in the Midwest,* was published in 2010.